DIY SURVIVAL

BEST HACKS FOR WORST-CASE SCENARIOS

COMPILED BY THE EDITORS OF
OFFGRID MAGAZINE

Copyright ©2022 Caribou Media Group, LLC

All rights reserved. No portion of this publication may be reproduced or transmitted in any form or by any means, electronic or mechanical, including photocopy, recording, or any information storage and retrieval system, without permission in writing from the publisher, except by a reviewer who may quote brief passages in a critical article or review to be printed in a magazine or newspaper, or electronically transmitted on radio, television, or the Internet.

Published by

Recoil Offgrid Books, an imprint of Caribou Media Group, LLC
5600 W. Grande Market Drive, Suite 100
Appleton, WI 54913
offgridweb.com | gundigest.com

To order books or other products call 920.471.4522 ext.104
or visit us online at gundigeststore.com

DISCLAIMER: Prices and details for items featured in RECOIL are set by the manufacturers and retailers, and are subject to change without notice. Please read all local and federal laws carefully before attempting to purchase any products shown in this guide or building your own firearms. Laws change frequently and, although our text was accurate at the time it was originally published, it may have changed between then and what's currently legal.

ISBN-13: 978-1-951115-82-1

Edited and designed by Recoil Offgrid Staff

Printed in the United States of America

10 9 8 7 6 5 4 3 2 1

CHAPTERS

Introduction P. 5

Food

Meat You Can't Beat: Canning Animal Protein P. 6
You Are What You Eat: How to Build a Six-Month Food Supply P. 12
Survival Charcuterie: Making Your Own Jerky P. 18
Grid-Down Chef: Use These Makeshift Cooking Methods When Conventional Means Are Unavailable P. 24
How to Pick Up (and Raise) Chicks: Egg-Laying Chickens in Your Backyard Can Be a Move Toward Self-Sufficiency P. 32
A Dish Served Hot: Building a DIY Parabolic Solar Cooker for Grid-Down Grub P. 44
Survival Spuds: Building Your Own Potato Patch P. 56

Hunting & Fishing

Improvised Angling: Forget Your Rod, Reel, and Tackle Box. In a SHTF World, You'll Have to Fish With What You've Got. P. 62
Feast Master: A Survivalist's Primer on Field Dressing and Butchering P. 72
Trap Triggers: Learn a Primitive Way of Procuring Small Game Without Expending Tons of Energy P. 78

Medical

On the Chopping Block: When is Amputation the Only Option? P. 88
Labor Day: What If You Have to Deliver a Baby Without Medical Help? P. 94
Back to the Suture: The OFFGRID Guide to DIY Wound Closure Methods P. 100
Antibiotic Alternatives: Plants, Poultices, and Pet Meds P. 112
Without a Hospital: What Do You Do When Conventional Medical Care is Unavailable? P. 118
Pill Bottle Perishables: Is it Safe to Consume Expired Medications? P. 126
Clean Up Your Act: Maintaining Hygiene Without Your Usual Conveniences P. 132

Water

Roof Tap: How to Make and Install a Rain Barrel P. 138
Not a Drop to Drink: ...Unless You Improvise With Your Own DIY Water Filters P. 146

Thinking Outside the Box

Off the Grid Everyday: Survival Lessons Learned From Society's Homeless P. 154
Survival Chop Shop: 10 Useful Items to Scavenge from Abandoned Cars P. 162
It Came From Space: 10 Uses for Emergency Blankets P. 172
Old News, New Tricks: Don't Toss Them Out. Newspapers Have a Lot More Survival Uses Than You Think P. 178
Paracord Preps: 10 Projects That'll Bail You Out When You're In a Bind P. 186
Swiss Army Survival: 5 Surprising Uses for the Original Multitool P. 198

CHAPTERS
(CONTINUED)

Survival At Home
Household Survival: Commonplace Items that Can Help in Survival Situations P. 208
Grid-Down Gardening: The Intersection Where Sustainability and Survivalism Meet P. 218
Backyard Survival Training: Practice for Worst-Case Scenarios in the Comfort of Your Own Home Before They Happen P. 226
Hydroponics Basics: What is it and How Practical is it in a Survival Situation? P. 234
Well Informed: Thinking of Building a Well? Here's What You Should Know P. 246
Winning the Germ War: Improvised Disaster Sanitation and Hygiene P. 256

Survival Outdoors
MacGyver-Level Pyro: 10 Ways to Start a Fire Without Matches P. 266
DIY Improvised Bucksaw: All You Need is a Few Parts and Some Ingenuity to Fashion a Practical Cutting Implement P. 274
Eat This, Not That: Edible Plants and Their Dangerous Doppelgängers P. 282
Delicious or Deadly? Wild Mushroom Foraging 101 P. 292
72-Hour Ziploc Bag Challenge: Lessons Learned from Three Days Surviving in the Desert with a Quart-Sized Plastic Bug-Out Bag P. 302

Weapons
Hunger Games: Build Your Own Survival Stick Bow P. 312
Improv Skills: Get Your Jason Bourne On By Turning These Five Common Items Into Self-Defense Weapons P. 322
Edge of Disaster: Improvised Knife Sharpening Methods P. 330
Pipe Dreams: The Pop-A 410 DIY Survival Shotgun P. 338
A Poor Man's Guide to Knife-making: DIY Bladesmithing Your Own Knife at Home P. 344

INTRODUCTION

There's little, if any, argument to be made that modern society places a high premium on convenience. Particularly in the wake of the COVID-19 pandemic, we have seen a massive pivot by companies big and small to place a premium on near-real-time door-to-door logistics. You can download apps on your phone to hire other people to not only do your grocery shopping for you but have someone else come into your home and put those groceries away, whether you're there or not. The lesson to be learned from this is that Newton's Third Law is not just for high school physics. Every action does, indeed, have an equal and opposite reaction. In this case, the opposite reaction is a severe degradation in our ability to figure things out for ourselves. While many will rationalize this by saying such skills are less necessary for daily life, that mindset makes our society exponentially more fragile, and makes general handiness even more vital. We have reached a point where even minor disturbances in complex, transnational supply chains can cause significant disruption in thousands, or tens of thousands, of lives.

The ability to function when immediate resupply is delayed or impossible has always been a foundational tenet of preparedness. More recently, as real-world disasters prove to be lower-intensity and longer-lasting, having the skill and knowledge to fashion tools and remedies on your own is especially critical. To that end, we set out to create a single compendium of easy-to-read, rapidly actionable Do It Yourself survival projects. It may be an unreasonable expectation to memorize every possible DIY survival skill and improvisation technique you could ever possibly have to use. But keeping a single, portable encyclopedia of such information is not.

We've collected and collated a wide array of DIY survival articles from across the OFFGRID canon to give you a buffet of tips, tricks, and hacks to get you through a gamut of survival situations in which you might not have everything you need pre-packed in a bugout bag. We made a point to shy away from arcane, obscure, or primal survival skills. For example, this book will not teach you how to flint knap igneous rock into crude arrowheads. Not that there's anything wrong with those skills. They're just not what the vast majority of urban and suburban dwellers will need to get through "low-intensity" crises – by which I mean, those disasters that fall short of a total societal collapse where Australian policemen in muscle cars fight bands of oil-hoarding marauders on motorcycles. You know the movie I'm talking about...

Some of these chapters will be fast-use skills you can use on the fly when a sudden emergency pops up: like how to turn common items into self-defense weapons, scavenge supplies from an abandoned vehicle, or even amputate a limb when there's no other option. Others focus more on the *pre* in preparedness – at-home projects you can work on and maintain now for if and when an emergency hits: like how to build up a six-month food supply, harvest rainwater, raise chickens for food, and start an edible home garden.

Whatever you think your disaster will look like, whatever it *actually* turns out to look like, the OFFGRID team is here to arm you with the skills and abilities you'll need to make your bad days a little bit better. As always, stay safe and get ready.

– Tom Marshall
Editor, RECOIL OFFGRID

1 › Food

Meat You Can't Beat
Canning Animal Protein

By Gordon Meehl
Illustrations by Ced Nocon

There's no debating it, the item taking up the most real estate in your emergency supply cache is food — boxes, bags, and bottles of it. We spend a lot of time, money, and effort making sure we have enough of what we hope is tasty sustenance. But, as we found out in our last issue's taste tests, even the highest-quality prepackaged, storable food leaves the palate wanting.

Animal proteins commercially packaged for long-term storage are at best mediocre meat-like chunks in an Alpo-like sauce, and at worst something akin to the sole of

a jungle boot. A couple of meals like this and you'll be dreaming of your favorite cut of beef or a delicately fried piece of yard bird. Well, just because the fan is covered in crap doesn't mean you're relegated to eating from an overly salted bag of carbs.

Canning your own meat (and other food stuffs) is a simple way to maintain some normalcy in your diet when things are less than normal. With the goal being to thrive — not just survive — having regular food is certainly a big morale booster. Besides offering you more palatable food, creating a supply of canned meat allows you to customize what you have on hand when the lights go out. If you want a higher protein menu and to avoid those carb-filled green bags, *can it*. If you need to maintain a low-sodium diet, *can it*. If you want to ensure what you're eating is kosher, *can it*.

Contrary to what some people think, canning meat at home is not a guaranteed invitation to botulism, nor is it some mysterious black art handed down through generations of frontier women. If you can boil water and have a few basic supplies, you can be canning like Ma Ingalls getting ready for the county fair.

One of the most compelling reasons to create your own shelf-stable food supply is the economics of it all. For about the cost of buying your family a mere five days worth of prepackaged food, you can have all you need to create months of long-term storable food for more than a few people. You need not buy expensive cuts of meat. Grocery stores drastically reduce prices as meat gets closer to the sell-by date. Cost drops significantly if you're bringing home meat you've stalked and killed yourself. You just can't find venison MRE anywhere, after all.

There's nothing complicated, expensive, or complex to buy to get started. All you need is a pressure cooker/canner (you can't can meat without one), some jars, lids, a few essential accessories, and a reliable heat source. Get yourself some meat, canning salt, and some of your favorite spices, and then you're good to go.

Pressure Canner: This is the heart of the process; you don't want to skimp on this. We really like ones made by All American. These heavy, cast-aluminum, American-made bombproof works of art are the Abrams tanks of cookware. A metal-to-metal seal eliminates the eventual need of having to replace gaskets or rubber seals. Simply put, if you buy the best, you'll never regret it.

In addition to the canner, you need something to put the meat in. Ball mason jars and lids seem to be the go-to containers for hardcore canners. They also make an accessories kit that makes your life a lot easier when cranking out your cache of canned gold.

The Process

Canning meat is all about the preparation. It's important to make sure everything starts off and stays clean. Prep properly and you'll eliminate chances for contamination. The goal is to avoid any type of bacteria that will give you the bubble guts, the trots, or worse. Clean the jars well, and while cutting your meat, have your lids and rings boiling. Prep the containers carefully and you'll end up with canned meat that may quite possibly outlast you.

Take a slab of the meat of your choice. Trim off any fat, skin, bones, and so forth. Yes, fat adds flavor, but if it gets on the lip of the jar anytime during prep or under heat, the lid will not get an airtight seal. No airtight seal means spoiled meat. The only exceptions would be if you're canning bacon (see sidebar).

Now that all the excess non-meat is removed, it's time to cube it up. We cut ours into ½-inch cubes, which tends to be on the small side, but at that size, it's easier to avoid getting bubbles between pieces when packing it into the jars.

Be sure to boil the lids and rings that secure the lids to the thoroughly cleaned jars. How many jars will you need? The simple rule of thumb is one pint jar for every pound of meat. You'll also want to start boiling about 3 inches of water in the pressure canner (don't put the top on yet).

Pack the meat in a jar till there's about an inch of headspace left at the top or about where the threads for the rings start. Add about ½ tablespoon of canning salt (found in any grocery store) to the top. Use the Ball magnetic wand found in Ball's accessories kit to carefully grab a lid and ring out of the boiling water. Slap the lid on the jar, and tighten the ring just finger tight. You don't want to muscle it on there; the lid tightens up under pressure.

Now the fun begins! Place the filled jars in the boiling water of the pressure canner. Read the instructions that came with the canner to get the particulars first, but the basic process is as follows: Fill the canner to capacity. Not enough jars of meat to fill the canner? Fill in the gaps with jars full of water. You need a full canner to get the proper results. Seal the lid according to the unit's instructions. Per the owner's manual, set your canner to 10 pounds of pressure (15 psi at higher altitudes). You'll be cooking the jars under pressure for about 90 minutes. Be advised that your pressure canner may recommend different times for different types of meats. Don't start your timer until the appropriate pressure is reached.

When the timer goes off, remove the canner from the heat (be careful because it's hot). Let the pressure go down to zero before opening the lid. Not waiting until the pressure is all gone is a quick way to have a bad day. Remove the jars, let them cool, and check them out. You're looking to make sure there's no air in the headspace of the jars and that nothing is leaking out. Check to make sure there's a slight indent in the top of the lid. Tapping the top gently should yield a nice ping. If there's any doubt, re-can.

So how long will canned meat last? When canned right, it'll last a heck of a long time. In 1820, Sir William Edward Parry made two artic expeditions. He took with him various canned meats. Though glass jars are superior, he used tin cans to avoid breakage and save weight. Long story short, a few of the tins made their way to a museum and were kept as artifacts. In 1938, more than 100 years after they were first canned, a 4-pound tin of roasted veal was opened, the contents were analyzed, and then it was fed to a cat. The results: The cat was fine, and scientists found that the meat was in near-perfect condition with most of its nutrients intact.

That isn't to say that 100 years from now your descendants will be cracking open a jar of great grandpa's venison, but there's every reason that you can keep a stockpile of your favorite meats long enough to last you through any harrowing times that may come.

Sources:

Can Manufacturers Institute
www.cancentral.com

All American Canner
www.allamericancanner.com

National Center for Home Food Preservation
nchfp.uga.edu

Offgrid Bacon

Rolling Your Own Bacon. Need We Say More?

Ingredients:
Raw or cooked bacon
Brown parchment paper, 12-inch wide
Brown sugar
Maple syrup
Canning supplies

One pound of raw bacon needs a 1-quart-sized jar to have enough room to can. But, 1 pound of cooked bacon fits perfectly into a smaller 1-pint wide-mouthed canning jar. We opt for cooking the bacon and saving the space, plus when you open the jar you can enjoy the bacon right then and there. What could be more awesome than that? Here's how I do it.

Rule of thumb: One (pre-cooked) pound of bacon per every pint jar you want to store. Go nuts and make a day of it and cook up as much as possible. You can use any bacon, but I suggest thick-sliced Amish smoked bacon if you can find it. We don't know if it's their lack of electricity or their expert 19th century farm craft, but the Amish make incredible bacon.

1. Cook the bacon until it's crispy, but not hard. It should still have some flop to it and should be flexible. Keep in mind it will still cook for a bit even after when you remove it from heat.
2. Put the cooked bacon on a paper towel to soak up the grease.
3. For every pound of bacon, lay out a 2-foot-long piece of brown parchment paper.

4. Lay the bacon along the centerline of the parchment paper, leaving space at either end.
5. Now for the yummy part. Lightly brush some hot maple syrup over the bacon, and then sprinkle on some light brown sugar. Feel free to experiment with other condiments;

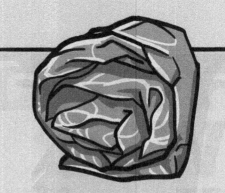

a light coating of hot sauce is pretty awesome, too.
6. Fold the excess paper along the long side toward the centerline and the leftover length on either side to the middle.

up with a bunch of bacon bits after rolling it.

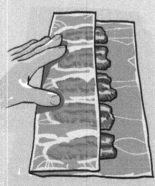

7. Now start rolling from one end. The roll should be snug, but not so tight that it bruises the bacon. This is why the bacon should be crispy, but not hard; if it's too brittle, you'll end

8. Your roll should be just the right size to fit perfectly into a wide-mouth jar.
9. Wipe the rim with a moist hot towel, and put the lid and the ring on the jar.
10. Process per your pressure canner's instructions.
11. You now have bacon for years to come.

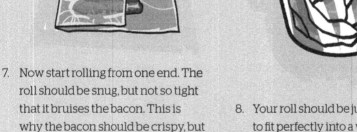

You Are What You Eat

How to Build a Six-Month Food Supply

By Tim MacWelch

You may find yourself asking, "Six months of food? Do I really need that much?" — especially when most people seem to be content with 72-hour go-bags and two-week disaster kits. But if you're reading a magazine like OFFGRID, you already know why long-term food storage makes sense.

A Katrina-level natural disaster, an economic collapse, or another Sept. 11-style attack — these and any number of similar catastrophes could wipe out your normal resources for food. In these types of situations, you'd have to rely on your own reserves, or devolve into a hunter/gatherer (and there are no guarantees with that menu plan). But maybe your problems aren't so widespread. Perhaps you're just suffering a personal crisis, such as a job loss or an injury that prevents work. For any of these situations, building a food reserve becomes a valuable insurance policy — one that you can actually eat.

Pick Your Food Plan

"Plan your work, and work your plan." A project like this can be a daunting task, so planning is one of the most important parts. You'll want to pay great attention to calorie content, methods of food preparation, storage conditions, and your own personal dietary restrictions. It's also helpful to plan out the meals and create a meal rotation. You don't need to plan 180 days of unique meals, but a two-week menu plan will give you some much-needed variety (unless you're buying a pallet of MREs or mixed, freeze-dried foods).

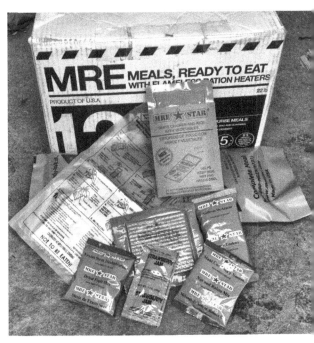

Finally, you'll need to decide which food preservation method best matches your plan. In this article, we'll look at four different approaches to building a food supply: MREs, freeze-dried food, canned goods, and dry goods.

1. MRE: Meals Ready to Eat (MREs) are a quick solution to build your food reserves, but they're expensive, bulky, and only last about five years. This approach is easy and no cooking is involved to prepare the food — it's truly "ready to eat" as the name declares. Each MRE contains approximately 1,400 calories, so two per day provides an average of 2,800 calories. You'll need 360 MREs (30 cases) for a six-month supply. For your daily ration, open up two MREs, pick through the contents to decide which items you want for breakfast, lunch, and dinner, then eat them when you'd like. Better MREs include a water-activated chemical heater, which would give you two hot meals a day. This is a great morale booster and perfect for those who are cooking-impaired.

COST PER DAY:
$16
COST FOR SIX MONTHS:
$2,880, plus shipping (though discounts may be available for large orders)
LONGEVITY:
Five-plus years

2. Freeze-Dried Food: Mountain House and many other companies provide a wide selection of freeze-dried meals and food items. They're even more expensive than MREs, but may last up to five times longer. Freeze-dried foods generally require hot water to prepare, and they're as bulky as MREs (yet without the weight). They're available in serving-sized pouches, larger cans, and even buckets. Four pouches a day will be needed to reach

though. They're even heavier than MREs, and their life span is only about five years as well (maybe less for pop-top cans). Check the calorie count when planning meals with canned goods. You'll need at least five cans per day to reach 2,400 calories. Roughly 900 cans will provide you with a six-month food supply, and these are the easiest foods to work into your normal meals.

COST PER DAY:
$10 to $15

COST FOR SIX MONTHS:
$1,800 to 2,700, with no shipping costs if purchased locally

LONGEVITY:
Five-plus years

2,400 calories. Oddly enough, the No. 10 entrée cans only contain about 2,000 calories each, yet cost over $30 apiece. The greatest asset to freeze-dried food is shelf life, with 25 years or more expected. You'll need about 180 cans or 720 pouches for a six-month food stash.

COST PER DAY:
$25 to $35

COST FOR SIX MONTHS:
$4,500 to $6,300, plus shipping (though discounts may be available for large orders)

LONGEVITY:
25-plus years

3. Canned Goods: Your average canned pasta, stew, and chili are more cost effective than MREs or freeze-dried food. They're typically ready to eat from the can without the need for extra water, and cans are insect and rodent proof. Canned goods do come with a few drawbacks,

4. Dry Goods and Grains: Cooking these foods and preparing palatable meals from them may be a bit of a challenge, but if you're familiar with cooking from scratch, this is the cheapest way to go. Dry pasta, rice, flour, dried beans, sugar, and many other staple foods can be stored for 30 years with negligible nutrient loss when properly packaged. They're also relatively easy to work into your regular meals. The drawbacks are that you'll need even more potable water than for freeze-dried foods, and you'll need to know how to cook. You can purchase these staples already packed in cans or buckets with oxygen absorbers and Mylar liners for maximum longevity. Or you can save a few dollars by buying the food in bulk and repacking it yourself. Depending on the staple food item, a 5-gallon bucket usually holds over 30 pounds of dry goods, which can represent over 40,000 calories. This means that 10 five-gallon buckets will hold enough staple foods for your six-month supply.

COST PER DAY:
$2 to $5, depending greatly on your menu plan

COST FOR SIX MONTHS:
$360 to $900, with no shipping costs if purchased locally

LONGEVITY:
30 years

Package Your Own Dry Goods

One of the easiest ways to package your food is in 5-gallon, food-grade buckets. If your budget allows, buy new 5-gallon buckets with regular lids. Purchase a few gamma (screw-on) lids as well, handy for accessing foods that will be used often, like sugar. If you're doing this project on a shoestring budget, ask for buckets from bakeries and restaurants — they may be free or only cost a few dollars a piece.

The bucket alone is good, but to still have edible dry goods after 30 years, you'll also need Mylar storage bags and oxygen absorbers. Smaller bags and several 100cc absorbers are great for rationing the food and for modular storage. The large "bucket liner" bags and 2,000cc absorbers are perfect if you want to dump a big bag of grain into a bucket and call it done. You'll need a total of 1,500cc of absorbers as a minimum for one bucket of grain, flour, beans, or pasta. You won't need oxygen absorbers in sugar, honey, or salt. They don't go bad, and sugar and salt will become a solid brick from the oxygen absorber (still edible, but you'll need a chisel to chop them up). Once you've figured out which staple foods will be in your bucket, place the Mylar liner in the bucket (even if your food is in smaller packages with their own oxygen packs), and fill it near the top. Add oxygen absorbers to total at least 1,500cc for the entire 5-gallon bucket.

Press the liner bag together and expel any air you can. Lay a 2x4 board across the bucket and smooth out the bag mouth on top of it. Run a hot clothes iron across the bag opening to heat seal it (you could also seal the bag with a flat iron for hair; no need for the piece of wood). Seal the bucket lid tightly and store it in a safe storage spot.

Build a Dry-Goods Menu Plan

Staple foods are easy to plan, if you have a shopping list and a menu. Here's a very simple menu, and the accompanying shopping list, for a three-week food supply that fits in a single 5-gallon bucket. Put together 10 of these buckets, and your six-month food plan is covered. Although a bit bland and monotonous, this basic menu provides 2,500 calories a day and only requires boiling to prepare, no oven baking required (which may not be an option in a grid-down situation). Just make sure that the shortening is stored outside of the buckets and rotated annually, as it will spoil. When packed with oxygen absorbers in a sealed Mylar bag, all of these dry goods should last for two to three decades.

Three-Week Menu Plan

42 Lunches and Dinners:
- 10 Plain Rice
- 10 Plain Beans
- 10 Pesto Pasta
- 12 Beans & Rice

21 Breakfasts:
- 7 Oatmeal
- 7 Grits
- 7 Cream of Wheat

Snacks
- Hard candy
- Sweetened beverages (tea, coffee, herb tea, etc.)

Shopping List for Each Three-Week Bucket
- 5-pound spaghetti pasta
- 11-pound white rice
- 11-pound mixed beans
- 2-pound sugar
- 1-pound hard candy
- 1-pound rolled oats
- 1-pound corn grits
- 1-pound cream of wheat
- 5 packs of pesto pasta mix
- 1 package of black tea, coffee, or herb tea
- 2 sticks of butter-flavored shortening (not stored inside bucket)
- Assorted salt, pepper, and dry seasonings as desired

Store it in the Right Spot

To get the maximum life span from your stored food, it's critical to store it in a food-friendly location in your home or bug-out site. The traits of a good food storage spot include the following:

› **Dark:** Light can damage some foods and shorten their life span.

› **Cool:** Heat is one of the most destructive forces to food. A few months in a hot garage or vehicle will drop the shelf life of your MREs to just a few months. Cool temperatures are critical to storage, and it's best if temps don't fluctuate.

› **Dry:** Moisture can allow mold and bacteria to flourish in stored food. Pick a dry spot to begin with, and package your food to keep moisture out.

› **Protected From Pests:** Hungry rodents can chew through MRE bags and plastic food buckets in a matter of minutes. Set mouse traps and rat traps around your food storage area. For greater security, place the food in metal containers like job site tool boxes, steel barrels, or metal garbage cans.

A dry basement, cool closet, or secure pantry works in most cases, though these are likely spots to be searched if looting occurs after a crisis cuts off your shopping trips. Consider mislabeling some bins of food or hiding food in floors, walls, ceilings, or furniture to give you a backup if your home is pillaged. Buckets buried in the flowerbed are another option in food security. Although this is more vulnerable to moisture and rodents, it offers protection from both house fires and theft. Use regular bucket lids when burying buckets.

It's All About the Calories

Consider 432,000 calories. In a world of dieting and calorie counting, this sounds like a huge number. But once you've done the research and the math, you'll see that this seemingly large number of calories only supports a sedentary man between the ages of 19 and 30 for a span of six months, using the USDA model of 2,400 calories a day. Sedentary females (and males that are younger or older) will require fewer calories, and of course active people will need a higher caloric intake. Calories should be your major concern when building a food storage system. Read the labels and add up the calories for yourself. Ignore the "servings per package" notations as they're often based on ridiculously small portions. For a short-term emergency, any food is better than none. But over a long-term crisis, a calorie deficit could have a major impact on your energy levels — and ultimately your survival.

Common Mistakes to Avoid

Mistakes are a natural part of the learning curve, but mistakes in food storage can be disastrous, leaving you with an empty wallet and an empty belly. Learn from the failures of others, and avoid these blunders yourself.

> **Forget the water.** Store several large containers of safe drinking water and the disinfection supplies to refill them over and over.

> **Store dry and wet together.** Jugs of water, cans of wet food, and any other containers of liquid should always be stored outside of bins and buckets of food. If they leak, the food may get ruined and you wouldn't know it until you needed the food (and opened it). I recently learned this one the hard way — a jug of water leaked inside a bin of dry food and converted it into a bin of black mold.

> **Food expires?** Write the expiration date on food cans and packages with a marker for easier inspection, and check your food seasonally for aging items.

> **Heap it up in a pile.** Stock your pantry like a store does, placing new items in the back and pushing older items forward. This helps to create an easy rotation of goods.

Survival Charcuterie

Making Your Own Jerky

Story and Photos by Tim MacWelch

Forget everything you've ever learned about food safety and the proper handling of meat. Ignore the sound advice you heard in cooking school. Disregard that appalling silly VHS training tape you watched before working in that restaurant. Throw all your ideas of sanitary food prep to the wind. The age-old process of making jerky is in direct opposition with the modern ideals of the time and temperature of safe meat storage.

We're going to take raw meat, trim off the fat, dry it out in the sun — and somehow, almost magically — it's going to be safe to eat later.

So whether you're a hunter, a protein lover, or a hard-core prepper, knowing how to handle raw meat is an important skill. But what if you've harvested a larger animal than you can eat in one sitting? Or several animals at once? How do you make sure your precious protein lasts longer? In this article, we're going to bring back a skill that's an oldie but a goodie, we're going to show you how to make your own traditional-style jerky.

All it takes is fresh raw meat and a dry day to learn some invaluable jerky-making skills. And if you haven't figured out yet that jerky production is a good skill to know, just ponder how you'd store meat in a grid-down or wilderness setting. No freezer or pressure canner is likely to be available. This leaves drying as you're only real preservation solution. Don't worry about homespun jerky being some horrible archaic food, like acorn mush. We've all slavered over the savory goodness of jerky. And with a little care and attention, you can make good jerky, too. Hungry for it yet? Let's prepare some now.

The Ingredients

The actual word "jerky" is believed to come from the Quechua word "ch'arki," meaning salted, dried meat. However, jerky has had many names across the time and diverse locations it has been made. Bull cheese, biltong, jerk, meat floss, kilishi, and other colorful names have been applied to this traditional staple food item. But don't think this is just some primitive tribal snack. Beef jerky has even been approved as astronaut food! NASA has supplied hungry space shuttle crews with this tasty, compact, high-protein snack since the 1990s. Here's what you'll need to start making jerky on your own.

Firewood: Hickory, mesquite, maple, and many other classic food-smoking woods are excellent choices for your firewood and smoke producers. Stay away from woods that produce a resinous black smoke, like pine, firm, and spruce. Also do your research to find out if you have any toxic woods in your area, and don't use those for cooking or smoking.

Fire-Starter: It's your call on this one. It could be the humble Bic lighter or a bow and drill set.

Meat: What kind of meat is jerky meat? It's whatever meat you have. Deer and beef are excellent, but virtually any edible animal will work. Just pay attention to the fat. It must all be removed before drying the meat. It must also be raw to safely last through long-term storage.

The Rack: A free-standing tripod with cross bars is my favorite type of jerky rack, though many things can work. Hang the strips from a handy branch or dangle them from a string. Set them on a window screen, oven rack, or dishwasher rack that you have taken outside. You could even lay the meat on rocks, concrete, bricks, or some other absorptive surface, though dangling in the air is usually the fastest way to dry the meat.

Spices, Seasonings, and Preservatives: Salt, pepper, vinegar, garlic powder, soy sauce, a wide range of spices and many other items have been used to flavor jerky and assist in the preservation of it.

The Steps To Jerky Heaven

Once your decisions have been made and your ingredients rallied, it's time to go to work. It's the hope of all jerky makers that the weather will cooperate on jerky day, but if not — there are options. Follow these steps and you'll make your ancestors proud!

Step 1: Start off with fresh, raw meat and cut it into thin strips. As you work, remove all visible fat and throw it into a stew or find some other good use for those valuable calories. Most people prefer tender jerky, which usually comes from cuts that are perpendicular to the muscle fiber (perpendicular to the bone that was in the meat). Other jerky makers, however, prefer to cut with the grain of the muscle (in the direction that it once stretched and contracted). Try some both ways on your first batch to see which you prefer.

Step 2: Add salt, sugar, spices, and/or vinegar to the meat. This can be done by sprinkling dry ingredients, soaking, or wiping on wet ingredients. The meat could also be soaked in a marinade or brine at this time. Make sure there is no oil in the marinade, as it will go rancid in the finished product. Some of these items, like the pepper, are just there for taste.

Other items, however, are there to help preserve the meat. Salt, sugar, and vinegar do a great job in discouraging the growth of bacteria, the primary organism behind spoilage. Salt creates a saline environment in the meat, which keeps harmful organisms from taking over. And vinegar creates an acidic environment, which helps to keep the bacterial hordes at bay. If you don't have any flavorings or preserving agents, move on to step three.

Step 3: Hang the meat on your rack, string it up with twine, or lay it out to dry. Do this in the sun, preferably on a dry and breezy day — and a few feet downwind of a tiny smoky fire. It's best if the frame or string of drying meat is mobile. This allows you to move the meat into the smoke if the wind shifts, and chase the sun as it travels. And never leave your jerky unattended, for a variety of reasons.

Step 4: Dry the meat until it begins to feel stiff and leathery. On a rack or flat surface, turn each piece so that any damp shady spots get exposed to sunlight. Continue drying, keeping the meat in the smoke, but not directly over the heat. Dry the meat until it becomes brittle when

Maggots!

Maggots! These little devils really add the "yuck" factor to the jerky-making process, but don't throw your precious food source away just because it's started moving again. Flies and their larvae are nuisances during the early stages of the jerky process, but they are easily repelled by using smoke or increasing your smoke output. Just remember to keep the meat bathed in smoke, yet away from the heat. Cooked meat spoils much faster than raw meat. And if some tenacious flies do make it past the smoke screen, simply wipe off the egg clusters (or moving maggots) and return the meat to the drying rack. You may not spot them at first, as the egg masses tend to get deposited underneath the jerky strips, but you'll usually find them when you turn the jerky over for the first time while drying. Then, once the meat gets a crusty skin on it, the flies tend to leave it alone anyway.

bent. Red meat will turn purplish-brown. White meat will turn grayish-pink.

If the weather takes a turn on jerky day or your meat hasn't dried all the way before dark, move all the meat into shelter and finish the drying process the next day. Don't leave it out overnight. The dampness is bad, but the scavengers are worse. It's probably going to be gone in the morning. In extended wet weather, you'll have to dry the meat with the heat of the fire. This will buy you a few days of storage before it spoils, as will using cooked meat for jerky in the first place. But it's not safe to store cooked, dried salted meat past one week.

Step 5: Store the finished jerky in a dry paper bag, cloth sack, wooden box, or some other breathable container. This keeps the jerky from sweating and helps it to last longer. If the weather is cool and dry, jerky like this may last for weeks or months. In humid weather, eat it as soon as you can, but stop using it if the meat becomes moldy or takes on a bad smell. Trust your eyes and nose when storing jerky under questionable damp conditions.

Conclusion

You were warned that safe food handling ideals would be thrown out the window in this article, and they certainly were — by allowing raw meat to lie about in warm weather. But consider the fact that many ancestral cultures used jerky as a valuable staple food item, trade good, pet food, and even as a currency. So if your power goes out while you have a deep chest freezer full of steaks, now you know what to do with your rapidly melting investment of meat — make a mountain of jerky!

Regardless of whether you are a bushwhacker, homesteader, or urban survivalist, the skill of jerky making has some serious benefits and there's no better time to start honing your skills than right now. Grab the rack out of your oven, hang salted meat all over it, and set it on a sunny balcony or deck to become the salty little jerky bits that they were meant to be. Enjoy!

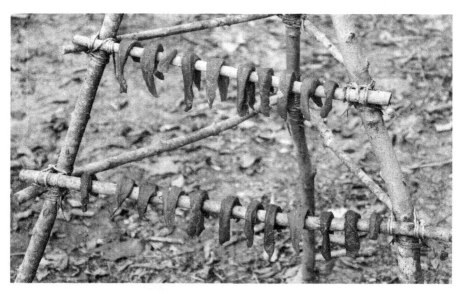

Best Meats

Don't feel like cattle and deer are the only creatures that can transform into jerky. Any raw meat from any edible animal species can be dried and preserved using the techniques listed here. But not all jerky is equal. The red meat and white meat mammals are certainly prime candidates for jerky, but edible birds, reptiles, and fish can turn into jerky as well. They may not be as appetizing as dried red meat, but they do work.

Fish jerky, wild turkey jerky, snapping turtle jerky, gator jerky, whatever jerky – all can provide nourishment, but perhaps not the dining experience you were hoping to receive. Freshwater fish jerky is probably the worst, being fairly awful under ideal conditions. While deer, beef, elk, moose, buffalo, and similar animals are global favorites and should be your top choice – if choice is an option. If not, then turn whatever beast you have into a salty spicy jerky. If you dial up the seasonings, it really dials down the gag reflex.

A Final Step for the Faint of Heart

When eating jerk, you're eating raw meat. This can bother some people. Around my camp, there is one bonus step before jerky consumption – this is some form of cooking. An easy and tasty way is to impale the dried meat strip on a pointy stick and toast it briefly over the campfire. This changes the color and the flavor (in a good way), and it kills any live organisms that are lingering on the jerky's surface or inside it. This extra step could be considered paranoid, but in many ways, it just feels right. Another common use for jerky is in soups, broth, and stew. The jerky can be pounded with a clean dry rock, until it is pulverized. Add this powder to hot water and simmer for half an hour. The resulting broth is full of somewhat tender slivers of meat and very welcomed on a cold day.

Grid-Down Chef

Use These Makeshift Cooking Methods When Conventional Means Are Unavailable

Story and Photos
By Jim Cobb

Let's see a show of hands. After a long, hard day, who doesn't like a hot meal? Yep, that's what we thought. Make no mistake, the aftermath of a crisis or disaster will require large investments of sweat equity in order to put things right again. From cleaning up storm debris to helping neighbors track down lost pets, you'll be burning quite a few calories. A protein bar and sack of trail mix won't cut it, not after the first day or so. You and your family will want to be able to prepare at

least some semblance of a real meal.

On top of being able to cook actual food, having a heating source means you can boil water for disinfection. Run the water through a coffee filter to remove sediment and dead bugs, then boil it to kill off all the nasty stuff you can't see that could surely make your day a whole lot worse.

When your oven, stove top, and microwave aren't viable options due to interruptions in utility services, you'll need one or more backup methods for food preparation. Even those who have stockpiled loads of dehydrated and freeze-dried meals will need boiling water to reconstitute them before eating.

Fortunately, there are several options available for off-grid cooking. Follow along, and we'll show you how to become a grid-down Gordon Ramsey.

Patio Grills

You do realize you can cook far more than just steak and ribs on a patio grill, right? Yes, that ubiquitous piece of equipment taking up space on decks and in backyards from coast to coast can do more than just turn chicken breasts into chicken briquettes. Whether yours is propane or charcoal, make sure you always have plenty of fuel on hand. For our gas grill, we like to have at least one, but preferably two full tanks sitting in the garage in addition to the one hooked up to the grill.

Watch for sales on charcoal, typically just before Memorial Day, Fourth of July, and Labor Day. It's a good idea to keep a minimum of four full bags on hand at all times. Charcoal is nice to have as a backup, even if you don't have a charcoal grill. The next time you're at the dollar store, pick up a few of the disposable aluminum baking pans, the ones that are a few inches deep like you'd use to bake a chicken. Fill the bottom of one with charcoal,

toss on some lighter fluid, and let her rip. Voilà — instant grill. Do this outside, of course. Trying this inside, say on your stovetop, will invite very bad things into your life. You can buy folding grill grates that work great to put over this type of makeshift grill.

Another helpful tip: Charcoal isn't the only fuel you can use in a charcoal grill. If you lack briquettes, bust up some dry branches and make a campfire inside the grill. Sometimes you need to think outside the box, right?

Patio grills are admittedly not the most efficient tools for boiling water or cooking pasta, but most of us already have them on hand so there's little to no extra investment involved.

2 Campfires

If you have a spot in the backyard for it, a campfire can provide nice ambience as well as the ability to cook a meal. If your backyard is more of postage stamp rather than a pasture, perhaps you have one of those patio fire pits that can stand in for the role of the campfire. Either way, you'll need plenty of fuel on hand, so don't toss every leaf, twig, or downed branch into your yard waste recycling bin.

Fair warning, though. If the extent of your campfire cooking ends at s'mores, get some practice before you truly need to cook a meal over an open flame. There's just as much art as there is skill with campfire cooking. Cook over the glowing coals, not over the actual flames. The heat will be higher, but far more stable.

Camp Stoves

What we might consider traditional camp stoves usually come in a couple different styles. The first is a single burner that rests on top of the fuel bottle. These are very popular with hikers and backpackers as they're small, light, and easy to pack. The other style is larger, roughly akin to a small briefcase. These will have two burners, which obviously allow you to use more than one pot or pan at a time.

As you shop around, pay attention to the fuel needed for each stove. Some use propane, others use butane, or perhaps unleaded gasoline. There are dual-fuel stoves, too. For our money, if we were buying a camp stove to use as a backup cooking method at home, we'd go with a two-burner propane-fueled model.

Why? Well, a simple 5-foot adapter hose allows you to connect the 20-pound propane tank from your grill straight to the stove. That way, you don't have to mess with the smaller tanks that are made specifically for these stoves. Cooking on these stoves requires no investment in special camp cookware, either. If you can use it on a gas stove in the house, you can use it on one of these camp stoves. The heat is easy to regulate, too, so you're less apt to burn your meal.

BioLite Stove

The BioLite Stove has been on the market for a couple of years now and is a remarkable piece of kit. In essence, it allows you to charge your cell phone or other device while cooking your dinner at the same time. The BioLite converts heat energy to electricity. This power is first used to run a small fan in the base of the stove, which greatly increases the efficiency of the BioLite, turning it into a small rocket stove.

Excess electricity can then be siphoned off and into your device by means of a USB port on the side of the stove. While you won't be powering your refrigerator with the stove, it'll let you keep tabs on news or weather reports via your smartphone.

Biofuel Stoves

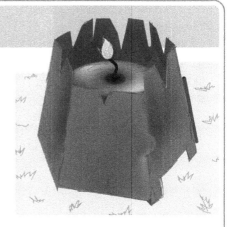

Biofuel means sticks, twigs, branches, pinecones, that sort of stuff. Think of a biofuel stove as a contained and controlled campfire. These stoves tend to be rather small, so your fuel won't be much larger than what you'd use for kindling in a normal campfire or fireplace.

The advantage these stoves have is their compact size. Stocking up on fuel means gathering up branches the storm brought down in your backyard. The stoves are easy to store until needed. The Vargo Hexagon Wood Stove, for example, folds up flat when not in use and will fit just about anywhere.

The downside, though, is that these stoves are pretty much one-pan-at-a-time deals. You won't be cooking any elaborate meals with these little stoves. But, let's face it, our need for calories in the wake of a disaster will far outweigh the disappointment of not seeing seven separate courses being served at the dinner table. One-pot meals will be the recipes of choice.

Fuel Tab Stoves

These are very similar to biofuel stoves in size. Instead of twigs and pinecones, though, these stoves use small hexamine tablets for fuel. These tablets burn hot, are smokeless, and store almost indefinitely under the right conditions. Despite the small size, one tablet will burn at least 10 full minutes and will bring 16 ounces of water to a boil in less than that.

One of the most common configurations of this type of stove is a folding model that, when closed, isn't much bigger than a deck of cards. As a bonus, extra fuel tabs will fit inside the stove for transport.

If you're lacking the stove, you can improvise by placing the fuel tab on an overturned tuna can or other surface. Place a couple of rocks or bricks on either side so you have something to keep your pan above the flame and you're good to go.

In my experience, you need a flame, such as a match or butane lighter, to get the fuel tab burning. A ferro rod won't light a fuel tab by itself. However, if that's all you have, take a small piece of tinder, such as a cotton ball, and place it on the stove. Place your fuel tab leaning on the tinder, then light the tinder with the ferro rod. A couple of boxes of these hexamine cubes aren't too costly, and if you keep them cool and dry, they'll last for years.

Alcohol Stoves

Alcohol stoves provide a steady flame, which can be an important consideration for those who aren't used to cooking over campfires and the like. However, these stoves can be a little more temperamental than some of the others we've discussed. Cold conditions in particular can prove to be vexing. Priming the stove, which involves warming the fuel prior to lighting, helps, but in some situations it becomes a case of lighting a small fire to warm your fuel to light your stove.

While the rubbing alcohol in your first-aid kit will burn, it isn't the best fuel for an alcohol stove. Far better is a bottle of HEET from the automotive department at your local discount retailer. Just make sure you get the yellow bottle, which is methanol. It will light faster and burn hotter and cleaner than rubbing alcohol.

You can find all sorts of videos online showing how to make an alcohol stove out of a soda or beer can. When done right, they do work fairly well. Both Vargo and Esbit make very nice alcohol stoves that aren't very expensive and are made to last. Another option is to take one of the ever-popular Altoids tins, fill it with perlite or vermiculite, then pour in a few tablespoons of alcohol. Light the vapors and you'll bring water to a boil shortly.

Foil-Pouch Cooking

One of the easiest meals to prepare over a fire uses nothing more than aluminum foil. Tear off a sheet about a foot long and coat the inside with nonstick spray or bit of cooking oil. Grab a bowl and crumble in a half pound of raw hamburger, a diced potato, a chopped carrot, and half a can of cream of mushroom soup. Mix it all together, then pour it onto the center of the foil. Sprinkle with garlic powder, salt, and pepper to taste.

Bring the long sides of the foil up, fold them together, and roll it down to the food. Then, roll up the short sides, making a nice compact package. Toss it right onto the coals of your fire for about 25 minutes or so.

Play around with different food combinations. The recipe above incorporates common ingredients, but there are many others utilizing various types of proteins and vegetables.

6 Solar Oven

There's little in life that preppers and survivalists love more than the word "free." Solar ovens allow you to cook your food using a free fuel: sunshine. These hot boxes are great at slow cooking your lunch or dinner. Provided, of course, it isn't the middle of the night.

There are numerous plans online detailing how to build a solar oven out of a cardboard box and some aluminum foil. It's important to pay attention to the placement of the oven to ensure you're gathering the most solar energy as possible. Rotate the oven periodically as the sun moves across the sky.

The drawback with solar ovens is that they aren't suited for any sort of quick meal. They're also very dependent upon the amount of sun peeking through the clouds. Because of these factors, your best option is to plan ahead and set it up right away in the morning so your food will be ready come lunchtime.

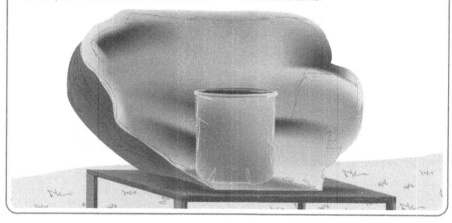

Cookware

In addition to the cooking solutions of your choice, you might consider investing in some cookware specifically for emergencies. Most of the pots and pans in the average household will not stand up to the higher heat generated by many of the stoves we've discussed, much less an open campfire or a charcoal grill. Plastic handles will melt and your pans could actually warp.

Any of the methods mentioned that involve a flame or coals may also leave a black residue on the bottom of your pots and pans. There's really no way around this happening but if you rub the bottom of the pan with a bar of soap prior to putting it on the fire, the soot will wash off easily.

Cast-iron cookware is the best way to go, if you can afford it and you don't plan on lugging it around anywhere. It's very heavy, of course, so it isn't really suited for the bug-out bag. On the upside, if you maintain it properly, a good set of cast-iron cookware can be passed down for generations. Bacon, cooked in a cast iron skillet over a campfire, is so good even the vegans in your group may break down and say, "OK, gimme a piece."

For those looking for something a little lighter, GSI Outdoors offers a great nesting set in the Pinnacle Base Camper Large, which includes two different pots, including lids, for boiling water or making soup, a good-sized frying pan, and a cutting board. As mentioned, everything nests together and fits into a nice carrying bag. There's even room to add in a couple of small utensils.

If you'll be cooking over a campfire at home, a tripod grill is a great investment. They allow you to place a few different pots and pans over the fire at the same time. You can also adjust the height of the grill to heat things up or cool them down a bit.

Keeping in mind that the most common cooking you'll likely be doing when on the road will be heating water — for disinfection or for adding to a dehydrated meal — a bush pot alone might suffice for the get-home bag. I like to have a stainless steel water bottle too, as that allows me to boil water while also heating up a can of stew or soup at the same time.

Off-grid cooking is not something you're likely to be entirely successful with the first time out. You're going to burn a meal or two in the beginning. You'll also run into problems keeping the fire going steadily, not cooking food long enough, or even dropping food right into the ashes. We all make mistakes; that's part of what makes us human. However, do yourself and your family a favor and practice using these stoves and other cooking solutions now, while you still have the option of having a pizza delivered if things don't go your way. ::

Like a Russian doll, the Pinnacle Base Camper Large from GSI Outdoors can reveal smaller treasures nestled inside.

Sources:

BioLite
www.bioliteenergy.com

GSI Outdoors
www.gsioutdoors.com

Vargo
www.vargooutdoors.com

How to Pick Up (and Raise) Chicks

Egg-Laying Chickens in Your Backyard Can Be a Move Toward Self-Sufficiency

Story and Photos by Jim DeLozier

There's nothing like eating truly fresh eggs. We know, the egg carton you buy at the local grocer says they're cage-free blah, blah, blah. But they're not nearly as fresh and tasty as the eggs you might get from a hen that just laid them that morning in your backyard. And they're even more satisfying because they came from *your* chickens. It's a process the whole family can participate in — it's a lot of work, but it's also a lot of fun.

No, this isn't *Farming Monthly*. But for many preparedness-minded folks, having a sustainable source of food on your property goes hand in hand with survivalism. That's why in this feature article we're flying beak-first into the topic of raising chickens.

Not everyone can raise poultry at home due to municipal codes and regulations, but that has changed a lot over the last few years. Many counties have passed ordinances stating that cities can't restrict people from producing food. Whether it's due to the growing hipster trend of organic foods or governments realizing the importance of sustainability, coops are sprouting up in urban and suburban areas more and more.

When we wanted to start raising chickens, we did a quick internet search for our county regulations and found that the city said no, but the county said yes (a maximum of six hens, but no roosters). The next thing we had to check was on our homeowners association (HOA) rules. Ironically, the HOA guidelines tried every way to say that we couldn't raise chickens without expressly forbidding it. We went ahead and bought some chicks and converted a playhouse into a hen house, to avoid calling attention to it. We generally believe it's better to beg for forgiveness than ask for permission. Also, the neighbors tend to be more supportive of your hens when you bring them fresh eggs — no one ratted us out.

After a year of covert chicken farming, we decided to move to an area where chickens were permitted and added many more.

Selection & Supplies

The first thing to decide is how many chicks and which type to buy. We advise you always buy more than one of any type of chicken and to be sure you have enough space. A general rule of thumb is to have at least 2 square feet per chicken, but we prefer about 6 square feet per chicken. We would also suggest that if you want to have six chickens, buy three each of two types or, at the very least, two each of three types.

The reason? Be prepared to lose at least one chick. As such, the tactical mindset of two is one and one is none comes into play here. If you buy two of each type and one dies, now you have one by itself. That doesn't bode well for solitary chickens, as we'll explain later.

Heat and Water

We bought a large plastic tub at a Costco for the incubator. Then we headed to the pet supply store to get some shavings for the bottom of the tub, as well as food and water dispensers.

You don't want your incubator to be too large; chicks can't manage their body heat very well, and it's easier to heat a smaller area. Some people prefer a red bulb for their lamp because it isn't as bright and lets the chicks sleep. Fill the bottom about

1-inch deep with shavings. It's important to place a thin brick, piece of wood, or a RCBS loading block under the water dispenser so fewer shavings go into the water as they "scratch" the shavings. If too many shavings make it into the water they clog the system and suck up the moisture, preventing the chicks from drinking. Chickens can become dehydrated easily, and this is a fast way to kill them.

Next, buy food and water dispensers with the canisters on top. Chicks can go through a lot of food and water in a day, and this helps to ensure they don't run out. The food they need when they're small is a fine crumble. If the crumble is still too large, run it through a food processor.

Take a piece of tubing and attach it to the top of the tub with cable ties to attach the heat lamp to. It doesn't need to be steel or even metal; any piece of wood or dowel will work. Attach it to the center or closer to one end, wherever is easiest and most secure. Do this so the light can be adjusted to be closer or further away from the chicks by rotating it up or down. When chicks are smaller, the light needs to be closer to produce more heat. When they're bigger, the light needs to be higher so they can move around freely.

As soon as their feathers start to develop, they can maintain their body temperatures better, but they can also fly the coop. If these are your only chickens and it isn't too cold outside they can go to their permanent housing once their feathers come in. If you have adult chickens or if it's still cold outside, it's better to build a small hen house for them that can be easily assembled inside the house.

Building the House

Let Home Depot cut the wood for you so you don't have to do it. Buy two 4x8-foot sheets of OSB or plywood (whichever is less expensive). The first sheet should be cut into four equal-sized pieces of 2x4 feet, and the second piece cut in half at 4x4 feet.

Also buy some punched angle bracket material to put it together. If you don't have an angle grinder, cutoff saw, or chop saw, you can buy these in specific sizes.

The finished sizes are approximately (four) 36-inch pieces and (four) 12- to 16-inch pieces. You'll also need a roll of painter's plastic drop-cloth, some 2½-inch drywall screws, short screws (½-inch), and some staples for your staple gun. Some sort of mesh covering to keep the chickens inside the small pen and the roof of the hen house (approximately 4x8 feet) may also be desired when you put them inside their permanent home. Bring the punch angle, short screws, staples, and the cut wood into the room with the chickens along with the staple gun and screw gun.

Create a box by first connecting two of the sides (2x4) with one of the shorter punched-angle sections and some screws. Repeat until all four sides are connected, then place the larger section (4x4 feet) on top of the four sides. Once this is in place, connect it to the sides with remaining sections of bracket material and more screws. When it has been secured to the sides, flip it over and line the bottom with your plastic drop-cloth and staple it into place, making sure the plastic material comes up the sides approximately 6 to 12 inches so that any spilled water or waste doesn't escape.

Place the new pen where you plan to leave it and then add your shavings. Once this is done, remove the tube or dowel from the tub, drill a hole through each corner wall near the top of the small pen, and attach it to the corner of the new pen. Choose a corner that's close to an electrical outlet and position the heat lamp on it. Put it under the top of the wall so it's closer to the chicks, providing more heat and so you can cover the pen with the mesh.

Put your chicks in along with the food and water dispensers, cover it with the mesh, and watch them grow.

Enclosure Tips

We've tried many different types of enclosures for the chicken coop/hen house. The premade pressboard units at box stores aren't very good. They tend to be small, difficult to clean, and poorly made. For the same cost you can purchase a

Chicks get cold and dehydrated easily, so we built a pen for them with a heat lamp, food dispenser, and water.

much better solution. Our current configuration is a 10x10-foot chain-link dog kennel with a walk-in gate that costs about $250 and took about 20 minutes to assemble with only two adjustable wrenches. It comes as four premade sections with two clamps on each corner. It's 6 feet tall, so we can walk in to clean it and fill the food and water dispensers.

As before, we buy the wood in lengths we can use without having to do much cutting. Build a frame for the roof out of 2x4-inch studs in varying lengths: (two) 12-inch, (three) 10-inch, and (three) 92 5/8-inch studs. Make sure when you lay out the frame for your roof, it remains 10 feet wide. It will actually be 12 feet, 3 inches long if done correctly, so it will hang over by 2 feet, 3 inches to cover your laying box. The third 10-foot stud will need approximately 3 inches cut off on one end to fit inside the frame. Once it's cut, lay it inside the frame, but don't attach it yet. Take the three 92 5/8-inch studs and place them approximately 2 feet apart (lengthwise), and butt them up to one end and to the piece you just cut.

Once they are properly laid out, secure them with the 2½-inch drywall screws. You should have an area 8x10 feet with full support for two full sheets and one half sheet of plywood or oriented strand board (OSB). This will provide shade and shelter the chickens when it rains or snows. Caulk the seams and paint the surface so it looks better and lasts longer.

The open area can be covered with wire mesh to keep birds of prey and other critters from getting to your girls. After all this is finished, line the perimeter of the enclosure with rocks. This keeps predators from digging in and the chickens from digging out. Chickens don't dig tunnels to escape, but they do claw and scratch the ground. Eventually, there will be openings they can use to get out.

The Egg Box

Next, build a three-sided box and attach it to the side of the structure into the end post and center post. Drill through the posts and use the 2½-inch drywall screws to attach the box. The top of the box should be hinged, preferably with a long piano-type hinge keeping it strong, so you can extract the eggs without having to go inside the hen house. Once the box is attached, cut the chain-link in a square where the chickens can go inside to lay their precious eggs.

Once the hole is cut, bend the wire from the chain-link back so the sharp ends are not an issue. Make a ramp for them

to walk up with small pieces of wood attached to it for traction. Connect it to the edge of the box with some drywall screws. We use buss-tubs filled with hay for their nesting and laying area. At first we had a separate tub for each hen, but they all laid their eggs in the same tub so now we have just two.

Compatibility

When you put chickens together, a pecking order will be created. While humans might use this phrase to describe a hierarchical organization, it originally came from the observation of chickens establishing dominance by pecking others and/or chasing them around. When introducing new adult hens to the coop, we put them in at night, and they seem to get along without issue. When combining your new chicks with your older chickens, a much longer process is required.

Birds of a feather flock together. You may have heard that as a child, but do you

Layers of Production

Some types of egg-laying chickens, or "layers," are more productive than others. However, egg size and frequency will fluctuate regardless of breed. This author chose his breeds based on egg output, disease resistance, temperature tolerance, and friendliness. Here are the types he owns and the approximate egg productivity:

〉 **Buff Orpington:** 180 eggs per year
〉 **Hybrid:** 280 to 300 eggs per year
〉 **Leghorn:** 250 to 260 eggs per year
〉 **Plymouth Rock:** 200 eggs per year
〉 **Rhode Island Red:** 250 to 260 eggs per year

Other popular breeds are Sussex, Ancona, Austalorp, Barnevelder, and Hamburg.

know what it really means? While civilization has progressed to some semblance of tolerance and acceptance, nature has not. Recently, this author's friends wanted to raise chicks. They bought three Rhode Island Reds and one that was possibly a Dark Cornish hen. After realizing they had allergy issues, the friends brought them to us. We merged them in with our three

Lesson Not Learned: This young Dark Cornish hen wasn't accepted by the older chickens in the coop and was viciously attacked. The author immediately separated her from the others, but she eventually flew over the barrier — yes, chickens can fly — and back into the hen house, where she was killed by the older birds.

Orpingtons, three Plymouth Rocks, and two bantams that the author's daughter absolutely had to have.

All was well in the tub and the small box, but when we put the young ones in with older hens, it was obvious that the Dark Cornish was not welcome. We sectioned off a portion of the hen house by putting a temporary kennel fence that segregated the young ones from the hens, yet still allowed them to get acquainted to each other. After a couple weeks of total separation, we allowed them to be together for short periods.

We keep a spray bottle close as a training aid for the older hens, giving a quick squirt when they peck the new ones too aggressively.

On the first day of this process we supervised closely for about an hour and left them alone for a short time to integrate. The Dark Cornish was brutally attacked by the six older hens, removing feathers, flesh, and tissue. We separated them immediately and put the Dark Cornish in solitary confinement to let her heal. Yet, she intentionally flew over the barrier to be with the other chicks. They continued the assault, so we separated her again. The Dark Cornish once again flew over the barrier into the area with the grown hens. Not surprisingly, she was killed.

Eggxpert Tip

After eating the eggs, mix the leftover shells with chicken poop and coffee grounds for an amazing base and combine that with compost to grow plants.

The rest seem to get along OK — even the bantams. The pecking order is being established, but there are no bloody chicks. Occasionally, one of the older chickens becomes a problem, attacking the chicks, and must be eliminated from the flock to preserve community spirit.

Living Conditions

Chickens can lay eggs for many years, but productivity will fluctuate and will steadily decrease as they age. You'll know which chickens are laying and which ones are not by the egg color. Interestingly enough, the white Leghorns lay white eggs, the tan hybrids lay tan eggs, and the Rhode Island Reds lay brown eggs. It's a little comical to see them separated into three groups by color, as birds of a feather flock together.

Extreme cold or heat can limit production, as well as stress or shortage of food or water. They need lots of protein and plenty of sunshine. We let our girls run around in the yard often. However, we used to let them "free range" all day until we started losing them to coyotes. Once a predator knows where your chickens are, they'll come back again and again until they're all gone.

Also, you don't want your chickens laying eggs around your yard. Let them out in the late morning after the laying has been done. Herding chickens back into the coop isn't any easier than herding cats. We use a long stick to help direct them back to the gate, but it doesn't always work very well. They'll hurry themselves back into the coop if you train them by giving them the remnants of fruit and vegetables. They literally run back in once they see the pie tin we use to carry the scraps of lettuce, apple core, grapes, fruit, or whatever we have laying around.

Handling Eggs

Our eggs are so tasty because they aren't refrigerated. A fresh egg will keep for weeks provided you follow a few simple rules:

- Don't wash them when you collect them. There may mud, dirt, feathers, or whatever on them when you collect them, but that's OK. There's a film on them called the "bloom" that will allow them to keep for weeks. Store them just as they are in a cool dry place (not in direct sunlight) with the pointy side down.
- When ready to eat, rinse them off in warm water to remove the debris and revel in the wonderful flavor of your fresh eggs.
- You'll need to refrigerate them if you want hard-boiled eggs. The shells are difficult to remove if they haven't been chilled before you boil them.
- Some people crush the shells and put them into the chicken food providing essential nutrients for them, but it's not recommended. Once a hen gets acquainted with the taste of the shells it might start pecking the eggs — even chickens love the taste of fresh eggs! Obviously, this can create a big problem. Again, a hen like this may need to be eliminated from the flock to preserve the integrity of the project.

Temperature

Some things to consider when raising chickens include temperature, moisture, snow, and other elements. Don't be afraid to leave them out in the cold — they have their own little down jackets. Their feathers are great insulators, so they'll be fine in

temperatures below freezing, even below zero. However, their water will freeze, and they'll die from dehydration.

We use an electric heater base that turns on automatically when the temperature reaches 36 degrees F. Conversely, when the temperature is above 80 degrees, they go through a lot more water, so you must keep their dispenser(s) full.

When it rains or snows, the ground can become saturated with moisture, which isn't good for chickens. During winter, place a tarp over the mesh portion of the roof and to cover one more side, keeping rain and snow out. Snow is much heavier and will accumulate on the tarp, which will collapse if not supported. Add some more studs to the section of the roof that's exposed so you can cover it with OSB during winter. After the ground has become moist from the elements, it tends to create a hard surface that the chickens cannot scratch.

This can be remedied with a pitchfork by churning the top layer and breaking it up.

Food and Water

The water dispensers should be elevated above the ground so they don't get muddy. We put them on large landscaping bricks, but you can use whatever you wish provided it keeps the water clean. While the chickens are "scratching" the ground they kick dirt into the water dispenser, turning it into a muddy mess that makes their water undrinkable.

It's better to cover their food dispensers and hang them from the roof or from a perch so the chickens don't sit on them. Where they sit is where they poop, and you definitely don't want poop in their food. We put one perch about 42 inches above the ground and another at about 18 inches above the ground. They have no problem getting to either.

Noise Concerns

Also, we were surprised at how loud our hens are. We thought only roosters made noise, but that's not true. Chickens can be heard from approximately 100 yards away. This is good information if you're trying to be covert about your chickens. In fact, we get excited when our girls are very loud because it often means a very large egg, but be aware of this in case you have neighbors who are sensitive about noise and might make a habit of complaining to the police. That could potentially put a stop to your entire chicken operation or possibly burden you with fines.

Like anything else, your experience may be different than ours, but you won't know until you cross that road. Get out there and make it happen!

The Chicken or the Egg?

How come this feature is only about the eggs? Raising table chickens (AKA meat chickens) is not all that dissimilar to raising egg-laying chickens except that they should be fed higher percentages of protein so they gain weight faster. We don't raise table chickens because we don't want to breed them, and it's not exactly cost effective to raise a bird for five to 12 weeks for *one* meal.

However, if you have the space and don't mind roosters (and their crowing), you can add a rooster into the mix – about six hens per rooster – and allow them to reproduce. If you want to raise chickens for meat without breeding them, it's less expensive to buy chicks that have not been sexed, usually equal numbers of males and females, and raise them for the table. Meat chickens are typically referred to as Cornish game hens when they're young, then as broilers or fryers (six to eight weeks old), and later as roasters (three to four months old).

Sometimes we end up with meat chickens by accident. Case in point: One beautiful black bantam hen with orange plumes turned out to be a cock. We figured it out when he crowed early one morning and never stopped. And because our local laws don't allow us to have roosters, table chicken he became. Eviscerating a chicken is too long to discuss here, so stay tuned for a feature on that topic in a future issue.

A Dish Served Hot

Building a DIY Parabolic Solar Cooker for Grid-Down Grub

Story and Photos By Michael Janich

The end of the world as we know it will also mean the end of pizza delivery and fast-food cheeseburgers. When your Happy Meal no longer lives up to its name, you'll not only have to worry about what to eat, but how to cook it without a functioning power grid. And one option you should consider for post-apocalyptic food prep is a solar cooker.

While not ideal when it's cloudy, in cold environments, or in a bug-out situation, a sun-powered cooker can work wonders in a grid-down scenario. Remember when a fire at a substation caused a power outage that crippled San Francisco for seven hours back in April? Considering how fragile our power grid is, it's not hard to imagine something similar happening on a wider scale — and for a longer period.

Enter the DIY parabolic solar cooker. "A para what now?" you might ask.

There are basically three types of solar-powered cookers: a solar oven, a solar panel cooker, and a parabolic cooker. (For info on the other two styles, check out "Daylight Dining," our buyer's guide on various commercial solar cookers, page 28.)

Parabolic cookers are like shiny satellite dishes that focus sunlight on a central point. Their concentrated focus can generate extreme heat quickly and can be used to fry food. (If you're thinking heat ray or Death Star, well, me too.) This design cooks faster and takes better advantage of short periods of sunlight, so it was the perfect choice for this DIY project.

Cardboard, and Lots of it

The inspiration for my parabolic solar cooker was actually a large cardboard box from an industrial shelving unit in my garage. Too big to fit in the recycle bin and made of the heavy, double-thickness corrugated cardboard that's a pain in the ass to break down, it ended up being the perfect "free" material for a reflector body. It was also typical of the material you might actually be able to scrounge in a TEOTWAWKI scenario.

I wanted to design the reflector so it was as large as possible, given the material on hand. Although a reflector can have as many panels as you want, the more you have, the more efficient it is. I also wanted the focal point to be above the reflector to provide easy access to the cooking pot. To do all that, you need to get your math geek on and discover the wonders of parabolas.

A parabola is an arc formed by a series of points that are equidistant from a single point and a line. For things like reflectors and satellite dishes, the single point is the focal point where the reflected rays will converge and the line is a straight reference line below it.

The Recipe

Here are the basic tools and materials you'll need to build this DIY solar cooker. Since the premise was to use scavenged cardboard as the basis for the reflector, the size of your scrounged cardboard will determine the size of your finished cooker and the dimensions of the other components, like 2x4s, plywood, etc. That's why no specific dimensions are given for them.

Tools
› Measuring tape
› T-square
› Spring clamp
› 550 cord
› Pencil

- Heavy-duty duct tape
- Utility knife
- Scissors
- Jigsaw
- Drill and drill bits
- Hammer

Materials

- ½-inch plywood (for the panel form)
- Two 1x4 boards (for the panel form)
- Sheet of paper
- Large corrugated cardboard box(es)
- Spray adhesive
- Heavy-duty aluminum foil
- Metal drywall corner
- Two 1-inch 8-32 screws with flat washers and nuts
- Three 6-inch ¼-20 carriage bolts with flat washers and wing nuts
- 2x4s (for the supporting frame)
- 3-inch deck screws
- Three lengths of ½-inch electrical conduit
- Grill grate
- Binding wire

Tee (Square) Time

To draw the arc of the parabola, get a rectangle of plywood a little longer than your planned panel length and about two-thirds as tall. The bottom edge of the plywood should be straight. You'll also need some 550 cord and a long T-square.

Take the length of your cardboard material and subtract 8 inches. Using that measurement and starting from the left edge of the plywood, measure along the top edge and make a mark. That will become the focal point. Anchor one end of the 550 cord to the focal point and attach the other end to the end of the T-square. The loop of cord between the focal point and the T-square, when doubled, should come a few inches short of the plywood's straight edge.

Starting with the head of the T-Square against the straight edge at the bottom of the plywood, place a marker in the cord loop and pull it tight. Now, slide the T-square to the left along the straight edge, keeping pressure on the marker so the 550 cord attached to the T-square stays perpendicular to the bottom edge of the plywood. As you do this, the marker will ride the string to scribe a parabolic arc.

If all that sounds too confusing, search the Internet for videos of "drawing a parabola with string," and you'll get a better idea.

The arc on the plywood is half the shape of your parabola, and the distance between the bottom of the arc and the focal point is its focal length. Measure that distance and write it down. Then, draw a line perpendicular to the plywood's bottom edge up to the focal point. The L-shaped area enclosed by that line, the arc, the left side of the plywood, and the bottom edge will be your parabola form. Cut it out with a saber saw, place it on the remaining piece of plywood, trace around it, and cut out another matching piece.

Use a piece of heavy-duty duct tape to secure the narrow ends of the plywood pieces together like a hinge. Fold a piece of paper once to get a 45-degree angle, then again to get 22.5 degrees — 1/16 of a 360-degree circle. Spread the wide ends of the forms apart until the interior angle matches the paper's 22.5 degrees, then measure the gap at the wide end and cut two pieces of board to that length. Tape or nail the boards in place, making a form for your panels (or the start of a really small skateboard ramp).

Cut a rectangle of cardboard as wide

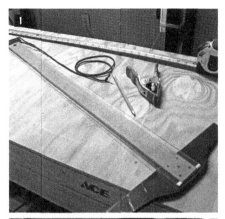

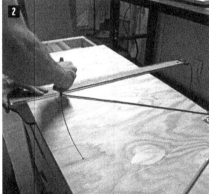

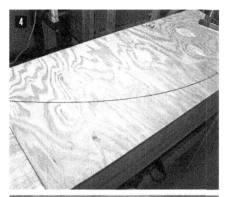

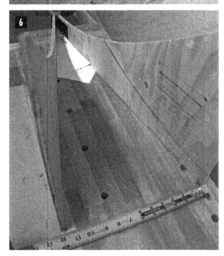

1. Hey, math boy ... these tools are how real parabolas are made.

2. & 3. Drawing the parabola to make the panel form.

4. Once the parabola form is drawn, cut it out with a jigsaw and make an identical second one.

5. To make a reflector with 16 panels, each is 1/16 of a 360-degree circle, or 22.5 degrees. Fold a piece of paper twice to get a reference.

6. Use the paper reference to set the angle at the apex of the form, then measure the wide end.

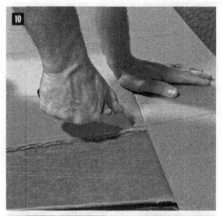

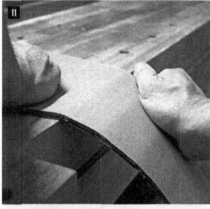

7. The finished form for marking the panel template.

8. Clamp a piece of cardboard to the form and trace both sides to make a template.

9. Use the template to mark the cardboard for the panels.

10. Carefully cut out the panels ... all 16 of them.

11. Crease the panels every couple of inches to create a curve.

12. A light coat of spray adhesive will allow the aluminum foil to stick.

as the back of your form and longer than its base. Clamp one end to the front of the form, press the cardboard down to fit the curve, and use a pencil to trace along the outside of the form on each side. These are your cutting lines for your panel pattern. Cut it out, then trace around it on your cardboard material, "nesting" all 16 pieces to minimize waste.

After cutting out all 16 panels, use the edge of a table to crease each one every few inches so they bend to fit the curve of the plywood form.

Shiny Things

For the reflective surface of the panels, hit the grocery store and get several rolls of heavy-duty aluminum foil. Apply a light coat of spray adhesive to each panel, then carefully apply the foil. I found folding it in half lengthwise, positioning the center, and then smoothing it from the center out worked best. Use the base of your palm or fingertips — not your fingernails — to keep it as smooth and reflective as possible. Then, trim the foil a couple of inches around the perimeter of the panel, notch the edge every few inches with scissors to create relief tabs, and stick the tabs to the back of the panel with more spray adhesive.

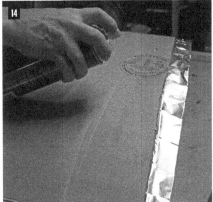

Begin assembling your reflector by using Gorilla Tape to attach the panels together. Start at the wide end, butt the edges together, and secure them with tape. Then align the narrow ends, match the curve of each piece, and tape that end. Add a piece of tape every 8 to 12 inches as needed to form a solid seam.

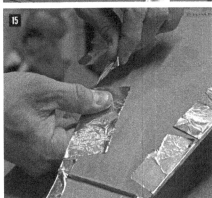

Don't try to build the entire panel at once; instead make two, two-panel pieces. Join them to make four, then eight, and

13. Use the soft bottom of your fist to smooth the foil and work from the center out.

14. Trim the foil around the panel, notch it every few inches, turn it over, and apply another light coat of spray adhesive.

15. Fold the tabs of foil and stick them to the back of the panel.

finally assemble both halves to form the whole dish. It helps to use a short support like a bucket or something similar to hold up the center of the reflector while putting the finishing touches on the tape job.

To support the reflector and allow its angle to be changed easily, contour a thin strip of steel or aluminum across the back so its ends extend an inch or so beyond the rim on each side. A cheap way to do this is to take drywall corner strip, hammer it flat to double it, and then fold the ends back for even more strength. Attach it with Gorilla tape and then reinforce the ends by drilling holes through it and the reflector near the rim on each side. Use machine screws, washers, and nuts to cinch it all together. Then, drill a ¼-inch hole in the center of each tab just above the rim to hang the reflector.

To close the hole in the center of the reflector and further strengthen its structure, cut a cardboard circle, cover it with foil, and drill a hole through its center and the center of the reinforcing metal strip. Use a 6-inch ¼-20 threaded screw, flat washers, and a nut to secure the circle in place and create a sun dial-like aiming post. When the reflector is perfectly aimed at the sun, the post won't cast a shadow.

Frame Up

The base for this solar cooker design is a simple 2x4 frame — braced T-shaped ends connected by another 2x4 across the bottom, all held together with wood screws.

Make sure the distance between the uprights matches the diameter of your reflector, and make the uprights almost as tall. Drill a ¼-inch hole in each upright half the diameter of your reflector up from the ground. To mount the reflector, place a long

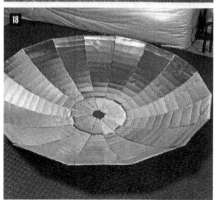

16. Attach panels edge to edge with Gorilla Tape.

17. Use something to support the center of the dish as you tape the panel sections together.

18. The fully assembled parabolic reflector.

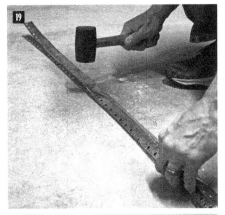

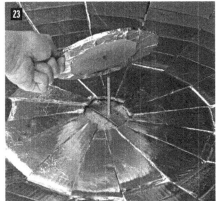
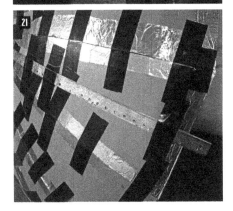

19. Flatten out some drywall corner to make the support strip. Any similar metal strip will work as well.

20. Drill ¼-inch holes in the tabs at the end of the strip to mount the reflector and allow it to pivot.

21. The support strip taped in place.

22. Attach the ends of the strip to the reflector with screws, washers, and nuts.

23. The center of the reflector is covered by a foil-covered cardboard circle secured with a long screw that also helps "aim" the reflector.

24. The frame for the cooker is a simple 2x4 structure.

¼-20 carriage bolt or screw through each hole in the upright and the tabs at each end of the metal strip on the dish. Use flat washers and wing nuts to hold them in place.

To make the cooking surface, get two pieces of ½-inch electrical conduit tube and an old barbecue grill grate. Use binding wire to attach the grate to the center of the conduit pieces so they are spaced about 4 inches apart. With the reflector hanging horizontally in the frame, place clamps on the frame uprights and set the grate assembly in place so the conduits straddle the uprights and are supported by the clamps.

Now, measure from the center of the reflector up to the grate and adjust the height of the clamps until the grate is at the focal point height (you wrote that down, right?). Once it's all set, use ½-inch conduit straps and wood screws to lock it in place.

The final piece of the puzzle is another piece of conduit or a wooden dowel roughly as tall as your uprights. This, plus a sturdy spring clamp, will allow you to adjust the vertical angle of the reflector.

Get Cookin'

To set up your solar cooker, place it on a level surface in an area of direct sunlight and orient it toward our massive star in the sky. Look at the sundial in the center of the reflector and turn the unit until the screw casts a shadow perpendicular to the conduits. Raise the reflector until the shadow shortens and eventually disappears, confirming the reflector is now pointed directly at the sun. Maintain that orientation and clamp the dowel or conduit support to the rim at the rear of the reflector to hold it in place.

In this position, the reflector should focus all the sunlight hitting it on the grate at the

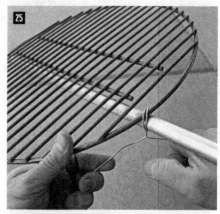

25. The cooker grate is made with electrical conduit and a grill grate.

26. Use clamps to get the cooking grate at the exact focal point before securing the conduit tubes with straps.

27. A simple dowel and clamp allow the angle of the reflector to be precisely adjusted.

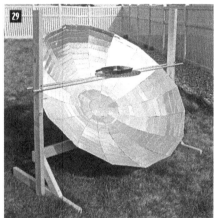

28. Use the "sundial" to align the reflector. When its shadow disappears, it's perfectly aligned.

29. Testing the parabolic solar cooker.

30. Anything that yields crispy bacon HAS to be good!

31. The DIY solar cooker got 1 gallon of water in this roasting pan up to 183 degrees F in just over an hour — plenty hot to effectively pasteurize it.

32. The start of cooking rice in a Dutch oven, sealed inside a roasting bag to maximize the greenhouse effect.

33. In just over an hour, the rice is perfectly cooked.

focal point. To confirm that, get a piece of paper and place it on the grate. Move it up, down, and under the grate and compare the size of the focused light at different heights above the reflector. It should be smallest and most focused at the exact level of the grate. If not, adjust the grate height to correspond with the most focused spot.

For the actual cooking, use a dark-colored pot or pan — ideally made of cast iron with a lid. Place it on the grate and let the sun work its magic. Check on the cooker periodically and reorient it as necessary to optimize its performance as the sun moves.

You can also incorporate the greenhouse effect in your cooking by enclosing cast-iron Dutch ovens in plastic roasting bags to retain heat and moisture even better.

As long as the sun does its part, this parabolic solar cooker definitely works and works well. In addition to cooking, it's a great way to quickly pasteurize water without burning fuel and an excellent addition to any off-grid plan. While it's not the solar death ray I was hoping for, I haven't given up hope yet. Maybe with some shinier aluminum foil .... ⚜

34. The finished parabolic solar cooker.

Solar Cooker Performance

You're hungry and it's sunny outside — so what exactly happens next?

To answer that question, I tested the solar cooker in mid-April in Colorado. The ambient air temperature was 62 degrees F, and it was a mostly sunny day. I put 2 cups of white rice and 4 cups of tap water in a cast-iron Dutch oven, put the oven in a plastic roasting bag (the big turkey-sized kind), stuck a thermometer in it, and put it on the cooker.

The tap water started out at 76 degrees F. In 20 minutes, it was up to 150 degrees, and in 40 minutes it was at 170. Just shy of an hour after the cooking started, the temperature inside the Dutch oven hit a max of 204 degrees, and the bag was filled with steam and condensed water. When the steaming stopped at about 65 minutes, I carefully took it off the grate and opened it up. The rice was perfectly cooked and delicious.

To evaluate its potential for pasteurizing water, I put a gallon of water in a roasting pan, realigned the cooker, and put it to work. It took about 70 minutes for the water to go from 74 degrees to the 149 degrees needed for pasteurization, and it maxed out at a respectable 183 degrees after about two hours.

Direct cooking using a cast-iron frying pan was also successful.

While definitely slower than flame-based cooking methods, it still managed to cook bacon to that delightfully crispy state. And when you've got crisp bacon, who cares if civilization is collapsing?

About The Author

Michael Janich is a U.S. Army veteran and a former intelligence officer for the Defense Intelligence Agency. As a POW/MIA investigation team leader, he worked in remote areas of Vietnam and Laos and has extensive experience making do with limited resources. An avid prepper, he was also the co-host of *The Best Defense: Survival*, a TV show on the Outdoor Channel. Janich is also the founder of Martial Blade Concepts. **www.martialbladeconcepts.com**

Survival Spuds

Building Your Own Potato Patch

By Alexander Crown

Did you watch, or better yet, read *The Martian* by Andy Weir? If you didn't, the premise is an astronaut is stranded on Mars and survives for over a year. He happens to be a botanist and engineer, both attributes help him in his survival on a foreign planet. In the book, the astronaut has a few vegetables to choose from to grow for his survival and he quickly selects the potato.

Nowadays the potato gets a bad rap. This is mostly attributed to the fast food industry frying them in oil. While delicious, this does hurt their nutritional value and add several unhealthy components to an otherwise nutritious food. When you look

Examples of russet potatoes not evenly watered during growth, resulting in large irregular lumps.

at the potato by itself, it offers good nutrients, vitamins, and minerals — all of which are invaluable in a survival situation or just good overall health.

You Can't (and Shouldn't) Have Just One

The potato is not a low-calorie food, which in a survival situation is a good thing. We all know caloric intake is essential during the strenuous events of a natural or manmade disaster and our starchy friend the potato aids in keeping your energy levels up. Spuds do lack sodium and fat, both of which can be added during the cooking process, so be sure you have a few salt packets in your bug-out bag.

Potatoes offer more potassium than a banana, which is something many people don't realize. Potassium is a vital electrolyte that helps the body regulate water balance and healthy blood pressure. Both of these are important in emergency situations when dehydration is likely.

Carbs are your friend during difficult times and again, the potato is lush with them. Eating foods high in carbohydrates when you know you're going to be exerting yourself is a great way to have energy on tap when you need it most.

The potato isn't going to offer the same protein level as a steak, but it does have a bit. So, if you get a chance to eat a squirrel while bugging out, be sure to get some supplemental protein when you can.

We all know that vitamin C is important to staying healthy and fighting off colds, so luckily a serving of taters has almost half of your recommended daily value. The potato also has noble amounts of niacin, thiamin, and vitamin B6 — all of which are beneficial for the heart.

Potato Planting

Growing potatoes is relatively easy. The soil used for potatoes should be loamy and contain little rocks and clay to allow maximum expansion. I generally use a

Kiss the Cook

Potatoes can be cooked in a variety of ways. Whether you're on the move, made it to your bug-out spot, or stayed put, you have several options for preparing potatoes for consumption. Here are some ideas for making your spuds palatable.

> **Fire baked potatoes:** Wrap potato in aluminum foil and place in hot coals of a fire. Rotate the potatoes every 10 minutes; they should cook in 40 to 50 minutes. Be sure to poke a few holes in the potato with a knife or fork so they don't explode when cooking.
> **Survival chips:** Thinly slice potatoes and pat dry to remove water. Heat an oil or fat and carefully place the potatoes in the pan. Cook for 2 to 3 minutes or until crispy, flipping the slices at least once for even cooking.
> **Grilled fries:** Cut potato into even wedges and grill over medium-high heat. Be sure and season with salt or other spices.
> **Dehydrated crisps:** If electricity is available, potatoes can be dehydrated. Dehydrated potatoes can be eaten as they are or used in soups. Slice the potatoes into approximately 3/8-inch pieces and blanch them, dry them thoroughly, then sprinkle with desired seasonings. Follow your dehydrator's settings for vegetables. Once they are completely dry, store them in an airtight container in a cool, dark place.
> **Boiled potato mush:** Start by peeling the potatoes (the skins can be used as bait for critters). Place the peeled spuds in a pot of boiling salted water. Boiling potatoes makes them soft and easy to eat. Boiled potatoes can be kept in a plastic bag and eaten while moving and you can drink the starch water. To make them more flavorful, be sure to keep salt, pepper, and your other favorite spices in your survival kit.

mixture of topsoil, organic compost, and peat moss. Potato plants should be started from certified disease-free seed potatoes. These are available at most garden stores and come in an abundance of varieties. I usually opt for Yukon golds, as they're easy to grow and have higher a yield for their size; however, I also grow purple potatoes and russets in case one variety experiences any sort of problems during the season. Choose the varieties that are familiar to you and correspond to your cooking methods.

Once the seed potatoes are purchased, cut them into cubes that have at least two eyes — the eye is where the plant will sprout from. Place these cubes into shallow rows of dirt and cover with about 1 inch of soil, with the cut side down. Give them a good watering to saturate the area. As the plants grow you'll need to continue to put soil on top of them to encourage upward growth and block out sunlight from the roots. Allow the leaves to be exposed to a few inches on top until the container is completely full. Once full of soil, allow the plant to continue to grow, making sure to water adequately. It's important that you water enough to reach the bottom of the container and don't allow it to dry out. Uneven watering will cause your potatoes to become misshapen and lumpy.

Containment

Potatoes can be grown practically anywhere and in almost any container. This year I have grown potatoes in two different places. One is the traditional raised bed (approximately 4-by-4-by-1 feet) and the other a plastic storage container (approximately 24-by-16-by-16 inches). Both containers start the same using the growing methods described previously.

The storage container is actually two containers stacked together. The inside container has large sections cut from the sides with drain holes drilled into the bottom. The outer container also has holes drilled in the bottom for proper drainage of excess water, so the plant does not drown during large amounts of rainfall. As the potatoes grow, dirt is piled on top until the container is full. Once full, the tubers continue to grow below the soil for the rest of the season. The container growing method yielded over 6 pounds of potatoes or about 18 servings. The traditional method, in a raised bed, produced roughly 16 pounds or about 48 servings.

A variety of containers can be used for growing potatoes, including old tires, burlap sacks, or something as simple as a garbage can — you are limited by your imagination. One of the benefits to

Plant potatoes cut side down with about 4 to 6 inches of spacing.

Side cutouts on the plastic container for easy access to potatoes.

the container growing method is that you now have mobility. If you find yourself needing to bug out and you have time, you can take your portable garden with you. One may also consider incorporating this into your bug-out plan and have extra garden materials staged at your bug-out location to continue growth. I would suggest staging the containers close to your parking spot if possible because a container full of dirt can be fairly heavy to move on your own.

Potato Pointers

Potatoes are relatively easy to grow in comparison to other garden plants, but they do have a few problems to be aware of. Pests, such as the potato beetle, may plague your plants. Physical removal of the beetle will help. Shake the plant early in the morning and kill all insects that fall off. For the container planting method, move the container away from the area once all insects have been removed. Diatomaceous earth can help keep insects away and kill the few that remain. Simply dust the plant, including the underside of leaves, and continue this process regularly.

Blight is another enemy of the potato and responsible for the Irish Potato Famine. It can be a serious problem for your plants. Blight is spread by the wind. Leaf tips will turn brown and wilt, spores form, and wind carries them to any nearby plants. Blight spores can also sink into the soil and infect your tubers, destroying them. The best way to prevent blight is to choose blight-resistant varieties to grow, also give adequate spacing to your plants in the event that one becomes infected.

Proper Storage

Once your hard work has yielded a crop, storing your precious spuds is easy. Potatoes need a dark storage area with ventilation and some humidity. Tubers exposed to light will turn green and quickly become toxic. Never eat a green potato, it can cause severe nausea accompanied with diarrhea and vomiting, both of which are extremely hazardous in a survival situation and will lead to dehydration. Humidity is important, as the majority of the potato is water. Generally 45 to 55 degrees Fahrenheit is adequate; however, storage at temperatures above this with no light can affect the color of the potatoes, making them gray or brown depending on the variety. They will still be safe for consumption, but will lose some of their weight and nutritional value.

Root cellars are the obvious ideal conditions for storage, although not everyone has access to those or will if bugging out. If you have used a mobile container garden, your bounty can be stored under the soil, it will be cool, light free, and relatively moist. Potatoes can also be stored under a sink or in a cupboard, in a bowl, or a perforated bag. The bag will provide more humidity and keep the potatoes from experiencing weight loss. Harvested potatoes do not need to be rinsed off prior to storage and leaving the dirt on will not hurt the vegetable.

Potatoes have been a staple for human diets since the 16th century. The relative ease of growing and cultivation made the crop an excellent choice for early farming techniques. The nutritional value and benefits of potatoes make them a good choice to be a part of your survival plans. The nature of potatoes allows them to be prepared in a variety of ways with different resources. Typically this is a familiar food for the young and old and can be a welcomed comfort in harsh times. ::

Sources:
www.cals.uidaho.edu/edComm/pdf/cis/cis1153.pdf
idahopotato.com
Bartholomew, Mel. All New Square Foot Gardening. Rodale Press, 2005

Use a tarp while harvesting to make clean up easy and to limit the amount of lost dirt. This soil can be amended and used for several years.

2 › Hunting & Fishing

Improvised Angling

Forget Your Rod, Reel, and Tackle Box. In a SHTF World, You'll Have to Fish With What You've Got.

By David H. Martin

Warning: This is not meant to be an exhaustive guide to improvised angling. Fishing in some regions under certain conditions can be extremely dangerous. Seek a professional guide or a reputable instructor for more information.

Our SHTF nightmare goes a little something like this: Outnumbered and nearly overrun, we hit the mag release on our AR-15 and let the empty magazine fall to the soft ground below. Ripping our final magazine from our chest rig, we slam her into the magwell and drop the bolt. "Last one," we whisper to ourselves. The last 30 rounds to fend off these blood-thirsty marauders, save our family, and protect the precious few provisions we have left.

But in reality, it'll probably go a bit more like this: Out of supplies and no signs of rescue coming, we drop our empty MRE packet and bury it in the soft ground below. Pulling the final protein bar from our chest pocket, we rip open its wrapper and scarf it down. "Last one," we say with a hint of desperation.

While the first scenario is what some preppers plan for (and maybe even fantasize about), the second one is much more likely. Imagine an injured hiker who didn't pack anything but water. Or picture a suburban family stranded in a broken-down camper with no mobile phone reception, having already eaten through their cache of ham sandwiches. If they think the only way to stave off starvation would be to hunt small game, they'd be overlooking a vast source of sustenance. If you can find a stream, lake, or river, you'll find not only potential drinking water, but quite possibly a source of abundant food.

In past issues of OFFGRID, we've explored traditional angling techniques and introduced the concept of a bug-out kayak from which to catch fish. But not every outdoor adventurer is going to have the inclination or the knowledge to pack a fishing rod, just as not every prepper will have the room to jam a tackle box in their bug-out bag. So, here we're going to delve into improvised means of catching fish, covering all sorts of methods — from the unconventional to the ancient.

Fish for Knowledge

If you read "Teach a Man to Fish..." in OFFGRID Issue 4, you know that a mini fishing kit can fit into an Altoid box. But

Survival fishing might require some improvised cooking. Soda cans can be splayed out and repurposed as a grill.

the low-cost nature of fishing gear allows for greatly expanded kits to be assembled and stored in multiple locations, from your home and your office to your daily driver and your kayak. This will enable you to take advantage of multiple environments, species, seasons, and waters, from ponds and upland freshwater to salty bays and coastal tidal creeks.

For anything longer than one night in the woods, less is not more when packing fishing kits. Yet, judging from a quick look at fishing gear on the market, the manufacturers' main objective seems to be to make them as small as possible with almost no line and few hooks or lures. But why settle for 30 feet of line when, for $7, you can grab a readymade spool of more than 3,000 yards of light monofilament? Add in a box of hooks and you're halfway to a good meal.

The key to it all? Understanding your target species and settling in for the long haul, to keep moving and harvesting fish as you go.

Learn your home species, and adjust your kit according to destinations. Ask yourself, "If I crossed the state line, would I be able to work my way home living on only fish I caught along the way?" Stepping off the grid should increase, not decrease, your confidence. And the best way to do that is to gain knowledge and develop skill through practice. Next time your wife complains that you go fishing with the boys too often, tell her you're doing vital research.

If 10 percent of the fishermen catch 90 percent of the fish, and 20 percent of the water holds 80 percent of the fish, the first thing you need is a decision matrix to eliminate the less productive waters and focus on more productive waters that you can still safely access. A decision matrix would look like this:

Your target species and time window

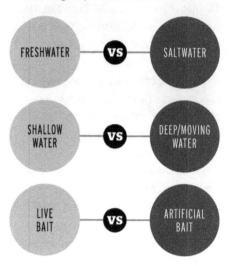

dictate your choice of tackle, and the tackle determines your movement and timing. Additionally, consider adding any of the following where it's legal and it makes sense: seines, cast nets, fish traps, bush lines, spears, or ancient techniques still practiced from bayou to backwater — everything short of dynamite.

Trust your instincts or you'll reduce your options. Stop reading the instructions and start reading the water, looking for those natural ambush points: bottle necks, choke points, sandbars, structural covers, or current lines that draw and concentrate bait flow, leading to small and large fish activity. Forget the trophy fish and focus on that small percentage of water that you can access safely and that holds the fish you need to survive. The key is to assemble a kit that enables you to work various levels of the water column, regardless of water body, for the target species, or make the tools you need.

Freshwater Techniques

Freshwater remains the common denominator. It can be a treatable source of hydration, a pathway to safe refuge, a barrier against potential hostiles, and an ambush point for life-sustaining fauna. Approach a pond, lake, river, marsh, or inland swamp almost anywhere throughout the USA, and you can count on a number of reliable "pan fish" species. There's bluegill, sunfish, bream or crappie, catfish, and regional fish — from trout to small-mouth bass. Look for spawning beds in the shallows during the spring, and keep your eye on cover vegetation holding ambush predators.

IMPROVISED FISHING POLE

Freshwater species readily hit ultra-light artificial lures like micro-jigs, spoons, and flies. So connect a synthetic lure to a hook and paracord and voilà. These species also like live bait — from worms and crickets to frogs and crayfish. Catch some little critters and suspend them from hooks that are tied to ultra-light monofilament or micro-braid lines. To rig these baits, just follow these easy steps:

1. Look for a light sapling, a length of cane, some bamboo, or a long, lean tree limb.
2. Cut and trim the selected branch, then harden it over campfire coals.
3. Tie in your ultra-light mono or micro-braid line about halfway up the pole, wrapping it in long spirals until you reach the tip.
4. Tie off the line and leave as much as you can flip out, about 12 to 20 feet. This way, if a large catfish or bass breaks your cane pole tip, you'll still be connected to your dinner.
5. Complete this classic rig by attaching a small No. 8 hook, split shot, and cork.

At night, standing on an overhanging river or creek bank, you can use your heavy cane pole, tipped with a heavy length of line to artificial surface plugs, to draw fish by the lost art of "jigger-poling." Swishing in tight figure-eight patterns and loops can sometimes trigger an explosive bass strike. Night fishing can be productive during the warmer months when you're on foot and fishing the shallows near shore.

FLOATING BAIT

No cane poles or bamboo in your bug-out locale? No problem. It's just a matter of observation and adaptation:

1. Check the shoreline for any floating vessel, like an old soda bottle or bleach jug.
2. Rig your floatable device with bait on 3 to 4 feet of line.
3. Attach a length of paracord or twine to your bottle and let it float across the lake, pond, or river, where you can pick up strikes away from the shore.

HANGING BAIT

Similar rigs can be suspended from tree limbs that hang over lakes or slow-moving

rivers, especially when you have live or cut bait. Be careful not to offer your entire line and hook set in a trotline arrangement unless you can afford to lose it all at once to a gator or an alligator snapping turtle.

NETS AND TRAPS

Rivers offer the advantage of allowing you to turn the current to your advantage. Send out worms, live or cut bait, or almost anything with scent to attract catfish. In moving water, creeks, and streams, don't rule out ancient techniques. Nets and traps are great for ensnaring bait, crayfish, or freshwater turtles. They're effective forms of passive fishing, allowing you to focus on other important tasks like filtering water or even sleeping overnight while prey get caught up in them.

For example, seine nets have been used all over the globe for millennia to capture seafood. Some resemble volleyball nets that are held down by weights on the bottom, but buoyed by floats at the top. Also, funnel-shaped traps can be crafted with nothing more than bait, a knife, some twine/cord, and tree branches that can be wrapped. Bamboo is best, but any light sticks that are flexible can be used.

Saltwater Techniques

Tools, tactics, and techniques vary more widely once you reach coastal waters based on species inhabiting estuaries, brackish rivers, mangrove islands, coastal beaches, shallow tidal bays, and barrier islands.

REEL IN THE BAIT

Saltwater is where live bait rules. Netted, trapped, or hooked bait is used to attract larger predators. Common coastal species range from schools of small snapper, mullet, or pelagic species that cruise sandbars, oyster bars, and beach troughs looking to munch on something smaller while avoiding something toothier. Start by working through the shallows to procure scented live bait, from clams and barnacles to minnows and sand fleas (AKA mole crabs). You can catch them using a seine, a wire screen, or a handmade bait trap. Also, hooking even smaller baitfish on tiny hooks and mono line can do the trick.

CUBAN YO-YO

No, this isn't the latest popular kid's toys; it's one of the simplest fishing systems one can use from a shore, jetty, or pier. This time-tested fishing device is a simple plastic spool with a concave channel capable of holding hundreds of feet of light or heavy line in various sizes. In coastal waters from Alaska to Florida, yo-yos are capable of taking trout, flounder, redfish, mangrove snapper — even small shark if you include some wire leader.

To use it, first quietly wade or stand in the shade of the mangroves, or at a low-profile spot where water movement shows signs of baitfish and feeding fish. To

cast using the yo-yo, pay out several feet of line with the hand spool. Then swing the hook, leader, and sinker or lure around your head like a lariat, and let her fly, allowing the spool to spin in your opposite hand, your reeling hand. A 30-foot cast is plenty.

Terminal tackle can consist simply of a line connected by small sliding sinker, swivel, a length of leader, possible cork bobber, and a baited hook.

To manage large and small fish, practice rolling your wrist one handed and fishing by feel with your opposite hand. Take care not to allow the line to cut you when using microfiber lines. When that large fish hits, a braided line can cut you to the bone. Never wrap your bare hand with any fishing line lest you risk a deep cut; use the spool. A glove helps prevent skin loss when the fish hits. (If you receive a line cut or a hook stab, treat it immediately by flushing, disinfecting, and bandaging, then keeping as dry as possible.) Prepare to loosen your grip and allow the fish to exhaust itself by playing it carefully. Too many fish are lost by attempting to winch them in, tearing the hook or lure from their lips.

If you're able to procure, by hook or crook, a small seaworthy row boat or jon boat for fishing offshore, the yo-yo will allow you to drop weighted baits or lures into the deeper channel edges, where reef fish or even grouper may dwell (along with passing pelagic species during fall or spring seasons). Be prepared to play the fish and if need be, stab it at boat side with a handmade spear. Given time, you may even rig a small landing net by steaming and bending branches into a loop, and cross connecting with paracord fiber strands, square knotted into a small mesh screen.

HAWAIIAN SLING

Depending on the currents, the season, or the water temperatures, you may even be able to dive for crabs or to spearfish using a pole spear or Hawaiian sling. "A what?" you might be asking. A Hawaiian sling is a poor man's spear gun and works like a combination of a slingshot and a bow and arrow, but instead of flexing a wooden or fiberglass bow to build up energy you pull back on rubber tubing. While they're commercially available, you can fashion one yourself, MacGyver style:

1. Obtain a sturdy shaft for a pole spear and sharpen one end (i.e. wooden dowel).
2. Tie bungee cord or surgical tubing in a 12-inch loop at the base of your spear.
3. Slip your hand up the pole, tightening the loop across the webbing between your thumb and trigger finger until you can grip the pole under tension.
4. Then point and release.

NETS AND TRAPS

The author fashions a fish trap out of bamboo. As a passive form of fishing, the trap funnels both bait fish and larger swimmers.

These devices work just as well in saltwater as they do in freshwater. Premade or crafted from paracord, a simple cast net or seine can gather both bait and larger keeper fish. If you have the capacity to carry a premade bait or cast net, this can reward you with one simple toss after mastering the ancient technique. Set nets framed by fish traps to funnel both bait and larger fish. If you're able to rip some screen or chicken wire from a fence or window, roll and form a cylinder to use as a bait or crab trap, then weigh it down, and bait with fish heads to keep the food chain going.

However, these require a large time commitment to make in the field, so consider staging a premade net in your boat, vehicle, or bug-out location.

Fish-Gone Conclusion

For long-term survival, the most well thought-out bug-out bags consist of core essentials surrounded by modular sub-component packs that may be added or deleted based on need, travel, and season. This holds true with angling supplies, too.

With each component, it's essential to know every element and how it works in the given environment you're in. Perhaps more importantly, it's vital to practice with it before it's needed. Just as you wouldn't wait until you're bleeding out from a gunshot wound before you try a tourniquet for the first time, you shouldn't add a single lure or tool to your kit without considering its cost, weight, safety concerns, and usefulness in the water. Instead of going entirely with the mini-fishing-kit-in-a-mint-box approach, consider how your off-grid adaptability and effectiveness will be greatly increased at very little cost by incrementally increasing the carrying capacity of your basic setup.

There are survival schools that will teach you how to survive by eating a worm. Or, if you go off the grid with grit and some knowledge, you can use that worm to catch an almost limitless abundance of fish. So save the Altoids, hero. You'll need them for kissing the girl once you've fed your clan long after the last MRE was devoured. ⁑

About the Author

Native Texan David H. Martin is a conservation-driven kayak fishing guide and firearms instructor based in Sarasota, Florida, where he charters coastal waters, mangrove islands, and remote rivers. Competing with sharks and alligators for his next meal, he hones and teaches survival skills needed for transitioning from potential urban threats to remote backcountry camps.

10 Worst
Angling Mistakes to Avoid

1) Don't Pack a Knife: A knifeless man is a lifeless man, goes the Nordic saying, and this is never truer than when working the water's edge. You don't want to connect with anything you can't disconnect from in a hurry – think getting tangled up with a fishing line, weighted fish trap, or even an anchor line. A fixed blade or a safety cutter like the Benchmade 9 CB will give you control over thrashing fish and save a trip to the emergency room when that unseen hook comes through the web of our hand.

2) Forget Edge Discipline: Almost any fisherman can show you the scar he got when his hand slipped on slime while cleaning a slick fish or when the blade ricocheted off a fish spine. Clean fish the way you'd sharpening your spear: cut away from your body.

3) Overlook Small Cuts: A knife is not the only thing that can cut you. The new micro-braid fishing line can cut to the bone when burning through your hand, leading to impairment and blood loss. Small hand cuts might seem insignificant, but can result in a red streak up the wrist, an early warning sign of an infection.

4) Go Deep: When wading, remember to keep it "shin deep, not chin deep."

The idea is to be predator, not the bait. Don't go for the trophy fish in deep waters without a boat, and just take what you need; small fish count, too.

5) Stay Unaware: Never turn your back on the water, especially at low light or nightfall. The water moccasin remains the most belligerent and malingering serpent at the water's edge, and the reason the .410 Snake Charmer shotgun was invented. And no one need be reminded about the dangers of crocs and gators.

6) Just Dive In: Your hiking stick works when wet. Don't attempt a crossing through moving water, even a seemingly smooth-flowing creek or channel, without probing the bottom. A safety line (i.e. a heavy rope) can provide a measure of security when crossing waters or maneuvering, scouting, or portaging river country. Recreational fishermen disappear every year, pulled down in their waders when stepping into a hole or slipping on a green mossy rock.

7) Ignore the Temperatures: Once you're wet, weather conditions can drastically affect you for the worst. It's easy to get so caught up in survival fishing that you forget to pay attention to your shivering body. When you're cold, you make bad decisions. Get a fire started at your basecamp before you realize that you have no dry spare clothing and your tinder is wet.

8) Clean Where You Eat: Clean your fish away from camp. If you can't use the entrails or head for cooking or baiting traps, don't bring it back to your bug-out base. Otherwise, you'll be sending out an aromatic invitation for raiders, from nuisances like raccoons to serious threats like bears.

9) Eat the Weirdos: Pass on any fish that acts disoriented or appears unnatural. Favor the firm, lively, and clear-eyed fighter. Prepare carefully and cook thoroughly. The fish will fall apart when done so plan on using a pan if you have one, or spreading out the fish on skewers or a grill. Even crushed beer cans make a good improvised oven or grill. A classic cooking technique is to wrap the fish in foil, coat in mud, then bury in campfire coals for about 30 minutes.

10) Pack Just One Line and Hook: Compared to ammo, whiskey, and cigars, the cost for ample line and hooks are low and their weight and bulk are minimal. Stock up well in advance, building in a variety of lines for any possible condition and having various kits set up for your different emergency packs.

Feast Master

A Survivalist's Primer on Field Dressing and Butchering

Story and Photos by Matthew Cosenzo
Illustrations by Joe Oesterle

In a world where millions go to the supermarket to get their meat, it's funny how many people have no concept of the work that goes into producing that perfectly wrapped and presented protein product. We can't count the amount of times we've talked with people who eat meat, but somehow find it distasteful that others spend their fall and winter hunting to fill their freezers.

With more and more people looking for organic and free-range animals to incorporate into their diet, what would happen if they couldn't just go to the store? For some, hunting an animal and processing it from start to finish is a way of life, whereas for others who never learned the sequence of tasks necessary to prepare an animal without contaminating the meat, their "Eww! Blood and guts!" reaction could cost them their lives in dire circumstances. It's not all macabre gore.

Field dressing an animal is a practice that's been handed down for centuries and a critical part of preparing what you've hunted for consumption. If you can filet a fish, you can field dress a four-legged animal.

The hardest part of the hunt begins when the animal hits the ground. The process of gutting and butchering can be daunting for the uninitiated. If you find yourself alone and miles away from civilization, that process can become even harder. But, like any task, it comes down to using the proper methods to get the job done. With practice you'll eventually realize it's not as gruesome as many people think. We'll focus on larger game animals such as elk, deer, or moose. The approach, steps, and care to be taken are the same for all animals of the same body type.

Tool Up

Everyone has their go-to knife or knives for the job. As with many other aspects of preparation, knife selection isn't a one-size-fits-all. Dressing requirements may change from when you're butchering in a controlled environment versus in the field. Over the last year we've found two blades that have remained in our packs through many rotations. The replaceable scalpel-style knives have been the rage in recent years — a newcomer, Wiebe Knives, stood out.

The company's Vixen model has a larger handle, allowing for better control and less fatigue in cold and bloody conditions, especially if you have larger hands. While the fine scalpel-style blade works in most scenarios, we still prefer a small fixed knife with a roughly 3-inch blade, because it offers greater control inside the animal — specifically when reaching in to cut the esophagus.

For a butchering and skinning blade, the author uses a simple, semi-flexible boning knife when working at home. They're cheap and durable enough to pop joints and scrape bones. We've used the Frosts/Mora knives for the better part of 10 years; their rubberized handles are nonslip, and their blades hold an edge very well. Remember to sharpen your knives after each use or replace blades on models with that feature. A dull knife is more dangerous than a sharp one. When you have to force your knife to do the work and it doesn't cut with ease, accidents happen.

And if you're alone in the middle of the woods with a severe laceration, you might not make it to dinner.

Gut Check

Out of all the processes involved, eviscerating or gutting the animal is the task that can be the most overwhelming. But anyone can make quick work of this task when done correctly. If you plan to completely butcher the animal in the field because it's too far or too difficult to haul it back to camp, hold off on gutting it. There are better methods of butchering in that situation, which we'll discuss later.

However, if you plan to leave it overnight (assuming the temperature is fairly low), gutting the animal and putting edible organs on ice is recommended.

For the sake of clarity, we'll explain things assuming the animal is on the ground rather than hung from a gambrel.

Position the animal on a slight decline, head uphill. With the animal on its back, prop the rear legs apart. If you're working alone with a large animal like an elk, it's easier to tie the legs to neighboring trees

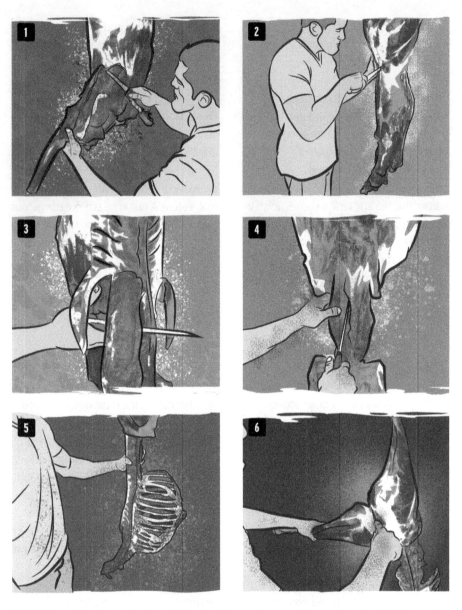

1. After hanging the animal and skinning it, use leverage to pop the shoulder from the joint. Be mindful of the curvature of the pelvis as you work your blade through.

2 and 3: Next comes the removal of the backstrap and the rib meat.

4. To remove the tenderloins, use your knife tip and fingers. They should pull free from the carcass with minimal effort.

5. A carcass with limited meat waste; just the rear legs remain.

6. Remove the rear leg in the same fashion as the front shoulder. Lessen the work by following the natural seams of the meat.

to assist in keeping the animal stationary and legs separated.

Using a basic scalpel-style field-dressing knife, make an incision a couple inches above the anus and cut a larger circle around it. The idea is just to free a larger circle of fur around the anus from the rest of the hide. Do *not* cut it free from the intestine. Leave this patch of fur connected and simply separate it from the remaining fur, as we can use this later to remove the entrails. Then, make a shallow cut around the middle of the abdomen just deep enough to penetrate the flesh without going too far into the membrane below it that protects the stomach and other organs. It doesn't take much effort to slice through the flesh, so take your time. Orient the knife with the blade facing upward — don't force it. Let the knife do the work and gently cut into the skin, which (depending on the animal) usually isn't more than an inch deep. You can work two fingers of your free hand into the initial cut to help pull the fur away from the carcass as you continue cutting upward toward the bottom of the sternum where the cut should end. You can then lengthen this opening by cutting back the other way toward the genitals to create one big continuous incision.

(Note: Depending on your state, proof of sex may need to be left on the animal for transportation, so check your local regulations.)

Now you'll have complete access to the lower body cavity. Reach up into the rib cage to cut the diaphragm, a thin membrane separating the lungs, liver, and heart from the digestive organs. Then reach past and cut the esophagus, which may be hard to see — when you reach in toward the throat it feels like a bony, round tube. When both hands are out of sight and inside the body cavity, pay close attention so that you don't cut toward your other hand. Go slowly and avoid lacerating yourself on any bone shards which may be displaced by a bullet.

With most of the organs free, work to pull the lower intestine back through the pelvis, making sure not to break the bladder. With just these few cuts, all of the organs should slide out fairly easily in one group.

You should also be able to pull the initial incision you made around the anus through the open chest cavity.

Another key note: You may see some examples of field dressing where the incision is made all the way up through the rib cage, opening the entire chest cavity. However, the less you cut, the less chance of dirt, leaves, and debris entering the cavity when dragging the animal or transporting it to a vehicle. This is another reason not to split the pelvis to remove the lower intestine and anus.

Thick Skinned

The key with any big game animal is to get it cooled down as quickly as possible. Skinning is just that, shedding the animal's coat to allow heat to dissipate. While we've hung deer-sized game unskinned and allowed them to age for multiple days, we've achieved a better product when skinning the animal and allowing it to age as an exposed carcass.

Attempting to fully skin an animal on the ground is best avoided, so all these procedures are described for an animal hung from a gambrel; they don't change regardless of animal size.

With the animal securely held in the gambrel, remove the hide from the rear legs, making incisions up to the knuckle. Peel the hide around and down until you reach the tailbone. Grabbing the tail and pulling away, it'll easily detach by cutting through the joint; be sure not to cut through the hide. With the hide free of the rear legs, using your blade and some brute strength, pull the hide down until you reach the shoulders. The key is to cut toward the hide and not into the meat. For the most part, the hide will pull free with little knife work needed.

Skinning out the shoulders can be a frustrating task given the weight of the hide and curvature of the shoulder. The area where the hide goes under the armpit can be a difficult spot.

There are two approaches to making this task easier. You can cut through the hide at two points inside the shoulders, giving you three separate sections and more freedom to work. Keep in mind, though, anytime you cut through the hide, you cut more hair, resulting in more to clean up later. It's usually easier to work the hide to the back of the shoulders and make an incision through the hide up the back of the leg to the knuckle. This lets you work the hide down and around each shoulder. Continue to work the hide to the base of the head. There's usually no need for a saw — with a knife and some twisting action you can easily sever the vertebra.

The Gutless Method

If you're miles deep into your hunting trip, you probably won't want to drag the animal out whole. Your best option is to work the animal one side at a time, removing all the meat without disturbing the internal organs.

With the animal on its side, make an incision through the hide, along the backbone, and up the neck. When cutting through hide, it's always best to cut hide to hair, that is, from the inside out. This helps prevent hair from getting on the meat, making it easier to clean and package later. Work the hide down, pulling and cutting as you go. In most instances the hide should pull free if the animal was recently killed and still warm. Start at the front shoulder, peeling the hide back as you would if the animal were hanging.

Work from front to back, peeling the hide and removing major muscle groups as you go. The hide will open like a flap, giving you complete access to the quarters, back straps, making removing the tenderloins easier. After all the meat is removed from one side of the animal, simply roll the animal to the other side and remove the hide and meat in the same order, front to back.

The Aging Process

Aging meat has been done for ages — for good reason. There are two main reasons to age your animal: concentration of flavor and tenderness. As meat ages, the natural enzymes in the meat break down the protein. This is simply a controlled rot, for lack of a better term. For this to happen properly though, you need to have the right conditions or you risk all your meat spoiling.

If you're dealing with a whole animal and don't have the luxury of a walk-in cooler, the key is temperature.

This author prefers the temperature to be no higher than 45 degrees F. Of course, if it's warmer or you can't hang the entire animal, you can age your animal in the fridge. Place the primal cuts on sheet trays lined with parchment paper then cover with plastic wrap. Age for up to five days if the animal is whole or quartered in the fridge.

Note: When aging meat in its quarters, you'll lose a bit more yield since more surfaces are exposed and more trimming will be needed.

Butcher It

This is a personal choice, and the process will vary due to what's needed. Some hunters turn both front shoulders into ground meat or sausage and leave the rest for steaks and roasts. Keep the meat in larger cuts, so roasts are fully trimmed and packaged and back straps are portioned in larger pieces rather than cut down to steaks. Larger pieces keep better in the freezer than smaller cuts, resulting in a better product months down the line.

When trimming and boning out the meat, you'll be left with scraps. You can immediately turn this all to grind, but you might consider keeping a pound of trim set aside to use later in a sausage. It might come in handy to prevent you from over grinding a sausage mix.

Pack It Up

Vacuum-sealing machines have become so prevalent and inexpensive, they're a no-brainer when packing meat. The clear bags are easily labeled, last longer, and the process is far quicker than wrapping cuts in butcher paper.

[Editor's note: If you decide to get one, see our buyer's guide in RECOIL OFFGRID Issue 10 for some shopping advice.]

Butchering an animal is largely preferential. Storing meat in larger pieces helps it last longer in the freezer.

Industrial meat and even internet-ordered groceries mean we're growing even further from the roots of the food chain. At least, if you're reading this, you've considered the steps to eviscerate, butcher, and package your own game.

For some, taking game to a local processor is the easier route. But you may find that resource isn't an option if the world goes to pot, so these skills will be valuable. You'll have to rely on yourself to do the dirty work of a trade many people have long taken for granted. If the need arises in a survival situation, you'll be much closer to self-sufficiency.

About the Author

Matthew Cosenzo is a graduate of The Culinary Institute of America, focusing heavily on field-to-table cooking. His passion for the outdoors combined with his approach to game creates a full circle experience. Cosenzo is always looking for the next challenge — be it on the range or in the field — to help him become a more efficient and educated hunter.

Trap Triggers

Learn a Primitive Way of Procuring Small Game Without Expending Tons of Energy

By Kevin Estela

You can't grill it until you kill it. This expression sends anti-hunter types into full-triggered mode. To some, there's a preconceived notion that living in the woods will only require eating nuts and berries. The reality of the scenario involves a much larger buffet line of small game and rodents that pack nutritious calories in little fur-bundled packages. Running around trying to hunt them expends more calories than will be returned — so the logical answer to the survival question is developing a series of traps that'll work for you when you rest or attend to other survival needs.

Check out the most popular survival books in your local bookstore or library, and you'll find any number of elaborate trap illustrations. Creating these traps may seem like a daunting task, but with enough practice, a rough working example can be made in short order. We've seen these books, and we've also seen what's often left out of written instruction. We'll break down some of the most common traps and focus on the trigger mechanisms to make them both more sensitive and more effective in putting meat over your fire. Check your local regulations as well before setting any traps.

Figure 4

The Figure 4 trap trigger is easily carved with nothing more than a blade and some hardwood. This trigger is most frequently used with a crushing weight, such as a rock or large round of wood, but pest control can be handled in urban areas with wood planks, pallets, and cinder blocks. Use dried seasoned branches free of rot, if you can. Green branches will contract as they dry and may split along the grain. If possible, select wood free of knots and about the thickness of a Sharpie marker to start. You can always scale your trap part components up or down. The three components — the upright, diagonal, and horizontal (these terms will make sense shortly) — can all be carved from a single stick. The thickest part of the stick is used for the diagonal stick, the thinnest for the horizontal, and medium thickness for the upright.

The key to carving the Figure 4 is to make precise cuts with the correct angles and orientation to one another. The vertical stick requires a chisel tip as well as a 90-degree angle. The diagonal stick requires a ramped notch on one end and a chisel on the other. The horizontal requires two ramped notches configured 90 degrees offset from each other. The three pieces of this trap trigger are held in place with opposing pressure. The angle of the diagonal stick and the length will vary the speed at which it triggers.

When carved correctly, the Figure 4 will be thrown out of the way when the trap is triggered. To make it more sensitive, keep the points of contact smooth without bevels or scratches. Don't drive the vertical stick into the ground, but rather rest it on a hard surface instead. The size of the weight will depend on the animal you intend to catch; for example, a 10-pound rock falling on a 2-pound animal will be sufficient to crush it. Placing a flat rock or setting the trap on a hard surface will increase the crushing force of your trap.

Pros: Simple knife-and-knowledge skill (just add sticks). Works well with "cage-like" traps, too.

Cons: Requires a deadfall weight

The Figure 4 trap trigger is adaptable to many variations of crushing traps. This trap has an additional weight added to the primary crushing log to increase lethality and effectiveness.

Paiute Figure 4

A variation of a Figure 4 with increased sensitivity is the Paiute Figure 4. This trap needs less carving, but requires cordage. In the Southwest states where the Paiute lived, Yucca fibers were easily processed into cordage with sufficient strength for trap triggers. In the modern era, paracord innards and jute twine can be substituted if your natural cordage making skills aren't up to snuff. Make sure your cordage has little to no stretch to prevent delayed action.

The Paiute requires a single chisel tip and ramped notch along with a single groove around the horizontal stick. If you're using reverse-wrapped cordage, the initial loop created can be looped around the toggle that wraps around the vertical stick. Where many survival manuals get it wrong is showing the Paiute trigger stick and toggle stick carved to perfect flats that maximize contact with one another at the expense of increased friction. To increase the sensitivity of the trigger and toggle, round the ends and smooth them out as best as possible.

Pros: Less carving than Figure 4, very fast trigger.
Cons: Requires cordage and a deadfall weight

The Paiute Figure 4 trap trigger requires less carving with the trade-off of adding cordage to the setup. The Paiute Figure 4 is an incredibly responsive and fast trap trigger; it works well with crushing traps and makeshift cage traps. A cage trap can be created to catch animals live, but must be weighted to prevent an animal from escaping.

The Simple Snare

A simple snare loop can be made from wire. Ideally, the wire should be the braided variety as it has greater resistance to breaking and the braid has a tendency to catch animal fur, adding a level of retention. Aside from the wire, the only other material necessary is a small twig or a stick that serves as a dowel. The process is easy.

1) Cut a small length of snare wire (approximately 18 inches). About 4 inches down from one end, place a dowel horizontally across the wire and loop the wire around three times.
2) With one hand pinching the dowel and the other the ends of the wire, twist it tightly a half dozen times.
3) Break the dowel in half and pull it from the loop. Don't let the loop close, but pinch it flat.
4) Bend the tail end of the working end of the wire to create an acute hook.
5) Thread the running end of the wire through the twisted loop and position the hook on the other end of the wire in line with the opening. The hook may increase the chances of hooking on the prey's fur and help close the loop.
6) Measure the size of the loop appropriately for the prey you intend to catch. The size of the loop should be approximately two to three fingers wide for a chipmunk or squirrel and four fingers for a rabbit.
7) Attach the running end of the snare wire to a good anchor. Make sure the anchor is affixed to the ground or a branch the animal cannot break free. If you have them, use a fishing swivel to prevent the wire from twisting and weakening.

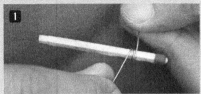
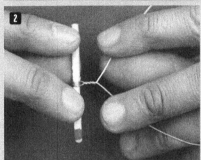
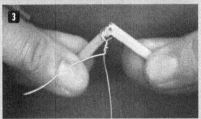
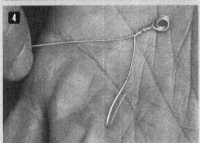
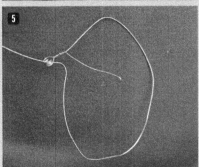

Goal Post

The goal post trap trigger is simple to construct with only three sticks and some form of lifting mechanism (bent sapling, counterweight, tensioned cord, etc). Cut two upright posts and carve ramped notches into them at the same height. Cut the upright sticks into digging chisels or a point. Using a blade, cut serrations in the space between the chisel tip and the notched ramps on each upright to grip the earth and prevent them from being easily extracted. The horizontal stick is the trigger pin; cut it to create two 90-degree angles opposite from each other on the two ends.

The goal post is set by pounding the upright sticks in the ground along a game trail. The width between the goal post will vary, but in general it should be slightly wider than the animal's body. Make sure the upright sticks are positioned with the ramped notches facing opposite directions inline with the game trail. This allows the trigger pin to fire from either direction. Placing the notches on the uprights facing the same way will only allow the trap to work in one direction. A single or a double snare can be suspended from the horizontal post. When the animal runs through the goal post and is caught through the snare, the trigger pin will be displaced and the tension from the lifting mechanism lifts the animal. Contrary to popular belief, the animal need not be lifted entirely off the ground. All that's needed is to lift the front legs. Lifting an animal completely off the ground and out of the reach of predators does have its place when they could also be in the area.

Pros: Very strong bidirectional trigger

Cons: Requires additional cordage for lifting mechanism

The Goal Post setup is a bidirectional trap trigger. Regardless of which way an animal runs through the Goal Post, it'll trigger. Whenever a lightweight snare is used, small forked twigs can be used to prop it open and hold it at the right height above the ground. A simple girth hitch can be used to create the snare loop with a simple stopper knot.

Toggle (aka the "L7" Trigger)

The toggle trigger is shaped and configured just like the letter "L" and number 7. This trigger works on the concept of opposing pressure to keep it from firing. This trigger mechanism can be carved from a single branch. Carve the ramped notches with minimal space from the 90-degree angle and the end of the stick. Bevel the ends of the "L" and "7" pieces to fit together better. Groove the opposite ends with an awl or carved knife tip to create a hole for cordage.

The toggle trigger is capable of holding an incredible amount of weight. It works well in various configurations, from a floating trigger pin to a staked version in the ground. Where the books have gotten it wrong in the past is showing an incredible amount of weight or force suspended with a toggle trigger on a set designed for an animal that can't trigger it. The friction between the two notched ramps can be alleviated by either working the beveled notches to points or by using a round twig as a "roller bearing."

The toggle trigger can be used for either snaring traps or for crushing traps. One easily constructed trap set is built with a rock suspended over the head of an animal, funneled into an area where one end of the toggle is attached to an attractant or bait an animal will tug on. When the toggle is released, the rock suspended above falls on top of the animal's head.

Pros: Easy concept to grasp
Cons: Can stick without "roller bearing"

The "L7" trap trigger utilizes two forked sticks that hook onto one another. It's very responsive and can be used for many setups, including fishing traps that set the hook when triggered. Forked "Y" twigs are used for holding snares at the appropriate height.

HUNTING & FISHING • TRAP TRIGGERS

Twitch Up

A classic snare trap trigger is the twitch up. This type of trap trigger can exploit natural forks in root systems, or carved forks can be pounded into the ground along game trails. The twitch up is very sensitive and can be scaled to any size to catch a chipmunk or an alien predator with dreadlocks by the leg. In case you're wondering, this is the one you'd use to lift a person upside down by the ankle like they do in the movies.

Pound a forked stick into the ground, with the same type of serrations described for the goal post. This forked stick needs to be secure enough to hold the force of the counterweight, and there needs to be enough room between the crotch of the fork and the ground for the trigger pin to clear. The trigger pin can be fashioned from a smooth piece of hardwood, bone, or antler. You can taper it like a cone, debark it, and round it so it slips with the

The classic twitch up works with a baited stick. When the prey disturbs the trigger stick, the toggle releases and the snare catches around the animal's neck, neck and front leg(s), body, or leg(s) alone. Note the "Y" twigs propping the snare loop open.

greatest ease. Attach the trigger pin to the counterweight with strong cordage, and attach the snare to the trigger pin as well. Pull the trigger pin through the forked stick and align the broad end with the end of the fork facing upward.

There'll be tension against the fork, and the trigger pin will want to pull through the fork. To prevent this, place a horizontal stick between the two tines of the fork and the tapered end of the trigger pin.

The horizontal stick can be tweaked to have a minimum amount of surface area touching it. This will increase the sensitivity. Place the loop of the snare under the baited horizontal bar and prop it up with small forked twigs. When the prey disturbs the baited horizontal bar, the trigger pin will release and the counterweight or bent sapling will pull the snare tight around one of the legs and lift the animal upward.

Pros: Extremely sensitive trap, adaptable to any size prey
Cons: May not react if parts are incorrectly sized and mismatched

Key chain split rings work well to redirect the pull from a counterweight with minimal drag. Logs work well as lifting weights in the woods and cinder blocks do the same in urban environments. With enough weight, a lifting trap can be scaled up for man-sized prey.

Platform Twitch Up

While the traditional twitch up is an effective and easy-to-make trigger mechanism, it relies on the prey eating from a baited stick. To increase the odds of success for this trap, a platform can be constructed over it. In this configuration, when an animal steps on the platform, the snare closes around the leg. This can be accomplished as easily as placing perpendicular sticks or a solid flat object like a piece of bark, wooden plank, or hard-ribbed leaves across the horizontal stick.

With more surface area, there's a greater chance to set off the trap. Unfortunately, this platform is more easily detected as it has a larger profile than the single horizontal stick used in a basic twitch up. A good trade-off is to make multiple snare loops for a prey to step in. Also, instead of creating a flat platform, alternating branches can be placed over the horizontal stick to resemble a "rooftop" platform.

Pros: Greater surface area for greater triggering effect

Cons: Larger footprint means easier recognition by prey

The platform twitch up snare setup requires no bait and fires when the prey steps foot on the platform. The twitch up pulls taut around the prey's leg and holds under the tension from the counterweight.

All of these trap triggers have their quirks and nuances to make them more sensitive and effective. Our photos show the basic traps without the clutter of "fencing" that funnels the animal in. This will increase the effectiveness of the trap. Of course, you could have the best trap in the world, but if it isn't in the right spot, it won't matter and you'll end up hungry. Don't try to half-ass your approach to game getting. If you're willing to learn how to make the traps to catch game, learn where your dinner lives, its habits, and the knowledge from seasoned trappers, you'll be able to bring dinner to you rather than you tracking it down. ∷

Universal Trapping/Snaring Best Practices

1. Funneling Using branches, rocks, and logs, create a funnel that forces your prey into your trap. If you can't bait your trap, funneling draws an animal into a setup they otherwise would attempt to avoid.

2. Multiple Traps Trapping works best on the principle of the more, the better. A single snare covering a rabbit hole may pay off, but multiple overlapping snares will increase your odds. The same concept goes for crushing traps – a minimum of six should be set with the expectation that just one will be effective.

3. Watch Your Eyes and Fingers Whenever you're setting a trap, there's a possibility you'll accidentally trigger it. Eye injuries or crushed fingers can happen. Respect your traps and what they can do.

4. Check Frequently Traps can be triggered inadvertently, and a trap that isn't set won't catch anything. Traps can be blown over by the wind, or they might just wound an animal, allowing it to possibly escape before you return. Traps should be checked every four to eight hours.

5. Dispatch Safely Ideally, snares will wrap a loop around an animal's neck and either snap the spine or strangle it. Ideal is rarely the case, and snares can sometimes catch an animal around the head and shoulder, around the trunk, or around one or both of the rear legs. If you catch an animal that's still squirming in a trap, you need a way to dispatch it humanely. A good forked stick will help pin it down or against a tree. A baton strike or .22 to the head will do the rest.

6. Reset Traps Animals are creatures of habit, and the instincts that drew the first animal to the trap you set may lead others there too. If your trap isn't mangled from the first kill, reset it and check it later.

7. Baiting Traps Baiting traps will improve your odds. Scavenged mushrooms, berries, nuts, and animal guts can be harvested in the wild depending on the usual diet is the animal you're trying to trap. You can also sacrifice some trail mix or a small bit of an energy bar to bait your traps.

About The Author

Kevin Estela has been a professional survival instructor since 2007 first at the Wilderness Learning Center as lead instructor and then with his own company, Estela Wilderness Education. Kevin is a ranked associate level instructor in Sayoc Kali, a purple belt in Brazilian Jiu-Jitsu under Sifu Chris Smith, and an avid firearms marksman and shooter. When not teaching outdoor skills, he's a full-time high school history teacher and founder of the Estela Wilderness Education Fund. Follow him on Instagram/twitter @Estelawilded or www.facebook.com/estelawildernesseducation

3 › Medical

On the Chopping Block

When is Amputation the Only Option?

By Curt Lang

If you haven't heard of Aron Ralston's horrific tale of survival, then you must be living under a rock — or at least been stuck under one, like him. Aron's ordeal of having his arm pinned by a boulder inside a Utah canyon made headlines across the world and has even been told through the lens of Hollywood in the Oscar and Golden Globe nominated film *127 Hours*. What makes his story so fascinating is his ultimate decision to perform self-amputation on his arm to escape and have any chance of survival.

Warning! This article is meant to be a quick overview and not a detailed guide on procedures relating to amputations. To be prepared for any emergency, we encourage you to enroll in a certified medical course or, at a minimum, a familiarization course.

Historically, amputations that were performed outside a hospital, called field amputations, have mainly taken place on the battlefield. In modern times, field amputations are mostly only needed for extrication purposes. Though very rare, field amputation cases are still reported due to car crashes, industrial accidents, and natural disasters.

Due to the high risks involved, surgeons and professional emergency response personnel perform the majority of field amputations. It is critical to remember that such a procedure is a one-way street with dangerous consequences. So before we go down that path, we must lay out the groundwork for making an informed decision. Amputations can only be done along the limbs (arms, legs, feet, and hands) and should never be done on the main trunk of the body nor — obviously — the neck.

When faced with limb entrapment, the first step is to make sure the victim is stable by checking all their vitals. Try to free the victim by using leverage or more manpower to move the heavy object and free the limb. If the victim is stable and time is not a factor for the victim's survival, then contacting emergency services and waiting for help is your best option. But if help cannot be summoned and there is imminent danger to the victim's life, consider the following. There are four main criteria used by medical personnel in the field to determine if amputation is necessary. In all cases, the victim has a trapped extremity that cannot be extracted within a reasonable time. Criterias one and two are situations where amputation is absolutely necessary, while criterias three and four are up to one's informed judgment.

Criteria For Amputation

CRITERIA ONE

The victim's vitals are diminishing rapidly, such as drop in body temperature or loss of blood, where removal of the victim is necessary for stabilization of vitals or transport.

CRITERIA TWO

The victim is in immediate physical threat, such as from fires, collapsing structures, and other dangers that require immediate evacuation.

CRITERIA THREE

The victim is initially stable, but shows signs of deterioration after time. Vitals become unstable as time goes by.

CRITERIA FOUR

The victim is stable, but extraction time may take hours or is indeterminable, and sometimes extraction is impossible without amputation.

Now let's assume that a nuclear meltdown has eliminated any surgeons within a 50-mile radius and the radiation has created a swarm of human-eating squirrels. Your buddy is pinned by a heavy object on his arm or leg and cannot be freed. Mutant rabid squirrels are hungry and rapidly advancing in your direction. This surely is a situation where amputation is the best option, and now you must take action.

Once the decision is made, your next challenge becomes obtaining the necessary tools. Ideally, you want to have anesthetics, gloves, a tourniquet, scalpels, saw, and antiseptic materials. However, depending on the situation, you will have to make do with what is available in your immediate surroundings.

Amputation is painful, so any type of anesthetics will help — but since it is not normally readily available, anesthesia is optional. Local anesthetics can be applied liberally around the area where the cut will be made. If sedatives are available and you are trained in proper administration of the drug, then sedation can help. However, sedation should be avoided if the victim will be too difficult to move after amputation or if the victim is required to remain mobile.

Tourniquet and Torsion

One item that is not optional and might be the most important step in a successful amputation is a tourniquet. Knowing how to apply a proper tourniquet is absolutely necessary to ensure that the victim will not suffer from excessive loss of blood during an amputation. Commercially available tourniquets such as the Combat Application Tourniquet (CAT) and the Special Operations Forces Tactical tourniquet (SOFTT) are available. Both use nylon straps that loop around the limb and use a turning rod mechanism to tighten the tourniquet.

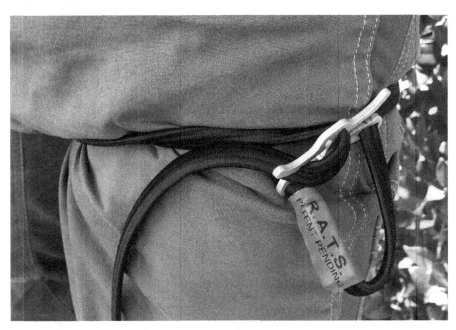

Overhand knot

Simple tourniquets can be made out of anything, such as belts, clothing, shoestrings, and towels. Aron Ralston used the rubber hose from his hydration pack as a makeshift tourniquet. The best tourniquets are wide, preferably over 2 inches, to provide pressure over a greater surface area. Do not use thin string or wires that can cut into the victim's skin and cause unwanted bleeding. If you need to use thinner materials, place a protective inner lining against the skin to prevent it from getting cut. The tourniquet should be soft enough to circumvent the limb and be able to tighten evenly around the limb.

The other item you will need is a torsion device, which is usually a stiff rod-like material. Basically, a strong wooden stick will work, preferably around 1 foot long. First, you will need to place the tourniquet in the correct position. An effective tourniquet should be placed a few inches above the trapped area of the limb. For amputations, do not place the tourniquet too close to the trapped area because there will need to be room for cutting the tissue. Also, never place a tourniquet directly around a joint because the blood vessels are protected from applied pressure.

Once the location is determined, wrap the tourniquet around the limb and secure it tightly around the limb with an overhand knot. Place one end of the torsion device

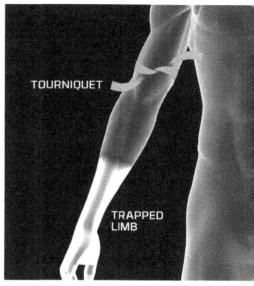

Once the location is determined, wrap the tourniquet around the limb and secure it tightly around the limb with an overhand knot.

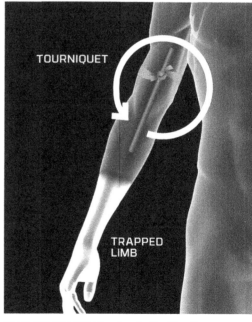

Place one end of the torsion device directly over the knot and secure the torsion device onto the tourniquet with two more overhand knots. Tighten the tourniquet by twisting the torsion device – in one direction only – thus increasing the pressure on the blood vessels.

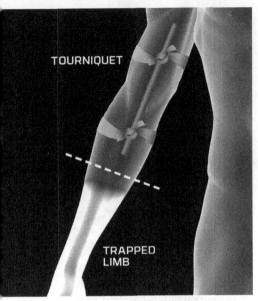

Secure the torsion device to prevent it from loosening by tying the other end of the torsion device against the limb using any remaining material.

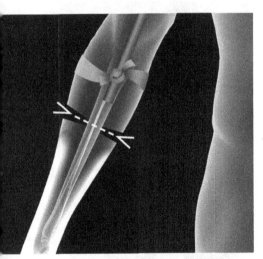

Using a sharp tool, make an incision into the flesh, and cut laterally to both edges of the limb. Continue to cut deeper and toward both sides until you reach bone. Cut the tissue around the bone and try to create a small gap in the tissue for cutting the bone. Using a stronger and sturdier tool, you will now cut through the bone completely. After the bone is cut, continue cutting the remaining tissue beneath the bone.

directly over the knot and secure the torsion device onto the tourniquet with two more overhand knots. Tighten the tourniquet by twisting the torsion device — in one direction only — thus increasing the pressure on the blood vessels. A sign of an effective tourniquet is the cessation of bleeding in any wounds beneath the tourniquet. In the case of amputation with no downstream bleeding, look for signs such as loss of color in the skin below the tourniquet. Now you will need to secure the torsion device to prevent it from loosening by tying the other end of the torsion device against the limb using any remaining material. It cannot be overstressed that an improperly applied tourniquet will greatly complicate an amputation.

Clean Cut

Ideally, we would want to reduce the likelihood of infection by sterilizing the amputation area and all tools with a disinfectant before the procedure. If you have sterile gloves, use them. In unfavorable conditions, try to keep as clean as possible by removing dirt and other grime from the area and rinse the tools with water. Infection can have serious consequences, so maintaining cleanliness is important.

In order to free the victim, a complete cut must be made through the limb. You will need something sharp to cut through the tissue and another tool that is sharp yet strong enough to cut through bone. Several options can be used to cut tissue, such as a kitchen knife or a pocketknife. The difficult part will be finding something that can cut through bone in a reasonable amount of time. A saw will work, as will a large serrated knife.

Using a sharp tool, make an incision into the flesh, and continue to cut laterally to both edges of the limb. Try to be as efficient in your cuts as possible to reduce the amount of time that the victim will have to endure the pain. Continue to cut deeper and toward both sides until you reach bone. Cut the tissue around the bone and try to create a small gap in the tissue for cutting the bone. Using a stronger and sturdier tool, you will now cut through the bone completely. Remember that the upper half of the arm and leg contains one large bone, while the lower half contains two smaller bones. After the bone is cut, continue cutting the remaining tissue beneath the bone.

Whatever It Takes

Complications can arise at any time during the amputation. Heavy bleeding from the initial incision site means that the tourniquet was not properly installed. Immediately stop with the cutting and refashion the tourniquet until the bleeding ceases. Applying a second parallel tourniquet directly near the first one can also increase its effectiveness.

If your tools will not cut through the bone, then brute force can be used to fracture it. This method was used by Aron Ralston to free himself. Using the site where the limb is trapped as the fulcrum, apply heavy force along the free part of the limb. This will create leveraged force, which can snap the bone near the fulcrum. When using this technique, make sure to secure the joint area (elbow or knee) with added support so that you do not dislocate the joint. A good snapping sound will accompany the breakage of bone and some tissue damage can be present around the break.

If this still does not sound like a horror film yet, then these other options might help make it so. In real situations you will have to improvise and make quick decisions. If you need to make your own sharp object to cut the flesh, try using a sharp rock or glass. This might not be the cleanest, but sometimes it may be your only option. If you have an axe or meat cleaver and know how to wield one, then make sure it is one clean chop. Got a chainsaw? No problem — that may work too.

After the victim is free, it is essential to remember not to remove the tourniquet, which is keeping the victim's blood from gushing out of the severed limb. Check the victim's vitals regularly and monitor for signs of shock. Keep the wound site as clean as possible and move the victim to a safe spot. Rest is always welcomed after a traumatic ordeal, but you should seek professional medical help as soon as possible.

Though the details might sound gory, matters of life and death require extreme actions to survive. By assessing your situation, knowing your options, and fully understanding the consequences, the decision for amputation can be important for survival. On a side note, if our hypothetical nuclear meltdown did not also eliminate all the lawyers in your area, then getting a written confirmation that your buddy agrees to receiving the amputation might help with any legal nightmares that might follow. By freeing your buddy, you've saved him from hungry mutant squirrels that were after more than just his nuts.

Warning! This article is meant to be a quick overview and not a detailed guide on obstetrics and child delivery. Consult a trained medical professional or accredited healthcare agency before even considering these techniques.

Labor Day

What If You Have to Deliver a Baby Without Medical Help?

Story by John Schwartze
Illustrations by Lonny Chant

When you realize you're going to have a child, it seems that the planning never ends. Selecting a name, shopping for clothes, and going to Lamaze classes are all part of preparing for the big day. But people often forget to plan for one outcome that happens a lot more often than you'd expect: delivering a baby before medical assistance can be reached.

We all hear about those stories on the news — the baby was in a hurry to get here or some complication prevented the mother from getting to the hospital and the delivery had to take place without a doctor or nurse. You may have heard about a woman who recently went into labor at a San Diego Padres game. The delivery came so quickly that it had to be performed at the stadium. Fortunately, the mother was lucky enough to be assisted by a nurse who happened to be there.

But what if she'd been somewhere remote, without the help of that experienced Petco Park staff nurse who happened to be a midwife as well?

Don't think it can't happen to you. If your car breaks down, you're snowed in, or just happen to be somewhere isolated and you have to deliver a child on your own, you need to know what to do. Your child's life may depend on it. Here at *OG* we believe in preparing for the *when*, not the *if*. Here we've put together some basic how-tos if you're alone and have to self-deliver or help the mother deliver and may only have small household items at your disposal to aid in the process. It should be reiterated that we're not advocating child delivery outside of a hospital setting; however, we know that emergencies do occur when medical help cannot be reached. We took the time to speak to some subject-matter experts to outline the steps to take should you be put in that situation.

Plan Ahead

First of all, it pays to be prepared. Don't assume you'll be able to reach the hospital in time — plan ahead, especially if you're nearing the due date or know you'll be in a location where reaching a hospital in a timely manner may be difficult. Certain airlines and cruise ships impose restrictions on traveling while pregnant and may require written permission by your doctor before allowing you to travel. These vary among companies and should be investigated well in advance. It's best to consult with your doctor before taking any extended travel, especially during the third trimester. Your doctor may recommend against it, particularly if any irregularities have been detected during your pregnancy.

At the very least, whether traveling or staying home, plan out routes to nearby hospitals. If you're traveling, are unfamiliar with the area, or will visit multiple locations, you should research hospital proximity for every stop you intend to make. The last thing you need is trying to figure out

Pregnancy Myths

Certain Foods Induce Labor

Rumors still persist that things like drinking castor oil or eating spicy food can induce labor. There is no scientific evidence to prove this. It's still unknown what exactly triggers the labor process to begin. Speculation still exists that having sex can induce labor, but this is still inconclusive.

Due Dates Are Accurate

Due dates can be inaccurate by weeks and even months. There is no guarantee that the delivery will occur nine months from the date of conception, give or take several days. This is, at best, an approximation. It's hard to pinpoint the exact date, so assume it can happen at any time and plan accordingly.

Baby Gender Develops During Pregnancy

The male's sperm determines the baby's gender. The fetus is not neutral during the pregnancy process and nothing can influence the baby's gender.

where to go and how to get there when labor has begun.

You'll want to prepare a go-bag with spare clothes and any medication you'll need to be on as directed by your doctor to safely continue during and after your pregnancy. Other essentials you should pack are diapers, baby clothes, spare food, baby bottle, and breast pump. Some people even forget that once they leave a hospital, they'll need a car seat for the baby. Best to have one of those beforehand.

Commercial OB kits are great resources to have on hand in preparation for a possible unassisted childbirth. The contents are sterile, available for purchase at virtually any medical supply store or website, and are relatively inexpensive. Assembling your own kit is another option (see sidebar on page 40 for content recommendations). It's advisable that you bring it with you or store some OB kits in places you may be staying. You can never be absolutely certain when the mother may go into labor, and you have to deliver at home, in the car, or in a location where no help is available.

It's also recommended you take an infant CPR course. If you plan on becoming a new mother or father — check out CPR courses in your area so you can better prepare yourself should you need to perform this procedure after the delivery if your baby is having difficulty breathing.

The Big Day

Let's say you are completely caught off-guard. An emergency forces you and your pregnant wife to leave home in a hurry, and her delivery date is quickly approaching. The next thing you know, you're staying in a secluded place with only basic household items at your disposal. Then the labor process begins, and the likelihood of reaching a hospital or paramedics is low. It's looking like you'll have to deliver the child because you have no other option. What do you do?

First of all, don't panic. Women have been successfully giving birth since long before hospitals and modern medicine existed. Stay calm and pretend you're back in log cabin days when it was common for women to deliver at home. If you have a phone and can call 911, do so and follow the instructions of the dispatcher so they can walk you through the process, and you can report any problems. There are various complications that can occur during the birth process. We can't cover every possibility, such as Caesarean sections, so the process detailed here is with the assumption that you are dealing with a normal baby delivery.

Pre-Delivery Prep

If you can't call for help and the mother starts going into labor, see if you can quickly assemble the following items in preparation for the delivery:
› Clean blankets
› Clean towels or gauze
› A couple lengths of string or small, clean clamps such as twist ties
› A clean, sharp knife or pair of scissors

"As labor gets underway, the mother will need to do what's comfortable for her. She may want to walk around, and if it's early enough, she can still eat and drink. Being hydrated and fed are important, especially if the labor is long," says April Schwartz, a 10-year paramedic who has delivered four babies in the field. "Keep track of the contraction intervals. When they are consistently three to five minutes apart for about an hour, the delivery is imminent."

Contractions occurring less than two minutes apart and the mother complaining of the urge to bear down are telltale indications that the delivery process is about to start. If you're seeing these signs, have the mother lie down and get comfortable. Lying down is not imperative, but when she begins to push this will help you be in a better position to deliver the baby. Your role is basically to assist the baby's birth. The process happens by itself and you'll need to help guide the baby as best you can.

Crowning

Begin by washing your hands thoroughly and wearing sterile gloves if possible. When you begin seeing the baby's head "crown" (presence of baby's head at the birth canal), the birth process is beginning.

"You never want to reach in and grab or pull," says Schwartz. Check to see if the umbilical cord is wrapped around its neck. If the cord appears to be wrapped around the neck, this can be problematic and prevent the baby from breathing. "Place two fingers under the cord and guide it over the baby's head so it's not wrapped, taking care not to force the cord by pulling it," says Joe Ferraro, a 15-year paramedic who has delivered three babies in the field and teaches EMS child delivery at a junior college in San Diego County. "You just want to loosen the cord as best you can and make space between the neck and cord as the delivery progresses."

If you are still unable to free the cord after trying to guide it over the baby's head, clamp the cord in two spots with clamps in the OB kit or by tying a couple lengths of string a few inches away from each other on the cord and cutting it in between the two clamps or ties. This will keep the cord from causing a constriction. If you have a sterile knife or scissors, they can be used to cut the cord. Usually the cord is not around the baby's neck and, if that's the case, the delivery will continue to progress normally.

If a shoulder begins to present, you want to apply a minimal amount of unilateral pressure so the other can come out. Tilt the head up slightly so one shoulder can be relieved, and then the other shoulder. Usually the baby is turned sideways during a normal delivery. You do not want to push

on the top of the baby's head — their cranial bones are very soft and pressure to the top of the head can cause brain injury. Just apply light pressure so it's not an explosive delivery. Do not pull or push the baby, just guide it as the head is coming out while the mother pushes.

Post-Delivery Care

Once the shoulders are relieved, the baby will begin to expel rapidly. Help gently guide it out to keep it from falling. Once it's out, you'll want to quickly warm and dry the baby. "Stimulation from drying it lightly, but vigorously will encourage the baby to breathe," Ferraro says. "Once it starts taking its first breaths, it will usually begin crying. The important step at this point is to keep the baby level with the vagina to keep blood flow regulated since the umbilical cord is still attached, unless you've already cut it to free it from the baby's neck."

The baby will appear somewhat bluish after the delivery, which is normal. Check the baby's pulse — a newborn baby's heart rate should be 120 to 160 beats per minute. "If the baby has a low pulse, appears sluggish, does not open its eyes, start crying, or breathing normally, they may need a few rescue breaths to see if they wake up and jostle," says Schwartz. "You can also try gently smacking the bottom of the baby's feet to encourage breathing." Be sure you're familiar with infant CPR before attempting this — like adult CPR, there is too much that can go wrong if you are inexperienced with the process. If there are respiratory difficulties, you can start CPR on the child or use the syringe bulb in the OB kit to suction the mouth and free it of any fluid or blockages. If the crying has a good strong tone and the baby is breathing normally, suctioning or CPR is not needed.

If everything appears to be proceeding normally, prepare to cut the cord. "Generally after the birth, the cord will pulsate for a couple minutes," says Ferraro. "Once it stops, clamp or tie it off 6 to 8 inches from the child and then another clamp 2 to 3 inches from that toward the mother. Once it's clamped, cut between the clamps."

"If no means to cut the cord are available, you can go about a day without cutting it, as it will shrivel up on its own," Schwartz says.

After ensuring the baby is healthy, breathing, and crying, it should be given to the mother for warmth and to begin breast-feeding. This process will stimulate the mother to stop contractions and bleeding, as well as feed the child. "The child will begin to develop passive immunities through the mother's milk," Ferraro says. The baby should be kept skin to skin with the mother as much as possible. The mother's smell will help the baby start to perk up and breathe better. Cover the mother and newborn with a clean, warm blanket. Babies can easily lose heat since their body is not ready yet to regulate temperature. Keeping the baby's head warm is important since they lose heat through their head. Softly applying a skull cap can help keep the baby warm, and these are usually found in an OB kit.

The placenta and afterbirth will deliver itself, and you don't need to pull it out. Once it delivers, the bleeding should be minimal. Try to stop any bleeding with sterile dressing or a clean cloth by applying a minimal amount of direct pressure – don't pack the vagina with any of these materials. Have the mother lay down and put her feet up to keep from fainting or excessive blood loss.

After the delivery is complete you should do whatever you can to reach a hospital, taking care to move the mother as little as possible since fluid loss will still be occurring.

Self-Delivery

If you are the mother, and have to deliver alone, you'll need to basically do what's been previously described as best you can. Put your hand down to guide the baby to make sure it doesn't fall. Assuming the delivery happens without complications, try to rest, let the placenta expel, and keep the baby at your level. Cover the baby, keep it warm, and nurse as soon as possible. Women who are alone and forced to self-deliver may choose to do it sitting or squatting – this is not unusual in other parts of the world. After the delivery, try to seek medical attention immediately.

OB Kit on the Go

You can buy premade OB kits, but if you prepare your own you should at the very least include:

- Clean blankets
- Sterile gloves
- String or clamps
- Sterile scissors or scalpel
- Alcohol pads
- Skull cap for baby
- Bulb syringe for suction
- Abdominal pads for bleeding control
- Dressings for a sterile field

Conclusion

Aside from these steps, there is not much else you can do until medical help arrives. The best remedy for the situation is to be prepared and not put yourself in a position where you may have to deliver the child without trained assistance. The more you can do to avoid situations where you may be unable to reach help in time, the better off you and your child are. If you're ultimately put in that position, best to stock up on the household items and medical training you might have to rely on. Better to have it and not need it than need it and not have it.

Back to the Suture

The OFFGRID Guide to DIY Wound Closure Methods

By Joe Alton, MD

Traumatic injuries occur in the tens of millions every year in the United States. According to the Centers for Disease Control and Prevention (CDC), close to 2-million victims of trauma require hospitalization annually. In normal times, trauma victims have the benefit of an infrastructure that allows rapid stabilization and transport to a modern medical facility. The off-grid medic, however, has no such access, but is even more likely to be confronted by traumatic injuries.

Warning! This article is for informational purposes only and applies specifically to long-term off-grid scenarios. Improper wound closure can cause more problems than it solves. Seek care by certified professionals wherever a functioning medical system exists.

In survival scenarios, mishaps related to activities of daily survival are bound to occur. Those unaccustomed to, say, chopping wood for fuel could easily end up requiring intervention by someone with medical skills in the event of an accident.

One of those skills is wound closure. The well-rounded medic should be familiar with the various methods and materials used in closing a laceration. More important still is the proper judgement as to when an open wound should be closed and when it should not. Having the necessary knowledge, training, and equipment is imperative to be an effective caregiver.

The Open Wound

An open wound is any injury that breaches the skin. Skin is your natural armor. It prevents the invasion of microbes into the body that could otherwise be life-threatening. Typical open wounds include:

Abrasions: An abrasion occurs when your skin rubs or scrapes against a rough or hard surface. A motorcyclist's "road rash" is one example, but most people have "skinned" their knee as children. Bleeding is minimal, but the wound needs to be scrubbed and cleaned to avoid infection. No closure is necessary.

Punctures: A puncture wound is a hole created by a projectile, nail, needle, or certain animal bites. Some punctures may not visibly bleed, but can be deep enough to damage internal organs and increase the risk of infection if closed.

Lacerations: For the purposes of this article, we'll define a laceration as a cut that goes through both the upper layer (epidermis) and the lower layer (dermis) of the skin. Skin lacerations expose the structures underneath to the risk of contamination. Accidents with knives, tools, and machinery may cause lacerations that slice through major blood vessels or even cut deeply into internal organs, like the liver. Bleeding can be extensive. Most lacerations these days are closed by a medical professional.

Avulsions: An avulsion is a tearing away of skin and the soft tissue beneath. Avulsions usually occur during violent accidents, such as crush injuries or shrapnel wounds. Degloving is another gruesome form of avulsion (don't Google that unless you have a strong stomach). In many cases, these wounds bleed heavily and rapidly. After assuring that bleeding has stopped, closure may be attempted at some point dependent on the amount of tissue lost.

Decisions: Primary, Secondary, or Tertiary Intention

When faced with an open wound, you can choose to:
❱ Close it right away ("primary intention")
❱ Keep it open and let heal on its own ("secondary intention")
❱ Keep it open for a time and then close ("tertiary intention")

Your choice will depend on the situation. Most wounds that you close (primary) heal just fine as long as the wound is flushed with clean drinkable water or a diluted antiseptic solution. This is known as "irrigation" and serves to clear out debris and germs.

Primary Intention: Closure by primary intention usually leads to edges that fit together neatly and, if done properly, drops the risk of infection significantly. It's important to know that, although skin heals very rapidly, deeper tissues like

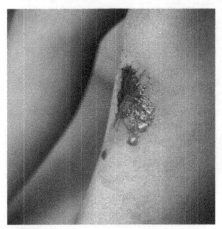

Skinned knees are a common form of abrasion. Typically, no closure is necessary; clean and dress the wound to reduce the risk of infection.

muscle and tendon take longer to heal and recover full strength.

For wounds that are jagged in nature, a portion of skin may require trimming, also known as "debridement." This makes the wound more symmetrical and assures the removal of dead tissue that would impede the healing process.

Secondary Intention: Healing by secondary intention leaves the wound open. It's preferred when wound edges cannot be brought together easily. An example might be a shrapnel wound, where large areas of tissue may be torn off. This may also be used for wounds with a significant amount of dead tissue (like bedsores), which requires debridement.

The process of a wound closing on its own is called "granulation" due to the granular look of newly forming tissue. The larger the wound, the longer it'll take to fill in. Other factors like the age and general health of the victim play a part in the speed of healing, as does the presence of infection.

These wounds are usually packed with moist (not soaked) sterile dressings, which should be changed at least daily and irrigated with clean water or a diluted antiseptic solution.

Tertiary Intention: Healing by tertiary intention is also known as a "delayed wound closure." In this strategy, the wound isn't closed immediately because of suspected contamination. It's treated like healing by secondary intention for a period of time so that the tissue can be closely observed for signs of infection. If no signs of infection are present after two or three days, the wound may be closed at that time.

Waiting to close is the more prudent

When to Remove Sutures or Staples

The longer sutures are in place, the higher the chance they may become embedded in the skin and cause scarring. On fine skin on the face, five days is often enough. On regular skin, like your forearm, a week to 10 days should do. Consider two weeks or more if the closure involves a joint, like the knee. If you're not sure about the strength of healing, take one or two alternating stitches out in the middle and observe for skin edge separation.

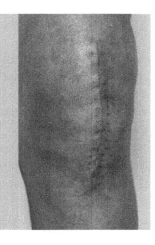

approach in many cases where infection is a common complication, like bite wounds. Leaving the wound open for a time allows pus and inflammatory fluid to drain and not accumulate below the skin.

A partial closure is sometimes performed with the placement of a drain. Drains consist of thin lengths of latex, nitrile, or even gauze placed into the wound to allow drainage. "Penrose" drains are a reasonably priced item that are still used in some operating rooms. Don't be surprised if a drain leaks fluid; be sure to cover any exposed areas.

Many open wounds should be treated with antibiotics to prevent infection whether you close them or not. Natural substances with antibiotic properties, such as raw, unprocessed honey may be useful in survival scenarios.

To Close or Not to Close?

That is the question, as Hamlet would say. It seems like common sense that we would want to close a laceration to speed healing and prevent infection. The decision to close a wound, however, involves developing sound judgment, something that takes some training and experience.

What are you trying to accomplish by closing a wound? Your goals are simple. You close wounds to repair the defect in the body's armor, to eliminate "dead space" (pockets of air/fluid under the skin which could lead to infection), and to promote healing. Although more an issue in normal times, a neatly closed wound is more cosmetically pleasing.

Closure options include sutures, staples, tapes, or medical glues such as Dermabond. Even industrial superglue has been used (they're both in the cyanoacrylate family), although the prescription product tolerates getting wet better.

Always use the least invasive method possible to close a wound. Steri-Strips and glues don't put additional holes in a person, but sutures and staples do. In certain areas, however, it may be necessary to use them. Joints like the knee and elbow are so frequently flexed and extended that tapes and glue are unlikely to hold a laceration together. These wounds should be closed if possible. For that, sutures or staples are required.

You'd think that all wounds should be closed. Unfortunately, closing a contaminated wound can do a lot more harm than good, and could possibly put your patient's life at risk. Take the case of a young woman injured some years ago in a fall from a zipline — she was taken to the local emergency room, where 22 staples were needed to close a large laceration in her leg. Unfortunately, the wound had dangerous flesh-eating bacteria in it, causing a serious infection which spread throughout her body. She eventually required multiple amputations (including her hands).

Despite this tragic case, some wounds are good candidates for closure after a good cleaning. Lacerations that are less than eight hours old are an example. Beyond that, it's likely that bacteria have already colonized the injury. Even the air has bacteria that can cause infections.

Another case that might call for wound closure is if a laceration is long and deep, cutting through layers of subcutaneous fat, muscle, or other internal structures. A muscle that has been ruptured or torn may not regain its function unless cut edges are approximated. You may also

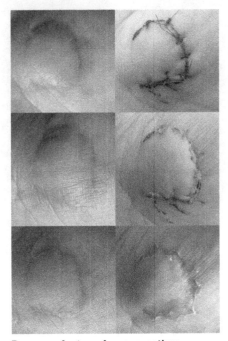

Progress of suture closure over time

decide to close a wound that gapes open loosely enough to suggest that it can be closed without undue pressure on the skin. The exception might be a puncture wound from an animal bite. These bites are loaded with bacteria and are often kept open.

Is the wound a simple laceration (straight thin cut on the skin) or an avulsion (areas of skin torn out or hanging flaps)? If the edges of the skin are so far apart that they can't be stitched together without creating undue pressure, the wound should be left open.

Wound Infections

Most wounds you'll encounter in an off-grid setting will be dirty. If you close a dirty wound, such as a gunshot, you have sequestered bacteria, bits of clothing, and dirt into your patient's body. Within a short period of time, the wound may show signs of infection.

An infected wound closure appears red, swollen, and is warm to the touch. In extreme cases, an accumulation of pus called an "abscess" may form. In these cases, stitches would have to be removed and the inflammatory fluid drained. If not recognized quickly, infection may spread to the bloodstream (a condition known as "septicemia") and become life-threatening.

The Suture Kit

Commercially produced suture kits, also known as "laceration trays" should contain the following items:
⟩ Needle holder
⟩ Toothed forceps
⟩ Hemostat
⟩ Small scissors
⟩ Gauze pads
⟩ Drapes
⟩ Antiseptic (such as Povidone-Iodine solution or Chlorhexidine; usually separate)
⟩ Sutures, absorbable and nonabsorbable

The above materials in the tray itself are usually labeled as sterile. Veterinary sutures are acceptable in a pinch as long as they're also sterile. If uncertain, the needle point may be exposed to heat until red hot, then allowed to cool. An alternative approved for nylon sutures by the National Institute of Health calls for 10 minutes of complete immersion in povidone iodine 10-percent solution. Rinse in sterile water or saline afterward.

One item missing from the list is local anesthetic. Agents like lidocaine with or without epinephrine are prescription drugs. Besides their anesthetic effect on soft tissue, they're also used for certain cardiac issues. An accidental injection of lidocaine into a blood vessel by an inexperienced medic can lead to life-threatening arrhythmias. Off the grid, anesthetic options may be limited to ice packs or topical ointments. Your experience with this may vary.

As for suture type, it's best to practice using an inexpensive non-absorbable suture like silk, which is, in my opinion, easier to practice with than some other materials.

Choosing A Closure Method

Let's say you've chosen to close the wound. When choosing a closure method, you should always use the least invasive method possible to close a wound. Surgical tapes and glues approximate wound edges well, but have little tensile strength. Sutures and staples are more invasive.

It's important to realize that you'll only have a limited supply of staples and sutures. If you're down to your last couple of sutures or the last stapler, feel free to mix different closure methods like alternating sutures and surgical tapes, or even adding duct tape improvised into butterfly closures when you've run out of medical supplies. You'd be surprised to see what qualifies as medical supplies when the chips are down.

There are several reasons why surgical tapes (Steri-Strips) and glues are used:
) They're less painful for the patient.
) Unlike sutures or staples, they don't require additional punctures of the skin. As such, there's less risk for infection.
) Materials are less expensive and more easily stockpiled.
) In a grid-down disaster setting, advanced closure materials like sutures and staples may no longer be manufactured or distributed. Conservation of these limited supplies is imperative.

Surgical Sutures: In certain areas, such as knee and elbow joints, it may be necessary to use sutures or staples. Sutures are needles and thread used to a sew a wound

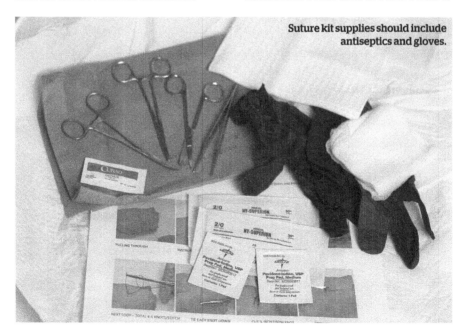

Suture kit supplies should include antiseptics and gloves.

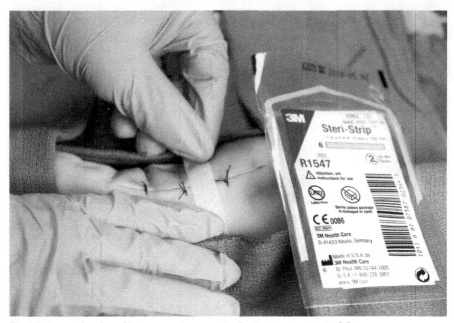
Steri-Strips can be placed between sutures or staples to conserve materials.

closed. Unlike staples, they can be used just about anywhere in the body. Some are absorbable; that is, they're meant to dissolve over time. For the off-grid medic, nonabsorbable sutures like nylon or silk will mostly be utilized for skin lacerations. There are, however, a wide variety of suture types available for just about any purpose.

Surgical Staples: Much like the staples used to hold paper together, they're almost as easy to place on the skin with a little training. Staple closures are strong enough to hold a wound closed over joints. A special removing tool is used for removal.

Sutures vs. Staples: Here are some considerations to help you choose between sutures and staples:

Sutures
〉 Can be used on skin or deep layers
〉 Best for jagged lacerations
〉 More skill required to perform well
〉 Can be performed alone
〉 Many materials from which to choose
〉 More time-consuming
〉 Any scissors can be used to remove, or no removal at all if absorbable sutures are used.

Staples
〉 Standard versions should be used for skin closure only
〉 Best for straight-line cuts
〉 Less skill required to perform well
〉 Best performed with an assistant
〉 Fewer choices (essentially, standard or large)
〉 Can be accomplished very quickly
〉 Requires special instruments to place and remove properly

Surgical Glue: Medical glues are cyanoacrylates meant for use in lacerations that don't need a tremendous amount of tensile strength. A good example would be a small laceration on the forearm.

Prescription medical glues like Dermabond hold up better to getting wet and are less irritating than regular superglue (which is also a cyanoacrylate). If you must use the industrial version, gels are easier to handle.

To use topical skin adhesive glue:
⟩ Approximate the wound edges carefully (best done with an assistant). If glue gets in the wound, it won't close.
⟩ Gently brush the glue over the laceration, taking care not to push any below the level of the skin.
⟩ Apply about three layers of the adhesive over the wound, preferably widening the area of glue each time after drying to increase strength of closure.

Although you'd use antibiotic ointment on most wound closures, avoid it in closures with skin glues; it breaks down the compound. The glue itself, however, helps protect the wound from infection.

Surgical Tapes: Surgical tapes are strips of sterile adhesive material used for simple laceration closure. A popular brand is called "Steri-Strips." Like medical glues, they work best on small lacerations upon which there is little stress. Placed with a sticky liquid called "tincture of benzoin," they adhere to both sides of the wound and pull it closed. Steri-Strips last for a few days and often fall off on their own. They can be used in between stitches or staples to provide more support or on top of glue closures.

How to Suture Skin

The process of learning how to suture should be hands-on. We teach it and found that there are few substitutes for having a physician show you how to stitch in person. Certification is rarely available, however, for those who aren't nurse practitioners, physician's assistants, or other medical professionals.

It's also important to realize that, off the grid, it'll be nearly impossible to duplicate the sterile conditions of an operating room. The best you can hope for is a clean environment that eliminates the majority of microbes.

You'll need something on which to practice. The best material I have found for teaching is a pig's foot. The skin of a pig's foot is probably the closest thing you'll find to human skin.

Wash your hands and put on sterile gloves. Place the pig's foot on a level surface and make a "laceration" by cutting straight through the skin with a knife or scalpel. You'll then perform a "skin prep." Paint the area to be sutured with a pad dipped in Betadine, Hibiclens, or other antiseptic. Alcohol may be used if nothing else is available. Start at the laceration edges and paint around them in an ever-widening oval. If you have enough materials, repeat three times.

Next, you'll isolate the "prepped" area by placing sterile drapes. The drape will usually be "fenestrated," which means it has an opening in the middle to expose the area to be sutured. If not, cut a hole big enough to see the entire wound. Taken together, we refer to this as the "sterile field." Local anesthesia would be given at this point if available.

Open your laceration tray and the suture packet cover. If you have sterile gloves, put them on now. Take the tip of your needle holder and grasp the curved needle in either the center of the arc (for skin) or one-third of the way from the string end to the needle point for deeper structures. Remove the needle and the attached string from the packet. Adjust the curved needle on the needle holder so that it's perpendicular (to skin) or slightly outward to the line of the instrument.

The needle holder is held in the dominant hand. If you're holding the needle holder in your right hand, the sharp end of the needle should point to your left and vice versa. For most purposes, the needle tip should point to the ceiling.

Now take your toothed forceps in your non-dominant hand and grasp the edge of the laceration where you wish to place the first stitch. Right-handers start on the right, left-handers on the left. Insert the suture needle at a 90-degree angle to the skin and drive it through that side of the laceration with a smooth twist of the wrist that follows the needle's curve. It should enter the skin no closer than a quarter inch from the edge of the laceration.

Release the needle but continue to hold the skin next to it with your forceps so that it stays in place. Re-clamp it, and pull through. Reload the needle on the holder and, going from the inside of the wound, drive the needle with a twist of the wrist through the skin on the other side of the laceration. If the edges are close together, this may be performed in one motion instead of two. If they're that close together, however, maybe you should have considered surgical tapes instead of sutures?

Pull the string through, leaving a small length on one side. This should leave you with a long side (the side with the needle) and a short side.

There are various ways to tie your suture, each with its own advantages and disadvantages. In our opinion, the ideal method for the survival medic:

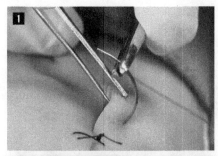

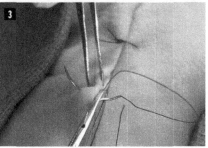

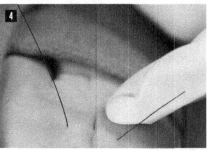

1. The needle enters the skin at a 90-degree angle.

2. Holding with the forceps, pass the needle through one side.

3. The needle goes through the other side.

4. Leave the end without the needle very short.

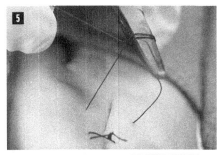

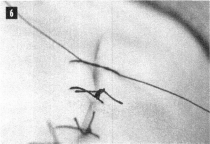

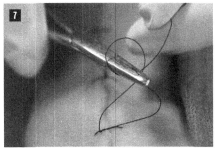

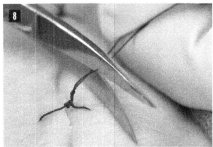

5. Loop the long end twice around the needle holder head.

6. Surgeon's knot in place

7. Each successive knot uses only one loop.

8. Perform several knots per stitch. Grasp both ends and cut at about ¼ inch from the knots.

) Has stitches that are independent of each other so that one faulty stitch by an amateur doesn't unravel the whole closure
) Conserves precious suture material
) Is easy to learn for the non-medically trained

This method is known as the "interrupted instrument tie."

Holding the needle holder loosely in the center over the wound, wrap the long end of the string twice over and around the end of the instrument. Then, open the needle holder end slightly and grab the very end of the short end of the suture. Pull it through the loop tightly to the other side. You'll form a square knot, also called a "Surgeon's Knot." Repeat the instrument loop several more times. Only one loop around the needle holder is required for every knot after the first. Four or five knots on top of each other should do.

Finally, grasp the two ends of the string and cut the remaining suture material ¼ inch from the topmost knot with your suture scissors. If you have a good supply of suture material, place each subsequent suture about ½-inch apart from the previous one, especially if over a joint (see below). In situations where suture availability is limited, you may choose to fill in areas between sutures with surgical tapes if the laceration isn't over a joint.

It's important to tighten your knots only enough to close the wound. Approximate, don't strangulate. Excessive pressure from a knot that's too tight will prevent healing in the area of the suture. You can easily identify sutures that are too tight — they cause an indentation in the skin where the string is. To complete your suture procedure, apply some antibiotic cream or raw, unprocessed honey. Then cover with a light dressing.

Once the closure is done, keep the wound dry and covered for 48 hours, checking it several times a day. Sutures or staples on the skin should typically be removed in seven days; if on the face, remove after five days; if over a joint, remove after no less than 14 days.

How to Staple Skin

After thoroughly cleaning a wound and applying antiseptic to "prep" the surgical field, you're ready to use your skin stapler. Your assistant will need two Adson's forceps to hold the skin for you. Position yourselves on either side of the patient. Both you and the assistant should wear sterile gloves.

Most staplers are held in the dominant hand the same way you would hold, say, a garden hose nozzle. Stand in a position so that you have an overhead view of the laceration to be closed.

Your assistant then grabs the edges of the skin with the two forceps. They'll then evert the edges (turn them inside out) slightly and gently press them together.

Hold your stapler at a 60-degree angle to the approximated edges and press firmly downward on the raised edges of the skin. The line of the laceration should be right in the middle of the line of the stapler.

Press the "trigger" of your stapler to embed the staple; then, release and retract. Check the staple placement and remove any that aren't appropriately executed. The skin should appear slightly "tented up" if the staple was placed correctly. Place subsequent staples ½-inch apart, especially in areas over a joint. If not over a joint, they can be spaced more widely apart, with surgical tapes placed between in-between.

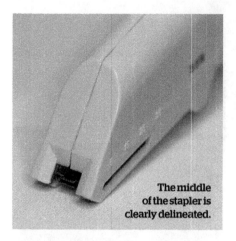

The middle of the stapler is clearly delineated.

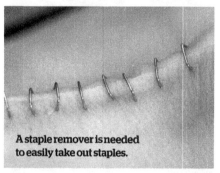

A staple remover is needed to easily take out staples.

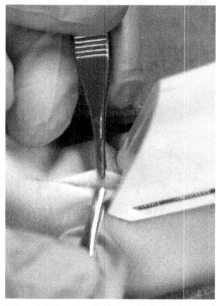

Adson's forceps are used to approximate the skin; the staple is then placed.

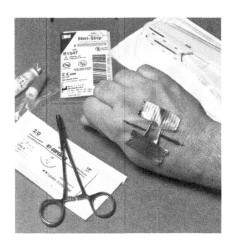

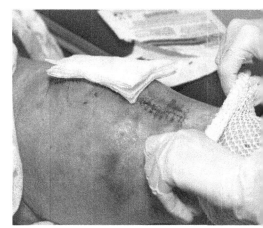

Various wound closure methods, including duct tape, staples, and Steri-Strips.

To remove staples, you'll need an instrument that's (unsurprisingly) known as a staple remover. This instrument is similar to office staple removers of bygone days. Place the "mandible" of the staple remover between the healed skin and the staple. Some brands contain two prongs on the lower blade and one on the upper. When the two prongs are under the staple, press the handles together; the top prong will press on the staple in such a fashion that the staple is easily lifted and removed. Repeat until all staples are removed.

Conclusion

It's important to realize that every surgeon may have their preferred way of closing a wound that differs from the above. Ask five surgeons, get five answers. Medicine is as much an art as it is a science.

There's a lot more that goes into proper education and training in wound closure than is found here, but with some commitment and determination, the off-grid medic can learn this important aspect of medical care.

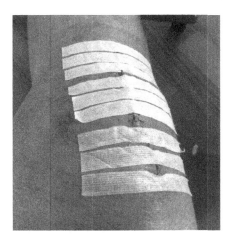

Suture Closure Aftercare

Most wounds closed with sutures should be covered with an antibiotic ointment and a nonadhesive dressing for the first 48 hours or so. Antibiotic ointments like Bacitracin or Triple Antibiotic reduce the rate of infection from 18 to 5-6 percent. These products, however, degrade surgical glue closures and shouldn't be used in those instances.

Antibiotic Alternatives
Plants, Poultices, and Pet Meds
By Dr. David Miller

A couple decades ago, I was backpacking in Central America and met a grad student who was studying the medicinal plants of the Mayan people. As a direct descendent of the ancient civilization, he wanted to know more about plants that were used back then and that are still available today. We had a great discussion, and he was kind enough to show me some medicinal plants. I asked him what he does when he gets sick and needs medicine; he replied

Warning! This article is meant to be a general overview and not a detailed guide on medical alternatives to be used in dire situations. Seek medical attention from a licensed physician before attempting any of these methods.

that he goes to the doctor and gets a prescription. Why? Because, that's the best medicine available today and is most efficient at treating illness. He added that the Mayans used plants because that was the best medicine they had available at the time.

That statement made quite the impression on me as a physician. I don't shun those using medicinal plants, but I always share this story when they direct the conversation that way. But what if you find yourself in a situation where access to modern medicine is limited, or non-existent?

Prior to 1850, infections were the most common cause of death. In the latter part of the 19th century, people like Lister, Koch, and Pasteur made advances that significantly lowered mortality due to infections. So, assuming you're up to date on your vaccinations and that smallpox doesn't make a comeback, the three biggest threats to surviving without modern antibiotics are pneumonia, infectious diarrhea, and skin infections. Fortunately, there are plants, poultices, and pet meds that serve as alternatives to treating infection.

Plants

It's important to know what plants are available in your area or bug-out location. What's present in the Midwestern United States may not be present in the Southwest. It's also important to identify plants correctly, as there are plants that mimic others and may not be helpful or could even be harmful (see *Eat This, Not That* in Issue 25 of RECOIL OFFGRID). Many of the plants used for medicinal purposes have both antimicrobial properties as well as anti-inflammatory properties. To be clear, don't use plants to stave off infection if antibiotics are available.

It's critically important to know what's available around you and what these plants look like in all seasons. There are plenty of books on medicinal plants and herbs, but a local plant identification class where you're shown exactly what to look for, what properties the plants have, and in what sort of habitat they typically thrive is the most helpful. By local, keep in mind that you may have to drive a few hours, but it's always worth your effort if it could save your life. There are numer-

Important Things to Remember

1. Know your local plants, their uses, and locations.
2. Understand which plants act as antiseptics and anti-inflammatories.
3. Don't rely on lesser treatments when better options are available (and warranted).

ous plants that can be helpful, but it's a good idea to keep a list of what you see in your area. If you wait until a scenario requires you to cram the material, it'll be way too late. Preplanning and education is the key.

Wild onions and garlic are easy to spot in the wild if you're looking for them. They can be helpful in fighting infection as well as inflammation. Whether you're eating them or using them topically in a poultice, they can be a valuable asset to have handy. Apple cider vinegar is also good to keep handy because it has many uses in a survival situation and is difficult to make/source in a hurry. It can help kill bacteria due to its acidity, and can help treat skin infections, bladder infections, and diarrhea. I'd recommend drinking 1 to 2 teaspoons in a cup of water twice a day to bolster the immune system. The water can be room temperature or warmed.

Tea tree oil is also something to keep handy due to its many potential benefits, including as an antibacterial agent to help with skin. For skin ailments, apply the tea tree oil directly to a closed wound, such as a boil, then cover with a bandage. This will help as an antiseptic to prevent further infection from getting into the wound. One drop of tea tree oil in a teaspoon of coconut oil rubbed on the wound twice a day should assist with healing and reduce localized inflammation. Keep in mind that tea tree oil can be toxic if ingested, and some people may experience irritated skin after applying it. Make sure to try a small test spot to see how your skin reacts.

Eucalyptus oil and camphor oil can be helpful in upper respiratory infections to help open the airways and break up some mucus. They can be used as a steam and inhaled or applied topically. The camphor can also be good for inflammation by rubbing it onto the skin in the affected area. There are many commercially available camphor combination creams (often mixed with menthol) available at your local superstore. Acorns can be easy to find and are a good source to use as an antiseptic for wounds on the skin. A handful of acorns in a pint of water is adequate to be beneficial. You can increase the efficacy of the liquid by crushing, then boiling the acorns. Don't drink the water as it can upset the stomach and cause abdominal pain. Instead, soak a cloth in the water and use it as a poultice or even a compress and place it on the affected area.

Poultices

The use of a poultice goes way back in time and can be a useful addition to your survival skills. A poultice is a paste made of plant material, used to relieve inflammation or as a drawing salve for infection. It's often placed on the injured area and covered with a cloth. Onions, charcoal, table salt or Epsom salt, or numerous herbs/plants (dandelion leaves, calendula flowers, and cayenne pepper) can be viable agents to cover a wound or area of inflammation.

As a general rule, use water as warm as you can tolerate without burning your skin to draw an infection and cold water to help with inflammation. Grind, crush, or pulverize the herb/plant/powder and add a little water to create a paste. You can then add it directly to the skin or onto a cloth if it irritates the skin. The best cloth would be cheesecloth. You want the paste to work on the skin, but not get too absorbed into the cloth. It's important that the poultice stay on for several hours to maximize effectiveness. You may need to repeat two to three times a day, depending on its efficacy and the severity of the wound. If you have an open wound or abrasion, application of honey is useful. This serves as a barrier to help protect the wound from debris and bacteria, but also acts as a topical antibacterial agent. We often will use medical-grade honey in wound clinics at the hospital as an adjunct to other modalities to treat wounds.

Pet Meds

When considering pet meds, you're really faced with a bit of a dilemma. First is acquiring the drugs. Fish antibiotics are available without a prescription from many online retailers. Unfortunately, you won't be able to buy them at your local retail pet store, as many of these medications are limited to distributors. With some foresight, however, an online retailer can have them to you in a few days. Many of the fish antibiotics are the same generic name and dose as for humans. This makes it easy for consumers in the self-reliance environment. Second, some folks question the safety and purity of fish antibiotics purchased online. Many are manufactured in the same facility as human antibiotics, but end up targeting a different market. The FDA doesn't regulate fish antibiotics like they do other meds, so it's often questioned whether they're safe to take. Impurities, concentration of drug, and absorption inconsistency are a few is-

ANTIBIOTICS AND THEIR USE

	TYPICAL ADULT DOSE	INFECTIOUS USES
Cipro	500 mg 2x a day	Urinary tract Travelers diarrhea Diverticulitis Anthrax Typhoid fever
Amoxicillin/ clavulanate	875/125 mg 2x a day	Sinus infection Skin infection Infected diabetic foot Cat/dog bite
Trimethoprim/ Sulfamethoxazole	800/160 mg 2x a day	Urinary tract Skin infection Travelers diarrhea
Doxycycline	100 mg 2x a day	Tick-borne disease Pneumonia
Metronidazole	500 mg 3x a day	Some GYN infections Giardia Diverticulitis with Cipro (moderate cases)

sues often cited as a concern. You should first try your local doctor for standard human antibiotics. Some physicians are open to writing a prescription to have on hand for emergency use.

The important part of taking any antibiotic is to know what you're treating with the antibiotic on hand. One antibiotic does not treat every infection. Taking an incorrect antibiotic may not treat the infection, and can allow the infection to progress as well as increase antibiotic resistance. This is why doctors don't like to treat illnesses with antibiotics if they're not needed, as antibiotic resistance has made it challenging to treat certain infections. The *Sanford Guide to Antimicrobial Therapy* is published every year and is an excellent choice to guide which antibiotic to use in a particular infection. Although this guide is directed towards humans, it would be valuable in guiding your choices in the lateral fish antibiotic market. I've kept one at my fingertips for the past 25 years.

When choosing which antibiotic to purchase (for your fish, of course), choose one that has a dose comparable to humans. The less "extra" ingredients, the better;

however, this still may not ensure it's free of impurities due to the lack of regulation. Next, get a variety of antibiotics, as one antibiotic doesn't work for every infection. For example, a drug for a bladder infection may not be the best choice for a skin infection. Last, please put some thought into the decision to use the antibiotic. This should not be taken lightly, and in a survival situation should be reserved for life or death circumstances.

In Summary

A recently published book by Dr. Joe Alton and his wife Amy of Doom and Bloom Medical called *Alton's Antibiotics and Infectious Disease* is easy to read and understand, and explores using antibiotics in an austere environment. It's well worth picking up if you want to learn more about infectious disease and options for treatment. Check online retailers for books on medicinal plants as well. Find one specific for your area/region or make your own reference based on what you see around you.

Plants, poultices, and pet meds are excellent alternatives if nothing else is available to you. Otherwise, see your physician if you're dealing with an infection. Pharmaceutical-grade antibiotics, if you need them, are the best choice for treating infections. For minor inflammation, you could certainly try plants and poultices, but I would caution you to stop these treatments if they're not working and seek medical help. Lastly, pet meds like fish antibiotics are an option if no other antibiotics are available. I would only use them in a dire situation and wouldn't take them in lieu of seeking medical treatment.

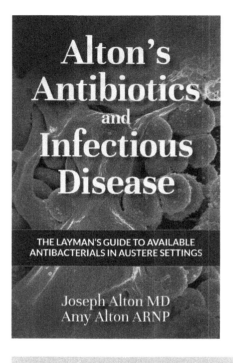

About The Author

David L. Miller, DO, FACOI is an internist in private practice for 20 years. His experiences away from the office have included time as a fight doctor in regional MMA events and as a team physician for 10 years at a mid-major university in the Midwest. Currently, he serves as the lead medical instructor for the Civilian Crisis Response team based out of Indianapolis.

Without a Hospital

What Do You Do When Conventional Medical Care is Unavailable?

By Dr. David Miller

We all do our best to be prepared in an emergency; however, there are always things we don't expect that may come up. We often take medical care for granted when disaster hits. The hospitals and physicians are usually there when we need them, but what happens when the hospital has been destroyed by a natural or manmade disaster? Remember Joplin, Missouri, in

2011 when an F5 tornado destroyed the hospital there? How about Hurricane Maria in 2017 that rendered 65 of 67 hospitals in Puerto Rico non-operational in the first few days after the disaster? There were 3.5-million people seeking help with only two functioning hospitals on the island. One month after the hurricane, less than half of those 67 facilities were operational. Are you prepared for that scenario? Do you have a plan?

I asked three experts in their respective fields what advice they'd give in a situation where disaster has destroyed medical facilities. Mark Linderman is a crisis risk manager for the CDC and takes a community approach to preparation. Kerry Davis is a former medic and nurse, and is the CEO of Dark Angel Medical. He focuses on teaching individuals skill sets and developing a plan to survive. J.R. Grounds is the leader of the Civilian Crisis Response Team and agrees with both Mark and Kerry in that individual skill sets are important; however, being flexible and working together are just as important.

Why is it important to be medically prepared for a disaster?
ML: There is a misconception that if something happens, the federal government will come in and save everybody. Depending on how widespread that disaster is, the government may not be able to help. A disaster happens locally first. The feds may be too busy helping elsewhere, and it may be some time before they can get to a smaller community. Communities need to understand what resources they have, how they're allocated, and how to respond if something happens. We need to care for ourselves first before the feds come in.

JRG: One of the problems is that before the outside help comes in, you can imagine that the staff at the hospital is being affected by the disaster. Maybe they can't even make it to the hospital. The local service providers are also compromised by the disaster. They may have emergencies at home as well. A hospital may be stocked with backup medical supplies and generators in preparation for a major catastrophe; however, the staff is a major resource that may not be able to get to the hospital.

KD: No one is coming to save you, so it's up to you.

When disaster strikes, what is the mindset for those going through the initial stages of the disaster recovery?
ML: Obviously, there is fear. Denial is also a huge factor in a disaster. A lot of people have to overcome that denial. Bitterness could play a huge role.

JRG: It's mass panic. Complete chaos.

KD: You have to remember the basic tenets of survival: fire, water, food, and shelter. Most importantly, have a plan. If you don't have a plan, then you are already behind the eight ball. Having a plan is being in the proper mindset. If you have a plan and know how to implement the plan, that will eliminate a lot of confusion.

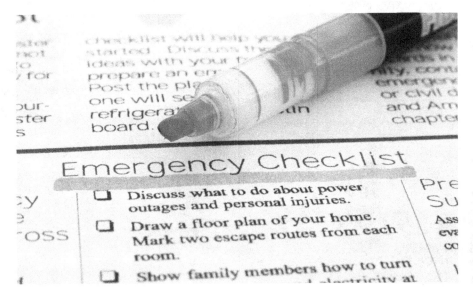

What can people do prior to the disaster to help improve their situation during a disaster?

ML: It's contingent upon the type of disaster. The biggest thing is that people should be sure they are up to date on the Tdap (tetanus vaccine). People should have a basic knowledge of first aid to help themselves or others. If the hospital is decimated, there should be protocols in place to address the situation with other agencies.

JRG: People have got to take more responsibility to deal with their current medical issues. Make sure they have medications, supplies, etc. They also need to be able to provide the short-term lower-level emergency care for themselves (e.g. bandages, anti-septics, splints).

KD: I think people are trying to become more self-reliant. I think if they know some basic medical stuff that will go a long way. Basic wound care is a big deal. Immuniza-

One of the problems is that before the outside help comes in, you can imagine that **the staff at the hospital is being affected by the disaster as well.**

tions are important. Make sure your tetanus is up to date. Dental health is important (see RECOIL OFFGRID Issue 27). Get an emergency dental kit. Have a reference library of books. Look at home remedies, because a lot of it works. Bioenvironmental stuff ... how to make clean water. How to use bleach. How to boil water. Basic field hygiene. In a prolonged disaster where people are dying, how are they going to dispose of the bodies? We may see the diseases of the dark ages — how are you going to prepare for that?

What medical supplies do you keep handy?

KD: We have analgesics, basic antibiotics

(Azithromycin, Ciprofloxacin, and Metronidazole). If you have these medications, make sure they aren't beyond their expiration dates. Lots of bandages, basic wound care, and dental care items (toothpaste, dental floss). Trash bags, toilet paper, feminine products, condoms, hydrogen peroxide, rubbing alcohol, basic suturing kits, skin staplers. If you know how to suture or staple, that's important too. Acetaminophen, Ibuprofen, and having pediatric doses of those medications are also helpful.

How often are you going through your med kit to know it's up to date?
KD: We do a quarterly inventory to make sure things aren't out of date. If something expires in that quarter, I will pull that and purchase an update for the inventory.

How many days of supplies should people have on hand?
ML: FEMA really tries to educate people that a three-day supply is adequate, but a disaster on a larger magnitude may require a much longer supply. Three days is a good start, but a more realistic view is that two to three weeks of supplies is needed.

If a disaster strikes and medical services are not immediately available, would there be any medical resources or facilities that would make sense as alternatives?
JRG: In Houston during Hurricane Harvey, the local hospital moved all of their critical patients to other facilities. We set up a tent with the National Guard infantry units and they didn't have necessary medical and decon staff. In a large-scale disaster like Harvey, there was a large geographic area to have the National Guard cover. Those units were being triaged themselves to areas where they could do the most good. The problem then was that the smaller areas were left to fend for themselves. The small

hospital was getting ready to go under water and their supplies were going to be compromised. They backed up a truck and loaded it with all kinds of medical supplies to take to the tent. We loaded stuff that we thought was important — bandages, insulin, diabetic supplies, nebulizers. We had a lot of resources, but the resources get triaged just like patients. If the resource is 10 miles away, but there is no way to get to it because of the flooding, it might as well be on the other end of the globe. The makeshift hospital that may be in a parking lot somewhere has to draw a line about who they might see because of the massive influx of patients. So when the secondary providers start getting that overflow of patients it can be very overwhelming.

ML: Emergency departments can be quickly overwhelmed during a disaster. There is a certain capacity that an emergency department can handle. If a hospital has been decimated, there are other resources available. Whether that is the Red Cross, churches, or universities, there are opportunities for assistance. Some universities can have nursing programs that can be valuable in a disaster situation. We have PODs (Places of Disbursement): open POD where people come to a location where, say, the health department has set up to care for people. There are closed PODs where universities that have nursing programs can help. These relationships are pre-established prior to the disaster. The urgent care center is also an option. Senior housing developments are a potential option, because they have nurses and medications that may be useful. Medical reserve corps (MRCs) should also be es-

> If a hospital has been decimated, **there are other resources available.** Whether that is the Red Cross, churches, or universities, there are opportunities for assistance.

tablished before the disaster. These consist of volunteers from the medical community who are important to establish.

Many people will want to help when a disaster strikes. Where should they go to be most helpful?
ML: You want to check with the local emergency management agency. You can also check with Red Cross, local churches, and walk-in clinics. Hospital and public health agencies get some degree of assistance and are required to have volunteer programs.

JRG: There will be some sort of incident command post that you can look for. If you see a tent in a parking lot, somebody in there will be in charge. Let them know what experience you have and what your credentials are, so that they can figure out how you can best be used. The other thing I would say is don't get your feelings hurt if that person doesn't immediately pay attention to you or put you right to work. They have to figure out how to incorporate you into the plan in a safe manner.

What about the surge of volunteers that shows up to help?

ML: Agencies have the best intentions, but their intentions convolute the process of response recovery. When we go down trying to help and it's not a part of the coordinated effort, there are now more people to feed, more places for people to stay. This diverts the efforts from people who actually need the help to people who are there to help. Now healthcare has to help people affected from the disaster, but also the people who are there to help.

> The biggest thing is having a plan, but be flexible.
> **Don't be so rigid you can't think outside the box.**

JRG: There are so many volunteers who just show up, and there isn't really a way to know what their experiences are or what equipment they have. So it becomes a situation where the volunteers can actually overwhelm the system. The person who's in charge on scene has to be responsible for the people affected by the disaster as well as the volunteers aiding in the disaster. The last thing they want is to need to take care of the volunteer as well. It's not that help isn't needed, but the chaos has to be managed. Also, find an organization that has experience in dealing with disaster services. Volunteer with them and get some experience.

Any final thoughts?

ML: The nature of a disaster is that it catches us off-guard so we have to be ready as a community. The community is the glue that holds us together and we have to remember that we are a national community as much as we are a local community.

JRG: You have to be able to take care of yourself. If you have a medical condition, you need to understand how your body will respond in that setting. You have to stay in the game to help as many people as you can.

KD: The biggest thing is having a plan, but be flexible. Don't be so rigid you can't think outside the box. There are a lot of gray areas. Plan ahead. Practice carrying your gear so you know if it's feasible to carry around. At least you are ahead of the guy who didn't plan. It's better to be proactive than reactive.

In Summary

When a natural or manmade disaster strikes, it may be a prolonged period of time before help arrives. Be prepared to fend for yourself. That means taking classes, developing skill sets, and formulating a plan for surviving the disaster aftermath. Make sure that you know what you are capable of doing in various conditions and train with your gear. Understand the emotional components after the disaster strikes and how you personally manage those within yourself and others. Maintain flexibility in your thinking as someone trying to survive the disaster as well as a responder trying to help others. As Kerry Davis said, "No one is coming to save you," and it's our responsibility to prepare and plan before disaster strikes.

About The Author

David L. Miller, DO, FACOI is an internist in private practice for 20 years. His experiences away from the office have included time as a fight doctor in regional MMA events and as a team physician for 10 years at a mid-major university in the Midwest. Currently, he serves as the lead medical instructor for the Civilian Crisis Response team based out of Indianapolis.

Pill Bottle Perishables

Is it Safe to Consume Expired Medications?

By Dr. David Miller

Here's the scenario: It's 5:30 a.m. and you go to the fridge to grab some milk, only to notice it expired a day ago. You hear a disturbance from the other room and, soon, in rushes your wife in a panic, "Don't drink that! It's gone bad!" Without even stopping to breathe, she grabs the milk and pours it down the drain.

In the *same* household, if you go to the medicine cabinet, you'll find medications that expired years ago. Why is it that food is immediately thrown out the minute it goes beyond the expiration date, but we keep expired medications "just in case?" Perhaps the easy answer is that we can always go to the store and get another gallon of milk before the sun comes up.

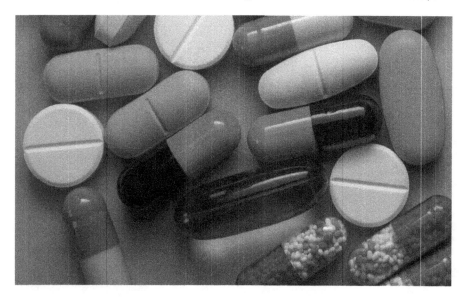

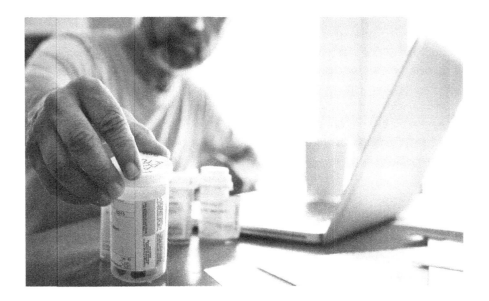

The more challenging answer is that you kept your wife up all night hacking up a lung, and she told you three days ago to go to the doctor (and you didn't). She will of course give the ultimatum that you go to the doctor today and get some medication, or else! Oh wait, she remembers that she has some cough medicine left over from when Johnny was sick ... "Here, try this." And all is better in the world. Thank goodness we kept that cough medicine for two years.

While this scenario could happen in any household in the world, it never happens in my household — because I have the best wife ever. However, I'll discuss some of the issues to consider when taking medications that have been salvaged from their imminent demise beyond the expiration date.

What Do These Dates Mean?

When talking about medicine in general, we always consider the risk-to-benefit ratio. In other words, if we consider options of a particular scenario, are the risks associated with our decision greater than the benefits? If so, we might elect not to pursue that particular option. Sometimes, we may accept the risk and proceed anyway. It's this scenario that comes to play when we take medication that has survived beyond its expiration date.

So what goes into determining the expiration date of a medication? According to the Food and Drug Administration, the expiration date of a medication is vetted by the manufacturer for the drug's ability to maintain its strength, purity, stability, and quality during its shelf life. The manufacturer of the drug must provide research data in this regard. Included in this process is the proper storage information for the drug in question. As long as the medication is stored properly, it should perform as expected up to the expiration date.

Once the drug has gone beyond its expiration date, several things can occur. The most likely outcome is that the medication is no longer stable or potent to do what it was intended to do. In essence, it may not work as well. Due to lack of stability, it's possible that the medication can break down into various components that may actually be harmful to the body. Although no pharmaceutical company that I have found has come forth with exactly what'll happen due to the instability, every single document on the FDA's website, and manufacturer's website, says that it can occur.

To evaluate this conundrum, the FDA has created the Risk Evaluation and Mitigation Strategy as part of the FDA's Amendments Act of 2007 to manage known or potential risks associated with a drug product. Part of that Strategy is to evaluate what happens beyond the expiration dates of medications. Back in 1986, the Department of Defense teamed with the FDA to enact the Shelf Life Extension Program. This was brought about to try to save the DoD money in replacing medications that had expired. It also increased the number of stockpile medications available in the event of necessity. Twenty years later, the Bioterrorism Act of 2002 created the Strategic National Stockpile, which built facilities to harbor medications targeting chemical, biological, radiation, or nuclear threats (CBRN). These medications also covered potential or emerging infectious disease threats. During President George W. Bush's terms, the legislation centered on increasing the ease of availability of medications during CBRN threats.

Post-Disaster Situations

So, thanks to the government, we have an understanding that medications, as related to the CBRN discussion, can be utilized beyond the expiration date. But how long? I'd always tell patients to discard any medications once they were a year old (some, like sublingual nitroglycerine,

So, thanks to the government, we have an understanding that medications, as related to the CBRN discussion, can be utilized beyond the expiration date. **But how long?**

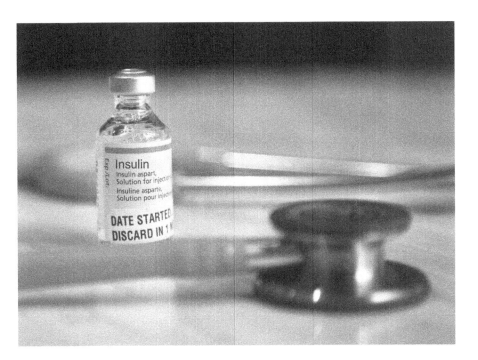

every three months). That really is nothing more than an arbitrary recommendation. It means that if you need that drug again and it has been a year since it has been prescribed, then I probably should see you anyway. It also assumes that the medication has probably not been properly stored and will not be as effective as intended. As usual, it was probably stored in the bathroom, where humidity and temperature changes vary considerably. If it's an antibiotic we're talking about, it may be that the reduced efficacy may not entirely rid the body of the bacteria and may increase the chance that resistance will occur when the bacteria re-emerges. Then, the antibiotic likely won't work at all. Perhaps you have infected other members in your household now with your crud and they too are resistant to the antibiotic.

If you're trying to avoid going to the doctor by storing your medications, please don't do it. Seek medical advice and expertise. However, if this is a true survival situation where chemical, biological, radiological, or nuclear threats have become a reality, then keep reading.

For chemical threats, we're talking about sarin and tabun in modern-day warfare. Historically, it also included mustard gas and chlorine gas. To counteract the effects of these chemicals we use atropine, pralidoxime, or a combination of the two. Atropine can be extended by four years beyond the expiration date, while pralidoxime has been extended up to five years. Further testing by the manufacturers could extend those dates further.

For biologic threats, agents like anthrax and botulinum toxin are frequently discussed. Two common antibiotics to treat anthrax are ciprofloxacin and doxycycline. The latter can be used six to eight years after the expiration date, while I have found no concrete recommendations for ciprofloxacin. For botulism, penicillin and metronidazole are the recommended medications. Penicillin, like ciprofloxacin, may maintain its stability long after the expiration date if stored properly. The same could be the case for metronidazole. In a survival situation, this may be a case where the accepted risk is worth the potential benefit if no help is otherwise coming.

Radiological and nuclear threats have their treatments based on symptoms. Potassium iodide is typically part of the stockpiled medications to reduce the risk of thyroid cancer in an individual exposed to radiation. The body absorbs iodine and doesn't care if it's irradiated or not. The potassium iodide competes for binding sites in the thyroid with the irradiated iodine. With less of the irradiated iodine being taken up by the body, the adverse outcome may be lessened. Potassium iodide has been shown to be stable for several years after the expiration date.

Other Threats

How about emerging infectious disease threats? These would be diseases like influenza where oseltamivir could be utilized in stockpiles. This is reported to have a shelf life up to 10 years beyond its expiration date. Other disease like Ebola, Zika, Chikungunya, and Dengue fever may not have specific treatments, but supportive care is important and could utilize a lot of resources in a major outbreak.

When those resources are scant in a catastrophe, there'll be more risk taken when it comes to medications. The risk of taking an expired medication might be worth it, but should be considered with caution. Nitroglycerine is a medication used by heart patients and usually comes in a small brown bottle with tiny white pills. These pills degrade relatively quickly when exposed to light, air, and humidity. Of course, use it if you have to; however, these really only remain viable for three to six months.

Planning for these types of situations in a controlled setting doesn't take much time and can **save a lot of angst when the stakes are high.**

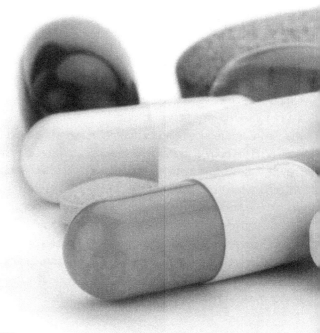

Another common drug is insulin, which can be kept at room temperature for about 30 days before it starts to lose efficacy. When refrigerated, it can be kept longer, but beyond a year, the potency is weakened and doses will need to be adjusted upward. This, of course, creates more variables in an otherwise difficult disease to manage. (For more on surviving in austere conditions as a diabetic, see "The Diabetic Survivalist" in Issue 24.) Other drugs that are in suspension, such as antibiotics, eye drops, and cough medicines may lose their potency faster due to lack of stability once they're placed in the suspension. It's generally not recommended to take these types of medications beyond their expiration dates.

Conclusion

Understand the risks and benefits of every decision you make, especially when it comes to taking expired medications. Periodically go through the medicine cabinet or closet to catalog what you have available, then work to procure more up-dated medication. Planning for these types of situations in a controlled setting doesn't take much time and can save a lot of angst when the stakes are high. Lastly, and most importantly, tell your wife how much you appreciate her looking out for you. ::

About The Author

David L. Miller, DO FACOI, is an internist in private practice for 20 years. His experiences away from the office have included time as a fight doctor in regional MMA events and as a team physician for 10 years at a mid-major university in the Midwest. Currently, he serves as the lead medical instructor for the Civilian Crisis Response team based out of Indianapolis.

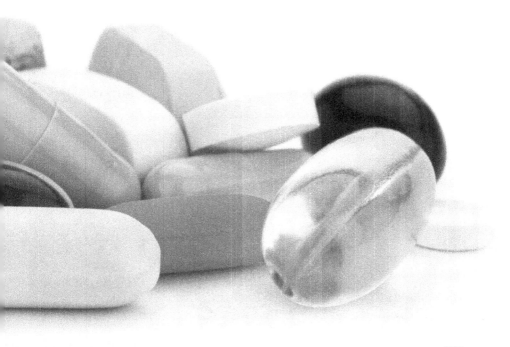

Clean Up Your Act

Maintaining Hygiene Without Your Usual Conveniences

By Dr. David Miller

If you've ever watched *Naked and Afraid* on the Discovery Channel, you've wondered about the hygiene on the show. Twenty-one days is a long time without a shower and soap. Obviously, they generally do fine, and it seems as if hygiene is downplayed on the show. It always gets me thinking, though. What kinds of issues would arise in that type of survival situation? How would I mitigate the atrocity of no soap?

First, let me start by saying that not having soap in that three-week period might not be as bad as you might guess. As long as you had water to clean with, you might be fine. In using your hands to scrub all of those 2,000 body parts, you remove debris and dead skin. This may keep the pores from clogging up to a certain degree and prevent inflammation in the pores of your skin. Some of these pores can have pustules and look infected, but usually don't progress in that direction.

Nature's Soap

Some of you might be thinking about making soap from hardwood ash and animal fat. The ash wouldn't be that difficult, and the animal fat would take luck and skill to acquire. But say you're adept and lucky. It can take some time to make bar soap — time that you might not be afforded in a survival situation. You could, however, mix the fat and ash in a pan that you cooked the animal in. It'd be great for washing the pan; however, the basic (pH) nature of lye from the ash might be irritating to someone with sensitive skin. It'd feel like a bad sunburn or worse. [See RECOIL OFFGRID Issue 30 about making soap from scratch.]

For a field-expedient solution, it's possible to crush the berries or roots of certain plants that contain natural compounds called saponins — soapberry (aka buffaloberry), soapwort, yucca, and creosote, to name a few. Upon mixing with water, these substances produce a frothy lather that was used historically as soap or shampoo. For more information, refer to our web article: offgridweb.com/?p=14084

Areas of Concern

Because most of the smelly parts on our body are also the most sensitive areas, and safely producing soap in the field may not always be viable, you'd be better off just using water on your body. You'll notice on *Naked and Afraid* that the participants are almost always given an opportunity to find water. It may not always smell the best, but it's available to make potable. I'm sure that a secondary reason is for bathing. You'll also notice that the contestants don't have rolls of fat like many of those in our citizenry. One of the problems with obesity is that the overlapping intertriginous areas are moist, hot, and rub against each other. These places, such as under the breasts, under belly fat, between the buttocks, and in the groin are common areas that are affected by poor hygiene and heat, and a foul smell can emanate from these areas. If left untreated, these areas can sometimes open up to create small wounds that may become infected by bacteria.

To treat these moist areas, air is probably the best weapon. Lying down and allowing the breeze to blow across those hard-to-reach areas will assist with keeping them dry and enable the areas to heal better. If you happen to be near a corn field, you could grind corn into flour and apply it to the areas. Again, this takes time and effort, probably more effort than is worth the time. And while corn flour isn't exactly the same as corn starch, it may be good enough to keep the affected areas drier. We usually recommend corn starch in our convenient environment if zinc oxide products aren't available. Apply this twice a day and wash, then dry, each time before application.

Another issue is that these warm, moist areas are ideal places for yeast to grow. This is what contributes to the funky smell that emanates from these intertriginous areas. Besides the smell, there may be redness, itching, peeling or cracked skin, and perhaps even small blisters. Although this isn't life-threatening, it's uncomfortable and you could also be susceptible to secondary infection when the skin breaks down. Hopefully your diet has been high in garlic to help boost your immune system. If you happen to find some wild garlic, you could either eat it or make a paste and apply it to the affected area. Let it sit for a few minutes, then rinse it off. You could do this twice a day. If you had a stockpile of apple cider vinegar, you could pour half a cup into a bathtub full of water, and soak. You could also try an apple cider vinegar compress by soaking a natural fiber cloth in the apple cider vinegar, then placing it on the affected areas for 15 minutes at a time. Do this twice a day until the area is healed. If there's infection in a wound, this is also a good remedy.

Apple cider vinegar can be used in part to make an improvised toothpaste.

Oral Health

Apple cider vinegar can also be used to make toothpaste. Use a ½ tablespoon of the vinegar with 1 tablespoon of baking soda, and add water to make a paste. Dental hygiene is often overlooked, but is super important to maintain healthy gums. Once the gums deteriorate, infection can settle in. The gums can be painful, red, swollen, and may even bleed. The teeth can also become painful due to infection, making it difficult to eat and makes a person pretty miserable. If there are no ingredients to make toothpaste, take a small branch from a pine tree (about the size of a pencil) and fray the ends. This can serve as a makeshift toothbrush. [Refer to "Off-the-Grid Dentistry" in Issue 27 for more information on dealing with dental problems when medical help will be unavailable for the foreseeable future.]

Female Hygiene

Ladies, urinary tract infections are also something that can bring misery in a survival situation. Symptoms of a urinary tract infection can include urinary frequency, burning with urination, incontinence, and fever. With poor hygiene, and with poor hydration, this can be a real possibility. Without the benefit of toiletries, you'll need to search for nature's bidet, like a babbling brook. Anything that you can do to wash away the particulate matter will help minimize chances of infection. Finding edibles to help your immune system (e.g. garlic, spinach, citrus fruits) can help in general. Edibles that can act as natural antibiotics (e.g. honey and Echinacea) may help, but shouldn't replace your stockpiled antibiotics. And be sure to stay hydrated.

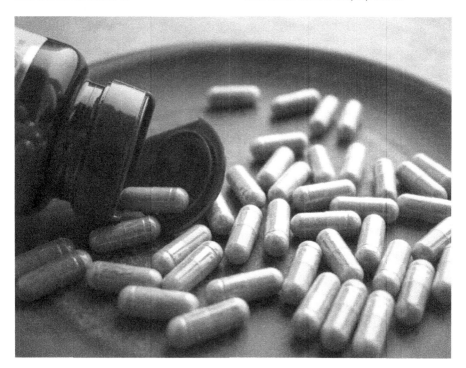

Ginkgo biloba tablets and certain vegetables contain progesterone, which can aid in managing menstruation during situations where conventional methods are unattainable.

Menstruation is another potentially troublesome issue in an austere setting. This was somewhat of a challenge for the military after Sept. 11, as the number of women in combat had increased. The idea was to suppress menstruation rather than accommodate hygienic practices that'd interfere with combat roles. There are options for menstrual suppression; however, these will require advanced planning. Your doctor can discuss a hormonal rod implant that provides contraception for around three years. An intrauterine device (IUD) can also be placed by a physician and stay in place up to five years.

For shorter term options, an intramuscular injection of hormone every 90 days is available. The end goal for these types of options is to stop menstruation from occurring. If that isn't an option for you, menstrual cups are available. Check out Eryn Chase's article in Issue 21 of RECOIL OFFGRID for an excellent discussion on wilderness hygiene. Edibles that contain progesterone include soy, broccoli, kale, cabbage, and gingko, to name a few, but the reality is that even though these contain very small amounts of the hormone, it's not likely it'll be strong enough to affect the menstrual cycle.

Conclusion

Hygiene in a survival setting may not seem like a priority early in the chaos and is often ignored due to other pressing issues in the dire environment (i.e. water, fire, shelter, food, and safety). Keep in mind that taking a few minutes to wash up and brush your teeth in those early days can prevent misery as the event draws out into weeks. Women will have extra issues to contend with, and planning may be the best remedy. The old adage of "an ounce

Menstrual cups can be another method to assist that time of the month in austere conditions.

Corn starch can assist in keeping certain areas dry that may be prone to fungal buildup.

of prevention is worth a pound of cure" applies here. Take some time to take care of your hygiene before minor problems become more of a pressing need. ::

About The Author

David L. Miller, DO, FACOI is an internist in private practice for 20 years. His experiences away from the office have included time as a fight doctor in regional MMA events and as a team physician for 10 years at a mid-major university in the Midwest. Currently, he serves as the lead medical instructor for the Civilian Crisis Response team based out of Indianapolis.

4 > Water

Roof Tap
How to Make and Install a Rain Barrel

By Martin Anders
Illustrations by Ced Nocon

City dwellers are well accustomed to — and largely spoiled by — the conveniences and wonders of modern plumbing. A twist of the wrist unleashes a never-ending flow of the wet stuff for drinking, cooking, bathing, cleaning, and more. The benefits and convenience of having large quantities of fresh water available to you at an instant are obvious. However, in an environment where clean water may not flow freely from the tap, those benefits become a necessary luxury and rare commodity.

On January 9, 2014, a massive chemical spill near a water treatment facility in West Virginia affected roughly 300,000 people

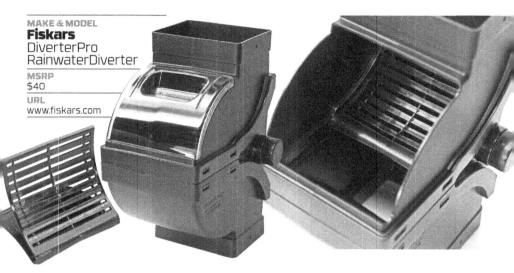

MAKE & MODEL
Fiskars
DiverterPro RainwaterDiverter

MSRP
$40

URL
www.fiskars.com

spanning nine counties. The root of that spill came from a single source, a company that produces chemicals used in the mining, steel, and cement industries. The chemical spilled was toxic enough that warnings went out to not use the contaminated water even after it was boiled.

Government officials immediately ruled area tap water off limits, bottled drinking water disappeared from store shelves just a couple of hours later, and the National Guard was called upon to truck in fresh water. Although the water was ruled safe to use about a week later, the effects of a regional water disruption were clearly felt. Considering the spill was an accident that originated from a single source, the consequences of a more widespread event would be more devastating. Surely the effects of a deliberate attack or large-scale environmental disaster on water resources in multiple areas would cause much more strain on clean water supplies.

This is where being prepared for the unimaginable comes into play. Unless you're blessed with a sixth sense, you don't have a crystal ball that tells you what calamities will fall upon you. You do, however, have the benefit of foresight and the ability to be proactive. There's no question that having extra water stored for a rainy day (bad pun intended) can be a lifesaver. Sure, storing water in bottles in your closet or garage are viable options, but if you want to store water in real quantities (like 55 gallons at a time) you'll need a viable alternative.

Our gardening friends have long discovered the easy answer to storing respectable quantities of water — best of all, the water is free. Rain barrels can be set up to trap and hold rain water. The water comes from rain collected on your home's rooftop and funneled directly into storage barrels. Garden aficionados store rainwater during the rainy months and use this water to keep their gardens watered — and their water bills down — during drier seasons. Adapting this concept to fit the survival mindset is simple enough.

Rain barrel kits are readily available at hardware and gardening supply stores. The methods of installation for our purposes are the same, with a couple of exceptions. While gardening water doesn't need to be potable, we need to take into consideration the drinkability of the water for survival purposes. Instead of using any old barrel, we want to use food-grade barrels, which can be found at restaurant supply stores and at various online retailers. Make sure you get one where the top can be removed so that it is easier to work on and clean.

Most rain barrel kits come with filters that take out large debris, but we want to add finer filters or mesh to further keep debris out. After all, the water is rolling down your roof into your rain gutter and finally into your barrel. If the water is being used to wash up or to do the dishes with, you should be good to go. If you intend on drinking or cooking with it, you'll want a separate water filtration system too. Boiling works, or you can get fancier with the many water filtration methods and gizmos on the market.

We took a look at the many rain barrel kits on the market and decided to go with a unit by Fiskars. We like how the Fiskars DiverterPro Rainwater Diverter fits different-sized rain gutters and especially liked the built-in filter that is easy to view, access, and clean. The filter's slats are pretty fine so we didn't need to enhance it any further. Also, when the rain barrel fills up, the water diverts back into the downspout and is directed away from your home as usual.

Barrel Preparation

Each kit differs slightly, so make sure you go through the instructions of your chosen kit carefully. Here, we detail the installation of the Fiskars diverter kit. We begin by preparing our food-grade barrel. You can choose a size that best fits your needs; we chose a larger 55-gallon size to maximize the amount of stored water.

What you'll need:
1. Food-grade barrel
2. Water spigot for ¾-inch opening
3. Trap adapter with nut
4. Teflon tape
5. Hose connector from Fiskars kit
6. Caulking
7. Power drill
8. ¾-inch spade drill bit

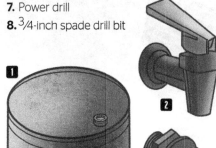
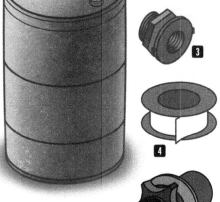
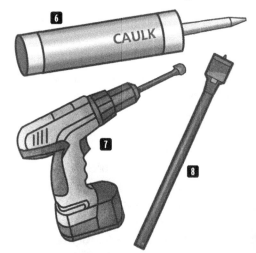

1

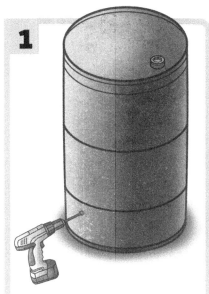

Being mindful of how much room you will need under the spigot to fill a water container such as a pitcher or bottle, use the ¾-inch spade drill bit to drill a hole at the bottom of the barrel for the water spigot. We drill our hole about a foot from the bottom.

2

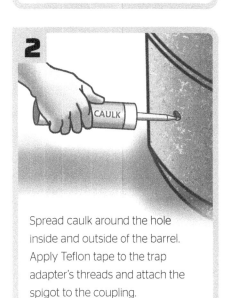

Spread caulk around the hole inside and outside of the barrel. Apply Teflon tape to the trap adapter's threads and attach the spigot to the coupling.

3

Install the water spigot onto the barrel and secure it on the inside with the trap adapter nut. You may need a wrench to get it on tight enough to avoid water leakage.

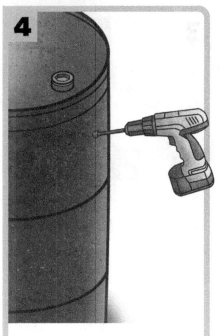

Near the top of the barrel, about 2 inches down from the lid, drill another hole for the kit's hose connector.

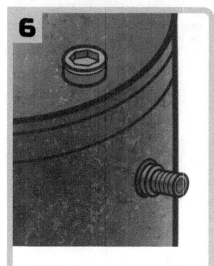

Install the hose connector according to the kit's instructions. (Basically, screw it onto the barrel snugly.)

Again, spread caulk around the holes inside and out.

Your barrel is ready.

Location Preparation and Installation

Select a location near your rain gutter's downspout. Rain barrels are very heavy when full of water, so you want to make sure the area is flat and firm.

What you'll need:
1. Fiskars DiverterPro Rainwater Diverter Kit
2. Concrete tiles
3. Marker
4. Tape measure
5. Shovel
6. Hacksaw

If the surface isn't flat, take the time to prepare the ground so that it is.

9 You want the barrel to sit on a firm surface. If the area isn't, lay down some hard material such as concrete tiles. It's a good idea to have your barrel slightly higher than ground level to allow gravity to help the water flow out, especially when the water level is low. If you want to put your barrel on a higher surface such as a platform, now's the time to do it.

WATER • ROOF TAP | **143**

Now saw the downspout at the same height as the barrel. (You might want to measure and mark the height before you begin sawing.)

Next, slide the Fiskars diverter up onto the upper piece of the downspout. Measure and cut the lower downspout piece to make room for the diverter. Reattach the remainder of the lower downspout.

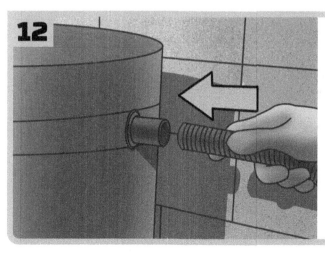

Measure, cut, and connect the connector hose to the barrel.

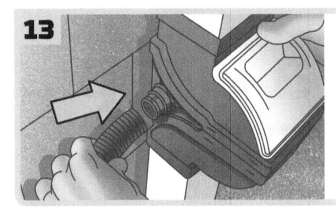

Then connect the hose to the diverter.

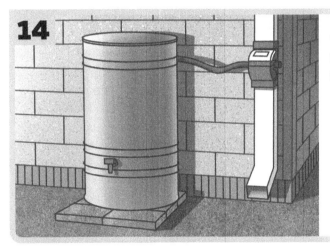

You're done. Now all you need is some rain.

More Storage

If you want to collect even more rainwater, you can daisy chain barrels together by attaching them together on their opposite sides with connector hoses. When one barrel gets full, it will overflow to the next. ⁞

Not a Drop to Drink...

...Unless You Improvise With Your Own DIY Water Filters

By Jim DeLozier

As noted by nearly every outdoor enthusiast and reputable survival teacher, clean drinking water is at or near the top of the priority list. There are many good reasons for this, so we want to help you be able to use and drink whatever H_2O you find in an urban or semi-urban environment during a crisis or post-crisis situation.

For the purposes of this story, we'll assume that you've practiced some common sense and found water from a relatively safe source — but you're not 100-percent sure if you should consume it. How do you know if it's safe to drink? Can you cook with it or drink it?

Consuming it straight from the source is definitely not a good idea unless you

want the runs, a crippling illness, or worse (see "Germ Warfare" elsewhere in this issue for more on microscopic pathogens). No doubt you'll need to filter the wet stuff... which is easier said than done if life as we know it has crumpled at our feet or gone up in a mushroom cloud. When commercially available filters aren't available, you'll have to roll up your sleeves and improvise.

Filter Materials

When attempting water treatment, you'll need to first filter it through different media to remove most of the particulate matter. Sift out the larger contaminants, then the smaller, then the microscopic. Once that's completed, you'll need to heat or treat the H_2O depending on available resources. Therefore, you'll need to obtain some items to repurpose for your DIY water treatment system.

Filter Media: You might not realize it, but there are dozens of everyday items lying around that could be used to filter water. Here are some common examples:
› T-shirts
› Towels
› Stockings
› Bandanas
› Pillow stuffing
› N-95 mask
› Coffee filters
› Fridge water filter

You could also use earthly materials, too, like gravel, sand, and charcoal. While they're not as abundant in concrete jungles like New York City (unless you happen to be inside a Home Depot when stuff hits the fan), they're great to use if you can find them.

Water Containers: Next, you'll need at least two containers that can hold H_2O. Consider any of the following:
› Plastic soda bottles
› Milk jugs
› Buckets
› Empty bleach bottles

You could even use pots or pans for one of the containers, but plastic works best because you can cut it or poke holes through it as needed.

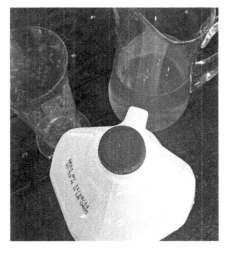

Filtering Techniques

First Filtering Stage:

1. Take a milk jug or large soda bottle, with a cap if possible, and remove the bottom by cutting it off carefully with a sharp knife or scissors.

2. If the cap is available, make a hole in it by setting it on a flat surface and placing the tip of a knife on the top of the cap. While carefully holding the cap, twist the knife around while applying pressure until you make a small hole. Once a small hole is in the cap, place it back on the bottle and turn the open side up.

3. Next, place the finest filtering element available, like a coffee filter, an N-95 mask, or tampon (see "Bloody Ingenious" elsewhere in this issue), at the bottom of the container (closest to the cap).
IMPROV: If there's no coffee filter or N-95 mask handy, you can substitute paper towels.

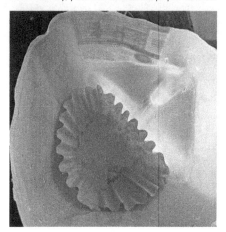

4. Then take the charcoal (if available), smash it into fine pieces, and place it inside the filter material. Cover the charcoal with about 1 inch of sand and cover the sand with about 2 inches of gravel.
IMPROV: Can't find enough gravel, sand, and charcoal? Replace them with cotton balls, cloth, or pillow stuffing.

5. Slowly pour the water you've found into the improvised filtration system so as not to disrupt the filtering elements. This should eliminate most of the sediment or particulate matter and prepare us to move on to the next step of filtration.

Second Filtering Stage:
1. Many homes have refrigerators with built-in water dispensers. Where there's a water dispenser, there's probably a water filter as well. Usually the filter is either a carbon or ceramic filter — both will work well for our needs. (Coincidentally, most businesses have coffee makers with either an in-line water filter or paper coffee filters.) Find the filter element and remove it. Usually it twists out of its receptacle by spinning it counterclockwise. The best type has a hole in only one end.

2. You will need two buckets (or some equivalent), one of which you must punch a hole in the bottom. Before you make the hole, identify the size of the threaded portion of the fridge's water filter — then carefully make a hole in the bottom of the bucket that's just slightly smaller than the threads of the filter.

3. Once that's done, place the threaded portion of the filter over the hole and, while applying slight downward pressure, turn the filter clockwise, allowing the filter to thread itself into the hole in the bucket. Once this has been completed, take your other bucket (with no hole) and place it beneath the first one to capture the water that comes through the filter.

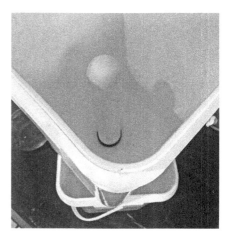

WATER • NOT A DROP TO DRINK... | **149**

4. Take the H_2O from your first filter setup and pour it into the bucket with the second filter, allowing it to flow through the ceramic or carbon filter into the container below. You have now filtered your questionable liquid twice. It should be fairly clean now, but if it's not clean enough at this point, repeat the process until the water is clear or nearly clear.

Treating or Heating

Once you're satisfied with the clarity of the filtered water, you can now heat it or treat it to be sure it's safe to drink.

Chemical Treatment: If you have access to regular household bleach (which you always should), you're in luck. Bleach works great at treating filtered water. It doesn't take much, so go easy. In fact, it takes about only two *drops* of bleach per quart of water or eight drops per gallon. Remember, a quart is equal to four cups, so a little goes a long way! Bleach kills 99.9 percent of all germs, so it's very handy. Iodine tablets could also serve the same purpose, but household bleach is more versatile.

8 DROPS OF BLEACH

1 GALLON OF WATER

Heat Treatment: However, if you don't have bleach on hand or want to take it to the next level, you can heat the filtered water to be extra sure it's safe to consume. If you have power or a camp stove, this last step is easy. But if you've just bugged out or are trapped away from home, you'll have to create a stove. For your improvised heating element, consider the following:

- Medium metal can, e.g. 1-pound coffee can
- 1-quart paint can (without paint residue)
- Small soup can
- Large ceramic coffee mug

Once you've found your desired improvised stove, set it aside. Next grab a roll of toilet paper and pull out the cardboard sleeve in the middle, without unrolling the paper. No, this isn't a magic trick. Grab the cardboard insert with your fingertips while holding the roll and simply pull the tube out of the center. (Save the cardboard for a different use — hey, any item can become a post-apocalyptic commodity if you're creative enough.) Compress the toilet tissue and place it inside the can so it's snug inside. If it won't fit, slowly remove layers of tissue until it does. If toilet paper isn't available, sub in a rolled-up washcloth or hand towel.

Next, pour denatured alcohol or 91-percent isopropyl alcohol over the tissue or cloth towel and carefully light the improvised stove. Be aware that the flame might be present, but not visible. The alcohol is what burns, and the tissue or cloth serves only as a wick. If you don't have denatured or isopropyl alcohol available, you'll have to use whatever flammable liquid is available.

Now pour your filtered water into a pot. You can't place the pot directly on top of your improvised stove, as it will restrict oxygen flow and extinguish the flame (a handy trick to remember when you need to safely put out the fire). Instead, position your DIY stove between two stacks of bricks (or empty ammo cans) and make sure they're slightly taller than the stove. Then place the pot atop the bricks. If you're outdoors, especially in the cold, it's important to block out the wind around

Heat water to 160° Fahrenheit

Temperature Test

One life-saving fact: Most organisms can't survive in temperatures above 140 degrees, which is especially helpful when heat treating water you've just filtered. But just to be safe, heat it up to 160 degrees. How do you know if the water is 140 or 160 degrees? It's not like you'll have a thermometer in a SHTF scenario.

When the liquid is heating, air bubbles form on the bottom of the pot. At approximately 140 degrees, the first little bubbles break loose from the bottom. The first medium-sized bubbles form and begin to release to the surface at approximately 160 to 170 degrees. This is important to know because on an improvised stove or with limited heating fuels, you might not get your water to a full rolling boil. Once you can count 10 medium-sized bubbles reaching the surface, you can be confident that the water has been properly treated.

your improvised stove. It takes much longer to heat the H_2O if you don't.

Make sure you heat the water to 160 degrees Fahrenheit, a temperature at which pretty much no germs can survive. (No thermometer, no problem, see the "Temperature Test" sidebar.) Obviously, it's important to let the water cool before attempting to consume it. And always be careful whenever an open flame is present and be cautious of any hot surfaces.

Financial Water Planning

You might be wondering, "How can I buy a water filtration system, a self-sustaining garden, and a solar-panel system for when the grid goes down – and still afford to pay the mortgage?" Stop! Those questions are much further down the road and *not* something you need to worry about yet.

Instead, focus on the survival priorities (food, water, fire, and shelter) and slowly integrate all of them into your lifestyle. For example, this author bought a ceramic water dispenser for about $30. It's the kind that holds 3- or 5-gallon bottles. In order to have enough water on hand for an emergency, he buys cases of 1-gallon bottles at the market. It's usually less than $6 for a case of six 1-gallon bottles – approximately $1 per gallon. He and his family go through about a case per week, so he buys a few cases at a time and marks the date on the sides. He cycles the water so no case is stored for more than 180 days. He adds to the cases by buying one more than he needs each time, until he has about 20 cases on hand. The cases can be stacked on top of each other so they don't take up a lot of space, but brings peace of mind knowing there are more than 100 gallons of water available at any given time.

Note: Be careful to purchase water only in clear containers for storage, because the opaque containers aren't designed for water and shouldn't be used if you can avoid it.

Another thing his family did was purchase three 55-gallon drums for water storage. This water can be used for cooking, cleaning, and bathing. He changes the water once a year so it's always fresh enough to drink in an emergency. He changes one drum in the spring, one in the summer and one in the fall so none of them go bad. Also, he adds a ¼ cup of household unscented bleach per 55 gallons to keep the water fresh.

So for less than $200 spread over a span of a few months, you can have a supply of water to sustain your family in a crisis. Remember, you can survive for weeks without food, but only days without water. Get moving and get your water plan into action.

Conclusion

Lastly, keep containers of powdered drink mix on hand, like Tang, Hi-C, Gatorade, Emergen-C, or hot cocoa. Why? One, it makes pond water taste a lot better, which is more palatable for your kids. Two, it adds electrolytes and potassium to the liquid, keeping you more energized. And, three drinking water alone could flush out necessary minerals if you're not careful, which can be dangerous in a long-term survival situation.

Whether you have a commercially available filter or had to McGyver your own from scavenged parts, filtering water can make all the difference in a crisis event. But it also takes common sense and the right attitude. Don't obtain H_2O from places that are clearly contaminated with toxins. Do stay calm and get creative with the resources in your environment. The proper mindset is the most important resource you have. So, stay positive, adapt, and find a solution...or you'll become part of the problem. ::

About The Author

Jim DeLozier – designer of the Survivor Trucks – is an all-inclusive continuity consultant who helps people prepare for anything and everything. Jim and his team design and build vehicles, structures, and shelters. They also train people in everything from martial arts and long-range precision shooting to power generation and hydroponics/aquaponics.
www.SurvivorTruck.com/consulting/

5 Methods of Water Disinfection

The Centers for Disease Control and Prevention list five methods for water disinfection.

1. Heat: Once water has been boiled up to 160 degrees Fahrenheit for 1 minute, it's safe to drink after it has cooled.

2. Filter: Filters that are sized between 0.1 and 0.4 microns will remove bacteria, but not viruses from water. Special hollow fiber filters can remove viruses, while reverse osmosis filters remove both bacteria and viruses and can also remove salt from water, handy if you find yourself around seawater.

3. Chemical: Tablets or packets of powder can be used to disinfect water. This method usually combines chemical disinfectants such as chlorine or iodine and may take several hours before all the germs are killed.

4. Ultraviolet Light: Measured doses of UV light are effective in disinfecting small amounts of clear water. Be careful when the water is not clear, as UV light is less effective in cloudy water.

5. Solar Radiation: Water can be disinfected with the solar radiation of sunlight. Fill a clear plastic bottle, lay it on a reflective surface (such as aluminum foil, shiny side up), and let it sit. The water will be safe to drink after at least six hours in bright sunlight. This technique only works with water that is clear, not cloudy.

SOURCE: http://wwwnc.cdc.gov/travel/page/water-disinfection

5 › Thinking Outside the Box

Off the Grid Everyday
Survival Lessons Learned From Society's Homeless

By Martin Anders
Illustrations by Ced Nocon

One doesn't have to go very far to find out how it would look to live off the utility grid. While most of the country is more or less stable (at the time of this writing), there are hundreds of thousands of people living nomadically in every city in the United States without the privileges of electricity and running water — let alone PlayStations and smartphones. They are our society's homeless, and they live off the grid despite living among us.

We have seen time and again throughout history all sorts of events that thrust people, once living comfortably, out of their homes and onto the streets. We're only one natural or manmade disaster away from ending up like the more than 600,000 people estimated by the U.S. Department of Housing and Urban Development to be living on the streets. So, in an effort to glean survival lessons from some of the most resilient people living without basic needs, OFFGRID headed into the heart of Baton Rouge, Louisiana's vagrant community.

This author packed up his notebook, a wad of $5 bills, and his concealed carry pistol and headed to skid row to conduct what would be some of the most, uh, "interesting" interviews of his career. The areas of town where the homeless congregate are already stripped of resources, far from any Barnes & Noble or gated community. Many of these displaced folks were here because of drug addiction, while others turned to drugs only after reaching what is, in essence, the end of the line. Regardless, finding a coherent participant wasn't always easy nor was our cause aided by the drug dealers, who made it clear that we were not welcome. Undeterred, we eventually found people of all ages who were lucid and sober enough to be interviewed. Though they didn't have many possessions, they did have a wealth of knowledge that could absolutely be applied to a survival situation after a disaster.

Primary Needs: Food, Water, Shelter, and Security

There's a lot of community support for the homeless. Most of their basic needs are met by local churches or shelters. But as you'll read later, these handouts may not always be an option. Though every interviewee survived differently, there were definitely some common themes.

Most everyone had a water container that they would refill by using hose bibs attached to businesses closed for the day. The types of food that they carried were nonperishable and prepackaged, and therefore didn't need to be refrigerated or cooked. When asked if they would steal food if the community could not provide it, the answer was a unanimous yes.

Thoughts on the subject of shelter varied greatly depending upon the situation and the individual's temperament. Some street people find clean beds at community shelters, but there's always more demand than supply. Also people entering a shelter (or a FEMA camp) will be subject to a search, so those not wanting to give up firearms, other weapons, and possibly medication will have to seek shelter elsewhere. Many of the homeless interviewed disliked the shelters because of the overcrowding and thievery — undoubtedly two problems that would be compounded in a disaster situation.

A partially disabled 63-year-old man we interviewed constructed a small encampment hidden deep in a wooded region, located far away from the densely populated homeless district. He chose this type of area to stay away from others competing for resources. But he also chose to set up his camp near train tracks because snakes, common to the area, dislike the strong vibrations created by passing railway cars. Being so far from resources required him to own and maintain a bicycle for transportation.

Meanwhile, a man in his early 20s used a drastically different approach: He solely occupied abandoned structures, constantly changed his routes, and only moved under cover of darkness to avoid detection. However, his austere nomadic existence limited his possessions to what he carried in his backpack and on his person.

A middle-aged man occupied a tent within walking distance of community resources, but remained on the outskirts of the densely populated area. One side of his "territory" was covered by a fence, while the others had a clear view of anyone approaching. In the colder months, he would move his encampment into the shelter of a nearby abandoned building. This man didn't try to hide his location, but kept his presence known, unlike his weapon, which was a rather sizable and rusty cane knife he kept hidden. He man admitted to being a multiple felon, was an imposing figure, and had narcotics in plain view. People like this are already out surviving on the streets, so should you find yourself among them, we suggest being hyper aware of your surroundings and distributing your trust sparingly.

Regardless of the type of shelter used, we noticed certain themes reoccurring throughout our interviews. Every man had some way of getting his sleeping area up off

Personal security is a constant concern for those living on the streets. This former gardening implement is now a self-defense tool.

of the ground — be it pallets, a mattress, or bedding material. Also, they all utilized some type of early warning system to alert them of approaching danger while they slept. Some placed broken glass or trash in the pathways of buildings. Others tied trip wires in the woods or simply blocked entrances with materials that would be noisy to move.

Those who chose to stay with other homeless people actually used some "challenge words" or code — much like the Allies did during War World II's D-Day when troops would challenge anybody approaching with the word "flash" and shoot if the password "thunder" wasn't given in return.

Lessons Learned

› About Food: Pack nonperishable food, as conventional cooking and refrigeration will be limited or nonexistent in a SHTF scenario. Consider purchasing meals-ready-to-eat (aka MREs), learning how to prepare your own canned food, or stocking up on commercially available canned food (see our "Meat Feast" feature story elsewhere in this issue).

› About Water: A container of some sort is a must for any survivalist, be it a plastic milk jug or state-of-the-art stainless steel water bottle (see OFFGRID's Fall 2014 issue for more).

› About Shelter: Because the location will depend on your specific situation and where you choose to set up camp, there's no single "best" type of shelter. But a roof over your head and a bedding area elevated off the ground is essential.

› About Security: In any dire scenario, be it homelessness or after a natural disaster, overcrowding is inevitable at shelters (whether set up by the government or charitable organizations), as is property theft. So, establish either a trusted network of friends (the kind your life depends on) or an early-warning system around your shelter. Self-defense tools are a no-brainer.

Secondary Needs: Medical, Hygiene, and Transportation

Once the basic needs were covered, we delved into additional needs that are not so immediate, but still quite important.

Medical attention is usually given out at clinics and hospitals, but what if there are none available? Or, as in the case with shelters, you don't want to be forced to give up your weapons or medication? From our observations, the alternatives aren't so pretty. Most vagrants either self-medicated or simply suffered through their ailments. Also, living on the streets without medical support appeared to get exponentially more difficult with increasing age.

On a related note, proper hygiene could have not only prevented some of the infections and medical issues we observed, but also could have served a secondary purpose of looking more presentable. And no, we're not talking about dressing up for job interviews. There appeared to be a fine line between looking too clean and healthy (thereby making oneself a target for the have-nots) and looking totally destitute (making one a target of those who prey upon the weak while also unapproachable to those who might be willing to offer help). Depending on the type of disaster you find yourself in, money might still be worth something. If you are displaced to an area not under distress, you may be able to work for cash, so you need to be approachable. If money is not worth anything, you can still trade your labor for things you need, which many of the homeless do. A general consensus was that begging or panhandling was not very effective, so you can't rely on handouts.

Another survival concept consistent among the homeless was the value of having cheap transportation — namely a reliable bicycle. Those homeless who owned a bicycle had a distinct advantage over those who didn't. *Every* street person we interviewed eyed our bicycle with envy, and all mentioned the importance of one. Why? Fuel may not be available, and roads are easily clogged by panicked motorists — but bicycles can go almost anywhere with nothing more than a little leg muscle. Plus,

Who Are the Homeless?

As the sad cliché goes, homeless people are hidden in plain sight. As a society, we tend to turn a blind eye when we see drifters begging for money or living under a bridge. Yet they continue to survive off the utility grid despite living among us on the grid. Here's a brief look at who they are, based on January 2013 statistics from the U.S. Department of Housing and Urban Development.

they're easy to hide or secure and allow a person to travel great distances quickly while expending little energy. These attributes allow one to obtain resources from farther away and help you get out of harm's way swiftly. The impoverished who owned bicycles also had a lock (preferably a U-lock), a small set of basic tools, and spare parts to keep their bikes reliable. One man suggested having a small bicycle trailer for hauling additional supplies and gear. (See OFFGRID's Spring 2014 issue for more on bug-out bikes and their accessories.)

Learning how to adapt is also strongly suggested. For example, the older man replaced a broken pedal with one fabricated out of a wooden block. If you find yourself off-grid, improvisation will be used in every aspect of your life, not just those regarding your bicycle.

Lessons Learned

⟩ About Medical:
Prepare some basic medical gear and know how to use it. Know where alternate medical facilities are (as hospitals might be overcrowded, overrun, or quarantined) and plan transportation routes to reach them. Also, if you have elderly relatives to care for, you'll need to plan accordingly.

⟩ About Hygiene:
Not only does improper hygiene cause medical issues to flare up, it can also mark you as a target. Don't look too clean, but don't look completely destitute either.

⟩ About Transportation:
Off the grid, bicycles are king. Without the need for fossil fuels or electricity, bikes can get you out of Dodge quickly and via many different routes.

Survival Priority: Backpacks

That's right. You read correctly — backpacks. We know how much you love them, so listen up. Topping the list of needs of the homeless is the backpack. The general consensus is that if you want to keep something, it should be kept on your person. Think vital items like your ID, cash, payment cards, and weapon(s). Depending on the situation, these items can give you access to resources, such as your bank account or government assistance should you be able to reach it. These belongings are almost impossible to replace in a disaster scenario. (Also, should there be some semblance of law and order, you'll want your CCW permit handy if you're carrying a weapon concealed.)

To carry all of your other needs, you should have a good quality, low-profile, medium-sized backpack. That means it should appear used and somewhat dirty. A huge pack that's glistening new with all kinds of goodies hanging off of it will definitely make you a target. Many of the interviewees related instances in which they were robbed. Others recalled how they often sleep with an arm through one of their pack's straps.

We asked all our interviewees, "If you could have a backpack filled with anything but cash and crack cocaine, what items would you want in it?" Not surprisingly, the 5 C's popped up in everyone's answers: a container for water, a cutting implement (such as a knife), cover (e.g. a tarp, tent, or sleeping bag), cordage (to secure items and make shelter), and a form of combustion (usually a lighter, though fires were seldom used because they attract attention).

In addition to the other items previous mentioned by the interviewees, some of the vagrants expressed interest in having a flashlight, a small radio, extra warming layers, extra footwear, extra set of clothes, writing implements, baby wipes, a small stove, and cooking and eating utensils. These are typical items most survivalists would have in a 72-hour go-bag.

Lessons Learned

> **About Backpacks:**

Few things are as essential as a good backpack, because it can carry all of your other vital kit (water, food, fire-starters, etc.). Find one that's medium-sized and low-profile to stay discreet, load it up, and keep it close to you at all times.

Takeaways

In addition to the critical gear already mentioned, many of the drifters we talked to suggest having things you can part with. Barter items — namely cigarettes, alcohol, and drugs (legal and illegal) — would be valuable to have in limited quantities so that you can trade with others you deem safe to negotiate with. (Obviously, the severity of the disaster and the condition of the government should be taken into consideration before obtaining anything illegal.) For example, if you're not a smoker, trading away a pack of cigarettes for creature comforts like toilet paper would be a huge morale booster.

All of the people interviewed for this story were visibly nervous. Life on the street is quite stressful — being properly prepared can reduce that stress in times of peril. These interviews gave us a small glimpse into what a future living off of the grid would be like.

We've certainly taken their lessons seriously, cross referenced them against our own preparations, and have adjusted our plans for TEOTWAWKI accordingly. We suggest you do the same, because it doesn't take much for average folks to end up on the streets — whether it's due to a sudden psychological affliction, the economic fallout of being fired, or a natural or manmade catastrophe that wipes out your community.

About The Author

Peter Palma is a freelance writer who served overseas as an infantry machine gunner and scout sniper in the U.S. Marine Corps. After leaving the service, he competed on TV's *Top Shot* during its first and fifth seasons. He currently resides in Louisiana, where he teaches basic firearms classes, is enrolled at Louisiana State University, and operates his weapons-cleaning accessory business, MS Clean.

How to Help

Aside from getting a chance to learn how impoverished people survive on the streets, you can volunteer at a homeless shelter or a nonprofit organization for plenty of other personally rewarding reasons. Below is a brief list of agencies providing assistance and information:

Invisible People: This nonprofit's founder used to be homeless and now dedicates his life to changing the way we think about people experiencing life on the streets. **www.invisiblepeople.tv**

National Coalition for the Homeless: A national network of activists, advocates, and professionals whose goal is to prevent and end homelessness. **www.nationalhomeless.org**

Project Night Night: This charitable organization donates age-appropriate care packages to 25,000 homeless kids every year. **www.projectnightnight.org**

U.S. Department of Housing & Urban Development: The online portal for the government's housing-related resources and assistance programs. **www.hudexchange.info**

Veterans Affairs: This U.S. agency helps veterans find housing, in addition to providing healthcare, job training, and other services. **www.va.gov/homeless**

Survival Chop Shop

10 Useful Items to Scavenge from Abandoned Cars

By Patrick McCarthy

In a long-term survival scenario, scavenging is essential. Sure, many of us have go-bags, or even stockpiles of emergency supplies, for when SHTF. However, sooner or later, those supplies will be used up, lost, or stolen, even for the most prepared among us. It's inevitable.

So, where do you turn when your supplies are dwindling? You could spend valuable time scouring buildings that have already been picked clean of resources, or you could look for something that literally surrounds us in everyday urban life — the automobile.

There are over 250 million cars and trucks in the United States alone, and each one is packed with useful survival items that are easily overlooked. From obvious resources, like gasoline, to more obscure parts, every abandoned vehicle you see is a veritable treasure trove of resources. You certainly don't have to be a mechanic to find them, and oftentimes, you don't even need any tools — you just need to know where to look. And that's where this guide comes in.

Before we get started, let's go over some general guidelines. First of all, choosing the right vehicle. Almost every make and model will have something you can scavenge, but everyday economy cars will generally be easier to work with and disassemble. Expensive luxury or sports cars may be less user-friendly and require specialized tools, making life difficult if all you've got is a multitool. However, keep an eye out for commercial vehicles, such as vans and work trucks, as they may contain items a passenger car wouldn't. Secondly — we know this is obvious, but we'll say it anyway — look for keys, and see if the car is in operable condition. There's no sense in tearing apart a car you could easily use for transportation. Now, let's move on to the actual scavenging.

Note: For demonstration purposes, we'll be scavenging from a common 2008 model four-cylinder Japanese sedan. However, virtually any type of passenger car or truck will do.

SCAVENGER LEVEL: MODERATE

Gasoline

Tools Required: Small-diameter rubber hose or a strong piercing instrument

Uses:
If you don't already know why gasoline would be like mana from heaven in a doomsday situation, you're better off putting down this magazine and going to www.darwinawards.com. If you have a functional vehicle, you'll want to replenish its fuel supply. Also, gasoline burns, and it does so very efficiently. Naturally, it can be used for starting fires, as an excellent solvent to remove grease and grime, and as a highly sought-after barter good.

How to Scavenge:
Due to its obvious value, gasoline is often surprisingly difficult to scavenge. Most new vehicles have a screen or valve that prevents the use of a hose to siphon from the gas tank filler neck. If you can find a vehicle from the mid 1990s or earlier, it may lack this security feature – but you'll need to pry the metal flapper near the opening out of the way with a screwdriver or stick before inserting the hose. If siphoning using your mouth, you also run the risk of serious injury from gasoline inhalation.

Assuming you don't care about damaging the vehicle, a much better option is to look underneath the car, find the fuel tank, and bore or punch a hole using a knife, awl, cordless drill, or other sharp instrument. Modern cars with plastic fuel tanks are ideal for this purpose, although it still can be done on older metal fuel tanks. Work with care, as you don't want to cause a spark. Note that you might need to punch a second air hole to help the gas flow more easily – a la those 2.5-gallon water jugs you get at the grocery store.

 **Tools Required:** None

Jack and Tools

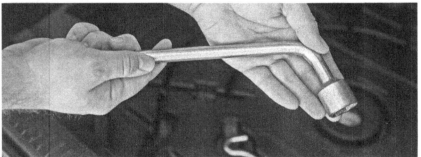

Uses: Almost every passenger car includes a jack and tools for changing a flat tire. Primarily, they can be used to remove the car's wheels and tires — we'll get into why that's useful in the next step. Secondly, the steel lug wrench found in most cars functions as an excellent blunt instrument, weapon, or prybar. It's definitely worth holding on to.

How to Scavenge:
Most cars store these tools underneath the trunk floor panel, although they may also be found underneath or behind the seats in some vehicles. The jack is typically also located near the tools. If you don't spot it immediately, check for storage compartments or removable panels in the trunk.

3 SCAVENGER LEVEL: EASY ⬡ ⬢ ⬢

Tires

Tools Required: None for spare tire; jack and tools for other four

Uses:
Ever see a tire burn? It creates acrid black smoke that's visible for miles. If you're in a survival scenario where rescue is possible, burning car tires is a great way to alert rescuers of your position. Note: Always remember to let the air out of tires before burning, or they may burst and scatter or put out your fire.

How to Scavenge:
Start by looking for a spare tire, as most vehicles have one inside or underneath the trunk. If the vehicle is missing the spare tire, or you need more tires for a larger fire, you can use the jack and tools (see No. 2) to remove the other four wheels and tires. One caveat: Removing a tire from its wheel is quite a chore with handtools, so hopefully you needn't roll them too far to where you plan to use them.

SCAVENGER LEVEL: EASY

Carpet and Upholstery

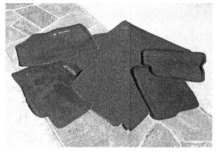

Tools Required:
Knife

Uses: Thick, soft, insulated fabric is always handy to have in a survival scenario. It can be used for warm bedding, blankets, or shelter against the elements.

How to Scavenge: Look for trunk liners, floor mats, and seat covers that are easily removable. If these aren't available, you may have to cut away the upholstery. The headliner is a great place to start, as it's usually one large piece of fabric.

Warning: If you're stranded in a cold-weather environment, you might be tempted to use the upholstery as kindling for a fire. Be cautious. They usually contain chemicals that turn into toxic fumes once burned.

 SCAVENGER LEVEL: EASY

Mirrors

Tools Required:
Screwdriver or prying instrument

Uses:
Automotive mirrors are large and high-quality, perfect for rescue signaling at long distances. They can also be used to start fires or to assist with personal hygiene (e.g. check for ticks, inspect an injury, or examine debris in your eye).

How to Scavenge:
Exterior mirrors can be carefully pried out of their housings with a knife or flat screwdriver. Interior mirrors can be unscrewed from the roof, or unclipped from their windshield mounts with relative ease.

Pick It Clean

When scavenging from a vehicle, always check the glovebox, center console, and other storage compartments for miscellaneous items. You might be surprised by what you'll find — bottled water, medications, first-aid kits, hand sanitizer, flashlights, lighters, pens and paper, tools, and more. In addition, vehicles have a lot of glass, wiring, and rubber hoses to be salvaged. You might even be able to use the vehicle itself as a temporary shelter — or disconnect and use the hood and trunk lids as roofing or sleds. Car parts and accessories have many uses beyond what they were built for, so your adaptation will be limited only by your creativity and ingenuity.

SCAVENGER LEVEL: EASY

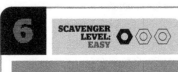

Battery

Tools Required:
Wrench or pliers, jumper cables (optional)

Uses:
Car batteries provide strong, long-lasting 12-volt electrical power. When combined with jumper cables or two lengths of large-gauge wire, they can be used to jump-start other cars, start fires, or even directly power lights (we'll cover that part later). If you're able to find a power inverter elsewhere, you can also use a car battery to power a myriad of AC electronics, such as mobile phones or radios.

How to Scavenge:
Pop the hood and take a look. Most of the time, the battery location will be obvious. Some cars hide the battery under a removable plastic cover, and a few luxury cars and sports cars relocate the battery to the trunk (where they may be hidden underneath trim pieces). If you've got jumper cables, you can connect them directly to the battery and touch them together for instant fire-starting sparks. If you want to take the battery with you, you'll need to disconnect the tie-down bar and terminal wires, usually with a small wrench or pliers. They are heavy, though.

Lights

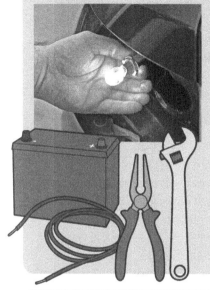

Tools Required: Car battery, wire, wrench, or pliers (if removing entire light assembly)

Uses: Automotive lights can be wired directly to a 12-volt battery for instant, bright light. An entire headlight assembly can be removed for focused light, or the bulbs themselves can be used to illuminate a wide area.

How to Scavenge: If you have a set of wrenches or needle-nose pliers, it may be possible to unbolt and remove an entire headlight with bulbs, but it'll take some time. If not, you can reach behind most car headlights and unclip or twist the bulbs to pull them out of the housings. Then cut two pieces of wire from the engine bay, and connect the positive and negative battery terminals to the corresponding bulb terminals for instant light.

Seatbelts

Tools Required:
Knife or cord-cutting tool

Uses:
Seatbelts are constructed of extremely strong, durable nylon, making for excellent cordage. If you need to tie something down, look no further.

How to Scavenge:
Simply pull to unravel the seatbelt from its reel, then cut. You can always use a knife, but we jumped at the chance to finally use the nifty seatbelt cutter on our multitool.

SCAVENGER LEVEL: HARD ●●●

Spark Plugs

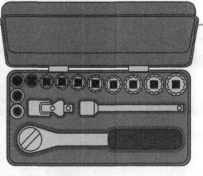

Tools Required:
Tool kit with ratcheting wrench, sockets, and extensions

Uses:
If you've got spark plugs, you've got a quick and easy glass-breaking tool. Just smash the white ceramic section on the plug with a blunt instrument, collect the larger chunks of ceramic, and you've got projectiles that can shatter glass panels instantly from a distance. It's much more effective and safe than trying to kick in a window or smashing a glass partition with a valuable tool (you wouldn't want to use, say, your flashlight as a hammer and risk damaging it, especially in a SHTF scenario).

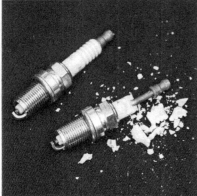

How to Scavenge:
The downside to spark plugs is that they're quite difficult to remove, even with basic tools. However, if you've got a standard hardware store tool kit with a ratcheting wrench, sockets, and extensions, it's doable. Our example car is a four-cylinder with coil-on-plug ignition, the most common style for cars newer than the mid-1990s. On top of the engine, one 8mm bolt is removed to take out a coil pack, and a ⅝-inch deep socket is used to remove the spark plug itself. Then just wrap the plug in a cloth and smash it to collect the ceramic pieces.

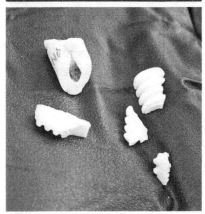

Motor Oil

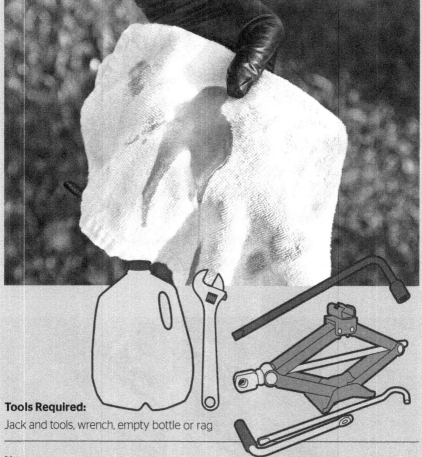

Tools Required:
Jack and tools, wrench, empty bottle or rag

Uses:
Motor oil is an excellent lubricant for mechanical items – including your firearms – hence its use inside car engines. It can also be used in an oil-burning furnace to provide heat (there are plenty of guides available online).

How to Scavenge:
For most passenger cars, you'll need to jack up the vehicle, although some pickups have enough ground clearance for you to crawl underneath. Remove the oil drain bolt with a wrench and drain some oil onto a rag or into a bottle.

It Came From Space

10 Uses for Emergency Blankets

By Martin Anders
Photos by Michael Grey

It's easy to bundle up in a scarf and jacket when the temperature drops. And packing a sleeping bag when you go camping is a no-brainer. But what if you end up stranded while on a day hike or have to flee unexpected danger after SHTF? Enter the emergency blanket.

This thin piece of Mylar film doesn't look like much more than a reflective sheet of flexible plastic, but it can retain life-saving heat if you're caught outdoors without shelter. Plus, it has a myriad of other improvised functions.

The amazing emergency blanket, also

known as a space blanket, was developed by NASA back in 1964 and has since become a mainstay in many emergency and first-aid kits — and for good reason. Emergency blankets take up little room, are very lightweight, and can keep you warm by efficiently preventing heat loss. Stash one in your backpack or vehicle's glove compartment and wrap yourself in it if you ever need a way to stay warm in a jiffy. Its powerful heat-retention properties are why marathon runners are draped in them after running their 26.2 miles and the reason its Mylar material was used to line the spacesuits that went to the moon.

Aside from making you feel like a toasty Pop Tart when wrapped in them, what else are they practical for? Let's examine 10 alternative uses for the blanket from space.

Insulation

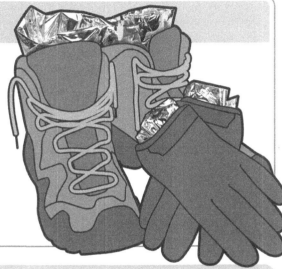

An emergency blanket makes a great insulator from the cold. Use it to help fortify your sleeping bag, if you're fortunate to have one, or cut a blanket up and stuff it into your shoes and gloves to help keep your tootsies warm.

Signaling

Emergency blankets usually come in a silver or gold chrome-like finish. Their mirrored reflective surface is great to bounce light off of to signal for help. When strung up on a tall object such as a tree, wind may cause it to move, creating a fluttering light reflection that may improve your chances of being detected.

3 Water Gathering

Because it's a large sheet of non-porous material, a space blanket is great for catching and collecting water. If it rains, you can dig a hole in the ground and line it like a mini-swimming pool to collect water. Make sure its edges are raised to avoid any dirty runoff. Or if you want to keep your water off the ground, you can tie up four corners onto a tree and use a rock to weigh down the middle. Water will collect at the bottom of this makeshift funnel.

Another alternative is to create a funnel or slide that can divert rainwater into a container. If you're contending with snow, you can shape the blanket into a cone and place snow into it. Then align your "snow cone" to catch sunlight so that the light generates heat to melt the snow.

4 Shelter

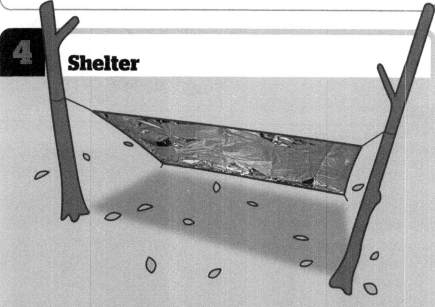

In conjunction with some paracord, duct tape, or even strips of itself (see Use #10), you can make a "lean-to" shelter by tying up two corners of the blanket up on trees and the other two corners lower to the ground to create a shelter from rain or the sun.

5 Heat Reflection

Mylar has a melting temperature of 500 degrees Fahrenheit so it is relatively safe in close proximity to open fire. Use a blanket to reflect heat from a campfire back into your aforementioned emergency-blanket shelter.

6 Medical

You can use an emergency blanket to fashion a makeshift sling to help better immobilize a broken or sprained arm or use it as a tourniquet in an extreme emergency. Use strips of it to tie sticks to a leg or arm create a splint for injured limbs. It can also act as an impromptu compression bandage if needed as well.

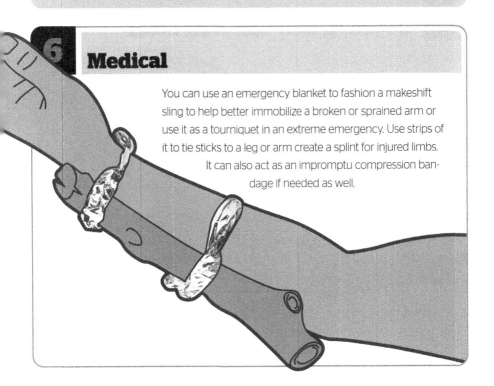

Waterproofing

Since the sheet is completely waterproof, anything you sufficiently wrap or shield from falling water should be able to stay dry. Use it to help keep the contents of your backpack dry by placing everything on the blanket then wrapping it prior to placing it in the pack. Keep yourself and your stuff dry by using a blanket as a tent footprint or groundsheet.

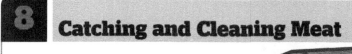

Catching and Cleaning Meat

Fish like shiny things, so strips of a blanket used as lures should better attract them than just a hook. Also, an emergency blanket makes for a clean and large enough surface on which to clean fish or field dress game. Keep the dirt off your meat!

9. Cooking

Fashion a blanket into a bowl shape and face it into the sun. Place very thinly sliced meat into it and allow nature to take its course. This works best when there is a blazing sun in the sky. Or if you opt to cook by flame, use pieces of a blanket to wrap up food for cooking near the fire. Not on the fire mind you, but place your wrapped food near the fire and it should get hot enough to cook what's inside.

10. Cordage

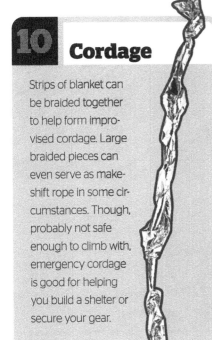

Strips of blanket can be braided together to help form improvised cordage. Large braided pieces can even serve as makeshift rope in some circumstances. Though, probably not safe enough to climb with, emergency cordage is good for helping you build a shelter or secure your gear.

How to Properly Use an Emergency Blanket

To be fully effective, an emergency blanket should be placed with the shiny side facing your body or any surface you want to keep toasty. This shiny side reflects about 90 percent of your body heat, while the dull side, which is not as efficient, only reflects about 65 percent of radiated heat.

Old News, New Tricks

Don't Toss Them Out. Newspapers Have a Lot More Survival Uses Than You Think

Story by Jim Cobb
Photos by Tammy Cobb

I don't know anyone who doesn't end up with a stack or two of newspapers or advertisements in their recycling bins each week. Even if you don't subscribe to the daily paper in your area, odds are there's at least one free newspaper that is delivered regularly along with a seemingly endless supply of ads, coupons, and classifieds. Some folks call this the local fish wrap. The point is just about everyone has unwanted printed matter lying around.

You could, and should, recycle what you don't need. But in these pages I'm presenting some ways you can repurpose it around the house, focusing on survival or self-reliance–related purposes.

Before we get into the projects though, let's talk for a moment about newspaper. Not all newspaper is created alike. There's newsprint and there's glossy paper. The glossy paper is what is typically used for advertising. Ya know, the shiny, full-color ads that are designed to draw you into the stores so you'll buy more junk you don't need or can't afford. Toss that stuff right into the recycling bin. We have no use for it here. What you want is the actual newsprint.

If for some unknowable reason you're that odd person who receives absolutely no newspapers at home, but you still want to try out some of these projects, you have a couple of options. You could ask a friend, relative, or neighbor to save some paper for you, of course. Or, you could head down to the local newspaper office and ask about "end rolls." These are rolls of clean newsprint that only have a bit of paper left. Trust me, each end roll will have plenty for our purposes here. Some newspapers give them out for free, others might charge a small fee.

Incidentally, if you have kids or grandkids, roll out enough clean newsprint for them to lie on, then trace around their entire body and head. They'll have a blast using crayons to draw life-size versions of themselves. It also makes for great wrapping paper for the holidays, just dress it up with some markers or stickers.

Plant Pot

This is a great project for the kids to do on those days when they complain about being bored. It requires newspaper, a bottle, and soil. There is a product on the market called a Pot Maker that works outstandingly well for this project. I highly recommend it. The mechanics of the project are the same whether you use the Pot Maker or a bottle. A wine bottle works great, but if that's not available, any bottle of similar size will work. The ideal bottle will have a concaved bottom.

Cut the newspaper into strips about 6 inches wide. The length will depend upon the size of your bottle. The strip will need to wrap completely around the bottle twice.

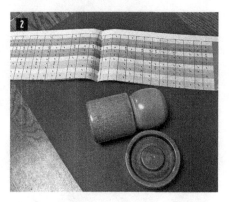
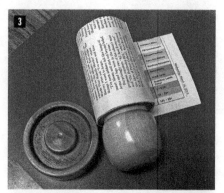

A plant pot made of newspaper is cheap and easy to make. Plus, you don't need to remove or replace it later because it'll decompose.

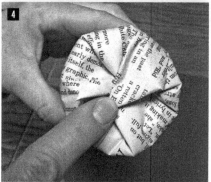

Wrap the strip around the Pot Maker twice. Fold that loose newspaper in and crimp the fold around the bottom edge of the dowel. Slide the pot from the dowel and fill with soil. The soil helps the pot keep its shape so be sure to fill the pots even if you don't plan on using them right away.

Once the seedlings are ready to be transplanted outside, you don't have to remove the pot. Just dig the hole and drop the whole thing in. The newspaper will decompose just fine.

Seed Tape

If you've ever planted carrots or lettuce, you know just how frustrating it can be to deal with those itty-bitty tiny seeds. We always just end up sprinkling the entire seed packet into a trench, resigning ourselves to the knowledge that we'll just be thinning the seedlings once they sprout and thus wasting quite a bit of seed. But, with a little effort ahead of time, you can use newspaper to cut down on the amount of seed you end up using in a season, thus extending your supply. Plus, you won't be doing nearly as much thinning as the plants grow.

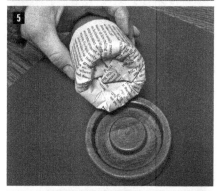

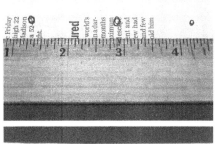
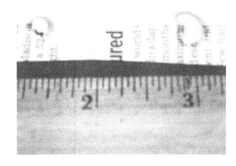

Start by cutting the newspaper into strips about 1 inch wide. Length is up to you, but I find it easiest to work with strips no more than 18 inches long. Next, make a glue using 2 tablespoons flour and 1 tablespoon water. The mixture should be fairly thick.

Read the instructions on the seed packet to find out the recommended plant spacing. If you don't have the original seed packet, do some research online. For our purposes, we'll say it's 1 inch. Lay out your newspaper strip and use a ruler and pencil to mark the seed spacing. Leave room on one end of the strip so you can label the strip.

Dip the tip of a toothpick into your glue, then use it to pick up one seed. One at a time, smear the glue and seeds on the strip at the spaced marks. Let the strip sit out until the glue has fully dried. Use a marker to label each strip with the type of seed. Roll up or fold the strips to store until needed.

To use, simply dig a trench in your garden to the appropriate depth, lay in your seed tape, and cover with soil. Water thoroughly, and you're done!

Garden Bed

If you have the time to wait, newspaper can be a tremendous asset in creating a new garden bed. Put down a few layers of newspaper over the entire surface of the planned garden bed, weighing the paper down with rocks or logs. Let this sit for a season and all of the grass and weeds will die off. This makes it much easier to till up the ground and get things ready for planting.

Fire-Starter

Having a reliable way to get a fire going can be critical to survival. Sure, there are all sorts of fire-starters on the market today and most of them work rather well. However, if you have a stack of newspaper and a few old candles, you can make fire-starters that work just as well as some and even better than most.

Roll a few sheets of newspaper together so the end result is about 1 inch thick. Use jute twine or some other type of cordage to tie the roll together at several points. Cut the roll into sections, each a couple of inches long. Be sure you have at least one loop of twine around each of these sections.

Submerge each of these sections into melted wax, and then set out to dry for a few minutes. To use, simply light the jute twine as though it were a fuse. You could also scrape a bit of wax away from a corner and light the paper directly. These fire-starters burn a good long time.

Toilet Paper

It isn't nearly as soft as Charmin, but it'll do in a pinch — and far better than trying to decide if those leaves look like poison ivy or not. You can make the experience a little more tolerable by repeatedly crumpling up the paper so it softens the fibers a bit.

Fire Log

As should be obvious to just about everyone, newspaper burns quite well. It is, after all, just wood pulp. There are gadgets and gizmos out there that will turn shredded paper into bricks or logs for burning. That's all well and good, but the method I'm going to describe requires nothing more than a small tub of water and a dowel.

Fill a basin or tub with warm water and just a squirt of dish soap. Separate the newspaper into sheets, then pile them in the water and let them soak for an hour or so. Drain the water and lay the sheets out in sections, overlapping them a bit. Begin at one end with the dowel and roll it along, wrapping the newspaper around the dowel. Keep adding paper until the log is about 4 inches thick or so. Slide out the dowel and your log is complete.

Lay the logs out to dry, which can take a few days to a few weeks depending on climate conditions. I wouldn't suggest using these exclusively in your fireplace or wood stove, but they can help extend your supply of firewood by using them here and there. They won't light right off a match, but will catch just fine off of some kindling.

Newspaper logs can supplement your firewood, extending your fuel supply.

These will produce a bit more ash than regular logs, but the benefit of increased fuel for the wood stove with little impact on your wallet will probably outweigh the inconvenience of one more bucket of ash to empty each week.

As a last resort, a rolled-up newspaper (and its Millwall brick variation) can be a decent improvised weapon when thrust into a bad guy's vulnerable bits, like eyes and throat.

Improvised Weapon

Newspapers for self-defense? What are you going to do, paper cut them to death? OK, newspapers wouldn't be my first choice for a weapon, nor my second, third, or even fourth. But, as a last resort, it'll do the job. How?

Take about five sheets of newspaper and roll them up as tightly as you can. The resulting baton will be strong enough to be used defensively against certain attacks. Offensively, you could swing it like a small club, but it's *way* stronger at the ends. Better to thrust the baton's tip into a bad guy's eyes, throat, or groin, or use the butt-end to hammer on vulnerable areas. Either way, your newspaper baton will certainly get an assailant's attention.

Sort of a variation on this theme is the Millwall brick. Roll the newspaper as before, then fold it in half. That's it, you're done. The striking surface is the fold. The more newspaper used, the harder and heavier the brick will turn out. You can make the weapon a little more lethal by adding a few nails to the business end of the brick.

This simple tool is the namesake of London's Millwall Football Club, whose fans were notorious for hooliganism. In the 1960s and 1970s, they allegedly used Millwall bricks to raise hell because pretty much every other improvised weapon had been outlawed. Where there's a will there's a way, right?

Insulation

You've no doubt seen the cliché in the movies of the homeless dude stuffing newspaper into his coat or pants, right? Guess what, it really does work to keep you warm. Newspaper, just like most of the puffy coat fillers you find on the market today, add dead air space between you and the outside chill. Your body heat warms that dead air, which is what keeps you from shivering. You may feel like the Stay Puft Marshmallow Man, but at least you'll be warm.

Newspaper also works as an insulating material around the home. When you find a cold draft coming in from the side of a window or door, stuff the crack with newspaper. It might not look all that awesome, but it works. Keeping out the cold outside air can be very important if your only source of heat is the fireplace during a power outage.

If frozen pipes are a concern, wrap them with newspaper. You can also run the taps at a light trickle to help keep things from turning to ice.

Boot Dryer

Wet footwear can be a serious issue and could lead to frostbite or worse in bad conditions. You can use newspaper to dry out your boots and shoes. Stuff loose crumples of paper into the boot until you can't fit any more inside and let it sit overnight. If the boots are really soaked, replace the paper with dry crumples after a couple of hours, then let it go until morning.

Conclusion

Even though they rarely carry good news these days, there is little in life more ubiquitous than newspapers — even in this Digital Age. Newspapers are so common we often overlook it as a useful resource. The true survivalist, though, tries to utilize everything and anything to achieve his or her goals. The survival uses of newspapers don't end here, as their limit is really just your imagination.

About the Author

Jim Cobb is a recognized authority on disaster preparedness. He has studied, practiced, and taught survival strategies for about 30 years. Today, he resides in the upper Midwest with his beautiful and patient wife and their three adolescent weapons of mass destruction. His books include *Prepper's Home Defense*, *Countdown to Preparedness*, and *Prepper's Long-Term Survival Guide*. Jim's primary home online is **www.SurvivalWeekly.com**. He is also active on Facebook at **www.facebook.com/jimcobbsurvival**. Jim offers a consulting service as well as educational opportunities at **www.DisasterPrepConsultants.com**.

Paracord Preps

10 Projects That'll Bail You Out When You're In a Bind

Story and Photos by Kevin Estela

Paracord is to the survivalist as ketchup is to French fries. Carried in hanks, bracelets, shoelaces, neck-knife lanyards, and all over, paracord is a staple piece of kit. But it's one thing to have some on hand; it's another to know how to actually use it. Many people look at paracord and see a piece of string.

We look at paracord and see endless possibilities to increase our survivability.

This is *knot* your average cordage article. We were provided with plenty of paracord from Campingsurvival.com, and we're here to take your skills and readiness to the next level with these RECOIL OFFGRID projects.

Warning! The content in this story is provided for illustrative purposes only and not meant to be construed as advice or instruction. Seek a reputable instructor first. Any use of the information contained in this article shall be solely at the reader's risk. This publication and its contributors are not responsible for any potential injuries.

Paracord Project #1

Trapo

Difficulty: 🌀🌀🌀🌀🌀🌀

FUNCTION
Weapon

HOW TO
Anyone who has seen the Steven Seagal movie *Out for Justice* knows what a rock in a sock is, even if they don't know why Ritchie killed Bobby Lupo. Here's how to make one out of paracord with a ball bearing. This version requires knowledge of how to tie a monkey's fist knot around a solid sphere.

Start by passing your paracord around the object enough times to cover it. For a 1-inch ball bearing, this is approximately six passes of paracord. Wrap your cord perpendicular to these passes six more times. Thread your paracord another six times to the inside of the second set of passes and around the first set of passes (there's a reason for the difficulty rating on this one, and you just read it). Dress up the knot by pulling it here and there until it tightens around the ball bearing. Tie the ends into loop that can be slipped around your wrist and flail away.

NOTES
We've tied these by hand without a jig and must admit it's worth the extra steps to assemble one. Not since puberty have you wished as much for an extra hand to help out in in the process. Just drill four holes, 1 inch square, into a wooden board and insert wooden dowels to hold your ball bearing for you.

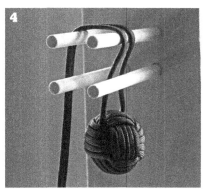

A monkey fist knot can be finished with any number of tied handles for a more secure purchase.

Paracord Project #2

Friction Saw

Difficulty: ●●●●●●●

FUNCTION
Cutting synthetic materials

HOW TO
All that's needed to create a paracord saw is a length of paracord (braided Kevlar cord works well, too, and that's why we carry it in our wallets) with a couple loops tied in each end, large enough for your hands.

With the saw tied, place it over whatever you plan to cut and run it back and forth, increasing the friction and heat on your work piece, while dispersing the heat over the length of the saw. This will cut through duct tape, webbing, PVC pipe, or just about anything synthetic.

NOTES
Watch your hands with this one. Your saw will be hot when you're done. The longer the saw, the more room to disperse the heat.

A paracord friction saw works by running the cord over a synthetic object like this PVC pipe. With enough heat, the saw will cut through even the thickest tubing, webbing, or synthetic cordage.

Paracord Project #3

Improvised Tourniquet

Difficulty:

FUNCTION
Stop bleeding

HOW TO
A tourniquet should always be applied "high and tight." That is, placed up high on the arm near the armpit or up against the crotch. In general, paracord sucks as a tourniquet, as it's too narrow to avoid causing damage to tissue. However, when multiple strands are tied as one, it'll work in a pinch.
 Tie a single square knot with multiple strands by passing left over right, tying a knot then right over left and tying a knot. Insert a tactical pen (or something else that will serve as a turnbuckle). If you can, put a key chain split ring around the strands first so you have a place to tuck that pen once tension is applied. Leave it on, and get your buddy or yourself to the emergency room.

NOTES
While you can do this with paracord, get in the habit of carrying a real tourniquet. They're cheap and highly effective. What's your life worth?

A single strand of paracord makes a horrible tourniquet. Multiple strands tied as one will work well to prevent bleeding out. Lock it all in place with a split ring and pen or similar object.

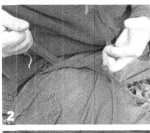

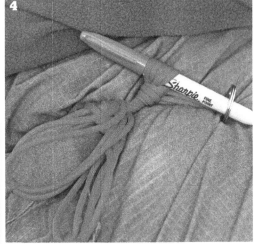

Paracord Project #4
Improvised Harness

Difficulty: 🔗🔗🔗🔗🔗🔗🔗

FUNCTION
Weight carrying (read advisory below)

HOW TO
You may need to escape a high rise or descend a cliff. If you have no other option, here's a solution. A traditional Swiss seat is tied with about 12 to 15 feet of flat webbing or rope. For comfort, you should use multiple strands of paracord unless you want that tourniquet effect from the previous project.

Once you have your cordage ready, find the center and hold it at your side by your waist. Pass one end around your waist and meet in the middle. Create a surgeon's knot with the two ends. Take the two ends and pass them under your ass. Put the ends over your shoulders and stand up to pull them tight. Pass the ends back through the paracord waistband you made and tie each off with a half hitch. This is the point where you'll feel a pinch between your legs. Remember, it's life or limb – or in this case life or sack.

Take the ends of your harness and tie them off with a square knot and backup knots, to your left if you're a righty and to the right if you're a lefty. Make sure your knot is on the opposite side of your brake hand. If you're wearing a sturdy belt, pass your carabiner through that too, making sure the gate opens toward you. The spine of the carabiner is where your munter hitch will be used for rappelling. The majority of your weight will be supported by your paracord leg loops. This works even better with flat webbing, but can work with what you have.

NOTES
Seek professional climbing and rope instruction before trying this one at home. Rappelling is inherently dangerous. However, even more dangerous than rappelling in an emergency is doing nothing when SHTF. That could lead to death.

Use multiple strands of paracord to create your Swiss-seat harness.

Keep the gate of your locking carabiner facing you when you clip in. This allows the rope to work against the spine of the 'biner instead of against the gate when you belay or rappel.

The author rappelling with a paracord harness. While you can do this, it isn't nearly as comfortable as a dedicated harness.

Paracord Project #5

1-2-3 Anchor

Difficulty: 🌀🌀🌀🌀🌀

FUNCTION
Vehicle recovery anchor

HOW TO
Cut six 1- to 2-inch diameter wooden stakes, measuring approximately 18 inches long. Pound the first stake into the ground at a slight angle in the direction you want your stuck vehicle to go. Don't make this angle too great. From your initial stake, pound the next two stakes about 1 foot further away on each side at 45-degree angles left and right.

From these two stakes, pound the final three stakes another foot behind, continuing in a pyramid pattern. For those of you who have played Beirut/beer pong, this will be a familiar pattern. Tie a length of paracord from the top of the first wooden stake to the bottom of the two stakes off to 45-degree angles. Tie paracord from the second row to the third row in a similar fashion. You can use a lark's head on the top and a rolling hitch and half hitches on the bottom. Attach your come-a-long to the first stake and to your vehicle. The 1-2-3 anchor works well since the stakes are supported by the following rows.

NOTES
Vehicle recovery can be quite dangerous, even fatal at times. Make sure your vehicle parking brake is on while securing your anchor and off when using it. A small hammer and come-a-long makes retrieval easier than resorting to a Spanish Windlass (the Spanish Windlass will be featured in a future issue of RECOIL OFFGRID).

1-2-3 anchoring requires cutting multiple posts and pounding them into the ground in a triangle stack. Having the right tools — such as a hatchet or kukri, cordage, small sledgehammer, and come-a-long — make self-rescue easier.

Paracord Project #6

Tripod

Difficulty: ●●●●●○○○

FUNCTION
Suspending objects and much more

HOW TO
Gather three poles and place them on the ground. They need not be the same length as the legs can be kicked out once assembled to make it stand straight. Wrap paracord around one of the poles with a lark's head knot to start the tripod lashing. Then wrap the three poles three or four times.

The strength of the tripod lashing comes from frapping, when you pull the paracord in between the middle pole and pole closest to you and pull it tight to constrict on the wrapping on all three poles. Do it a second time between the middle pole and the pole furthest from you. Finish the tripod lashing by taking the end of the cord and securing it to the remaining end of the lark's head knot.

NOTES
Tripods can be used to suspend stew pots over the fire, to build raised beds in wet conditions, as camp furniture, or as the framework for a hauling "crane." Anyone who wants to build advanced tripod projects should also know how to make a square lashing.

Tripods are staples in traditional woodland basecamps. They can be used to create raised beds, camp kitchen potholders, camp seats, and jerky smokers.

Paracord Project #7

Bottle Carrier Net

Difficulty: ●●●○○○○○

FUNCTION
Holding bottles, containers, potted plants, etc.

HOW TO
Measure eight lengths of cordage by placing it under your bottle and holding the ends over it. It should measure approximately three times the height of your bottle. For the bottle used in our tutorial, this meant approximately 6 feet in length for each cord.

In our example, we cut eight lengths of cord out of a 50-foot-long hank. The last 2 feet were used to create a handle. Attach the eight strands to your split ring with lark's head knots. The trick to this bottle carrier is tying knots with strands of cord adjacent to one another.

Tie the first overhand knot tied 3 inches from the ring, putting the knot on the side of the bottle rather than under it. From here, each knot works its way up the bottle every 1.5 inches. Try to keep your knots spread out consistently or it'll look like rubbish. Continue working up the bottle until you get to the top. Finish the carrier by tying four of the strands together as one handle and the remaining four as the other handle.

NOTES
This same pattern can be used on almost anything box-like or cylindrical in shape. Make sure your split ring can handle the weight, or use a welded ring available at hardware and boating stores. If you don't like overhand knots, you can use square knots instead.

Water bottle net carriers are more time consuming to make than they are difficult. Make sure to make your knots evenly spaced; your first knots should be alongside your bottle, not under it.

Paracord Project #8
Turnbuckle Rattler

Difficulty: ⚭⚭⚭⚭⚭

FUNCTION
Camp alert system

HOW TO
When constructing the turnbuckle rattler, look for two sturdy trees with minimal flex in their trunks. This won't work well with small diameter saplings. Take a length of paracord and wrap it around both trees. Tie an overhand knot in the paracord, leaving tail ends to your knot as well as very little slack in the loop you just created.

Just about one foot above the loop you just tied around the trees, tie another loop. From that, suspend a length of paracord down from the center in the gap between the trees and attach a few aluminum cans.

Cut a small wooden dowel from a tree branch or sapling. Put this dowel between the gap in the trees in the original loop and take up the slack in the loop by cranking the dowel end over end, increasing the tension. Slip a paracord loop over one end and attach it to a tripwire. When an unexpected guest enters your camp, they'll trigger the turnbuckle rattler, striking the cans and alerting you to their presence.

NOTES
The difficulty rating in this trap is derived from the trigger and tripwire mechanism. A simple 90-degree toggle is all you need, but that requires knife carving knowledge and skill. When setting this alert system, watch your eyes. This device is under tension and disrespecting it can lead to accidental triggering.

Never be surprised in your camp by constructing a turnbuckle rattler with discarded cans commonly found in the woods. Use the trigger and tripwire of your choice to set up this makeshift alarm system.

Paracord Project #9

Sling

Difficulty: ●●●●●○○○○

FUNCTION
Weapon

HOW TO
Paracord makes a great sling. For starters, determine what you plan to toss. For this tutorial, we're using golf balls. On one end, create a loop for your middle finger. About 2 feet from this knot, create a pouch out of duct tape, a couple pieces of leather, or flat webbing.

Tie a second piece of paracord to this pouch; make it as long as the other side with the middle-finger loop. On this end, create a knot you can pinch. If you're skilled at braiding, an entirely paracord version can be made with a web pouch. To streamline it, you can whip the paracord to the pouch with the inner strands.

NOTES
This is easy to make but difficult to master. Try tossing this horizontally, vertically, or in a figure eight path. With enough practice you'll be ready to kill that giant or challenge your skills.

Slings are centuries old and still extremely effective if they can be mastered. A word of advice: Wear eye-protection and duck when your friends try this for the first time.

Paracord Project #10
Stretcher/Travois

Difficulty: ✦✦✦✦✦✧✧✧✧

FUNCTION
Moving an injured person

HOW TO
Prior to starting, cut two poles at least one-and-half times the length of the person to be carried. If you're making a travois, make them twice as long if you can. The poles should be sturdy and have minimal flex. Place them parallel to each other and as wide apart as your patient for a stretcher; cross them about a quarter of the way down in an "X" for a travois.

Tie your paracord to one pole, then directly across from it. About 25 feet should be enough to hold a patient. Don't cut your cord! Continue zigzagging down your poles then back up again creating web work. Secure the end of your paracord and cover your web stretcher with a camping pad. It can be used without a pad, but for patient comfort, hook them up if you can.

NOTES
A non-paracord version of a stretcher can be made with just a blanket and poles. Whether paracord or blanket, learn ways of helping your buddies out and teach them so they can help you in case you're the one who screws up.

Sometimes, help can't make it to you, and you must get a patient to help instead. With a couple stiff poles and some paracord, you can create a makeshift stretcher or travois.

Beyond Paracord

The 550 paracord is the industry standard when it comes to cordage. It's a great baseline of comparison for other types of ropes. For example, tarred bank line is referred to as "thinner than paracord," and jute twine is said to be "not as strong as paracord." As outdoor enthusiasts, we hold 550 paracord in high regard, but there are times when other options may be better. Here are a few other cordage options to carry next to the hanks of paracord in your pack.

Braided Kevlar: This line is ridiculously tough. Thinner than 550 paracord, it has much more strength pound for pound. It's harder to cut and knot, but the tradeoff is packability.

Jute Twine: You don't always need 550 pounds of breaking strength, and there are times when you want to tie something up in camp and not worry about taking it down. Jute twine isn't synthetic and can be left behind to biodegrade. That'll make the tree huggers in your group happy.

SpiderWire Braided Line: This fishing line is the only type we trust. If you can catch a 50-pound freshwater fish, you're a stud. All other fish can be landed without worrying about breakage with this super line. Rather than using one of the inner strands of paracord, use this dedicated line. Just watch your fingers if you hook onto a fish and it runs. It'll slice your skin like a laser.

Dental Floss: Wicked strong, pre-rolled into cute spools, and dentist-approved, this is handy cordage. Waxed floss is great for whipping lines that'll unravel, and it also works well for setting up traps. When visiting your dentist, ask for samples. Rip them out of the packaging and tuck them into your pack pockets.

Sources:
Camping Survival > www.CampingSurvival.com

Swiss Army Survival

5 Surprising Uses for the Original Multitool

Story and Photos by Steven Paul Barlow

In this age of titanium folding knives, state-of-the-art bushcraft blades, and $500 tactical tomahawks, it's easy to overlook one of the best survival tools that most of us already own: the little red knife with the corkscrew.

A Victorinox Swiss Army knife is a small toolbox in your pocket. Have you ever cringed watching someone break the tip off his tactical knife while trying to turn a screw or pry a lid? Perhaps you've seen someone work up a sweat damaging or dulling his big blade while chopping or batoning a sapling, when a small saw blade would have sufficed? Tasks are often easier when you use the right tool. Swiss Army knives are available in many models, giving you lots of tool combinations to choose from without having to carry an entire toolbox. And no, not all of them feature corkscrews, and not all of them are red.

We've used this multitool in the woods and around the house, to prepare tinder, fashion snare triggers, tighten screws, strip wires, file corroded wires, open cans, repair toys, make an alcohol stove from a tuna can, and clear shooting lanes while hunting. Once, on a high-profile detail as a police officer, this author even used the scissors on a Swiss Army knife to self-administer an emergency haircut when a grouchy superior officer went on a rant about "non-regulation" hair.

When it comes to matters of survival, a Swiss Army knife can be a lifesaver, too. Here we highlight five of the most unexpected uses for everyone's favorite little red multitool.

Survival Use #1: Start a Fire

In a survival situation, you need to be able to make fire. You might carry a lighter and a ferrocerium rod with you, but those aren't the only sources of ignition. Our backup fire-starting kit uses a small piece of steel wool, the battery from a tactical flashlight, and, yes, our Swiss Army knife. The knife holds the battery in place and also forms most of the electrical circuit.

Step 1: Store a piece of steel wool inside your Swiss Army knife. Here's an easy way to do this. First, open the bottle opener and can opener on each end of your knife. Take a piece of steel wool and twist it in your fingers until you have a strong, twine-like piece just shorter than your knife is long. Push this inside the knife using the tweezers or toothpick, then close the can and bottle openers on top of it.

Step 2: When you're ready to start a fire, open the can opener all the way, but open the bottle opener just halfway, so that it's perpendicular to the rest of the knife. Remove your steel wool from inside and untwist some of it. You won't need much.

Step 3: Place several strands of steel wool into a tinder bundle about the size of your thumbnail. A cotton ball with some shredded paper mixed in works well.

Step 4: Remove a CR123A or similar battery from your tactical flashlight. Place the flat, negative end of the battery against the upright bottle opener. Lift the front of the battery slightly, and slowly close the can opener until it rests against the top of the battery, leaving a slight gap between the can opener and the positive nub of the battery. The battery should now be held in place by those two Swiss Army tools.

Step 5: Holding the knife upright in one hand and the tinder/steel wool in the

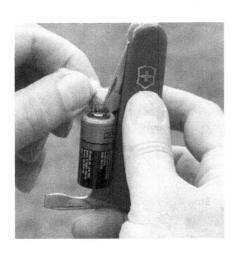

other, position the strands of steel wool so that it touches the positive terminal of the battery and the can opener. This completes the electrical circuit. The current will run from the battery through the knife to the steel wool and back to the battery. The steel wool is so fine that it'll heat up rapidly and begin to glow, until it catches the tinder on fire.

Note: Like many survival techniques, this requires practice, both to get the steel wool glowing hot and then to fan or blow the right amount of air onto a resulting ember in the tinder until it bursts into flame. This caught the author by surprise the first time he tried it, burning a thumb. Make sure you have other tinder and kindling ready nearby to keep your fire going.

Survival Use #2: Build a Stove

There are many ways to make various types of alcohol stoves. Our favorite — and one of the easiest — uses a small potted meat can with two rows of holes punched around the top rim. The cook pot sits right on top, and the flames jet out of the holes. But what if your Swiss Army knife is your only tool? No problem. Here are two simple stoves you can make, one with a tuna can and the other with the bottoms of two soda cans.

Tuna Can Stove:

Step 1: Using the can opener on your Swiss Army knife, open the can of tuna, but don't completely remove the lid.

Step 2: Eat the tuna. It's good for you.

Step 3: Fold the lid back into the can.

Step 4: Fill the can with methyl alcohol — either denatured alcohol from a hardware store (used as paint thinner) or Heet brand gas-line antifreeze (the one in the yellow bottle). You can find Heet in most

convenience stores.

Step 5: Place a couple of small stones (flat tops preferred) on either side of your stove to serve as your pot support.

Step 6: Light the stove. The flames will shoot through the gaps you cut between the can rim and the lid.

Step 7: Place your cook pot across the stones. Ideally, there should be an inch or less of space between the stove and your pot.

Soda Can Stove:

Step 1: Begin with two empty soda cans with concave bottoms. Using the reamer tool of your Swiss Army knife, bore 6 to 10 holes in the bottom of one can, being careful not to let the reamer blade close on your fingers. The metal on soda cans is thin, so boring holes isn't difficult.

Step 2: Cut the bottom inch off both cans. Use the reamer blade again so that you can keep your other knife blades sharp for other survival tasks.

Step 3: Fit the two bottoms together — the one with holes in it goes inside the other one. You'll need to bend the edges slightly to get it started, then you'll be able to push them together. The fit will be snug.

Step 4: Your stove is done. Fill it with methyl alcohol through the holes you made. Light the stove. Use stones as a pot support as you did with the tuna can.

Notes: Burn time of these stoves is usually 15 minutes. They'll boil two cups of water in 8 to 12 minutes. If yours doesn't, try adding holes to the stove, placing the cook pot closer to the stove, or configuring a windscreen around the stove. Build time for each stove is about five minutes. For the tuna can stove, that time also included eating the tuna.

Survival Use #3: Craft a You-Haul

A travois is an A-frame of wooden poles used to haul heavy loads. Historically, they were pulled by horses. But you can construct smaller ones where you provide the horsepower. They can be handy if you need to move camp, haul out downed game, or get an injured companion out alive. You'll need the saw blade on your Swiss Army knife to construct it.

Step 1: Cut two branches about an inch in diameter to a length of 6 to 7 feet. These will be used for the outside of your A-frame. Lash them together to form two sides of a triangle.

Step 2: Cut one crossbar about 1½-feet long to lash near the top of your A-frame. This will be your pushbar.

Step 3: Cut two or more longer crossbars and lash these at intervals across the base. You now have a travois.

Step 4: Strap your load to the crossbars near the base.

Step 5: Step inside the A-frame and pick it up so that the push bar is along your waist. Hold on to the frame and start walking.

Note: You can lash the pieces together with paracord if you have it. If not, get out the Swiss Army knife again. Whittle the ends of the crossbars into a triangular shape to fit dovetail notches that you cut into the side pieces as outlined in the next item. It's time consuming, but it works.

Sharp Trivia

+ Lots of Tools: The Swiss Champ, the flagship of the company's gadget knives, has 33 functions. It's made from 64 different parts and takes 450 different operations to manufacture.

+ What's in a Name? Founder Karl Elsener began using his deceased mother's name, Victoria, as a trademark in 1909, the same year the company was given permission to put the Swiss emblem on its knives to differentiate them from imitations. In 1923, the company switched to using stainless steel and used the name Victoria Inoxyd, with inoxyd being a shortened form of the French word for stainless steel, *inoxydable*. By 1931, the company combined the names, and the company has been called Victorinox ever since.

You can attach two pieces of wood using a dovetail notch, made using the saw blade of a Swiss Army knife. This dovetail technique can be used when cordage isn't available. For example, the author used sticks dovetailed together to form a pot stand.

Survival Use #4: Saw a Dovetail Notch

How do you join two pieces of wood together without cordage? Use the Dovetail Notch. Basically you cut a triangular notch into one piece of wood, whittle the end of the other into a triangular shape, and fit the two together. You can use this to make a frame to hang a kettle from a campfire or to fit poles together when building a shelter — anything you need to improvise in the field when cordage is in short supply.

Step 1: Using your Swiss Army knife's saw blade, make three cuts about halfway into a piece of wood where you want to make the notch. The first cut should be straight down. The other two, one on each side of the first, angle away.

Step 2: Use the saw and knife blades to remove the wood between your cuts, leaving a triangular notch that's narrow at the top and wider toward the center of the wood.

Step 3: Take the other piece of wood and carve the end into the shape of a triangle. Cut a little at a time and keep checking the fit to the notched piece until you have a tight connection.

Note: You can further secure the pieces by melting pine sap into the connections.

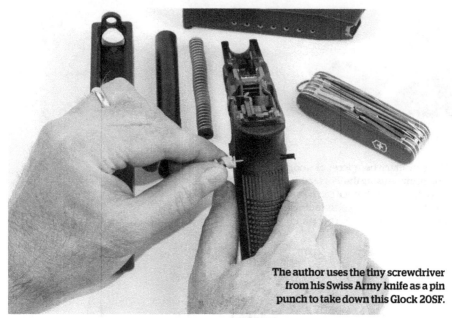

The author uses the tiny screwdriver from his Swiss Army knife as a pin punch to take down this Glock 20SF.

Attaching a length of paracord to the parcel hook of a Swiss Army knife makes a handy improvised pull-through bore cleaner. Patches can be cut from a cotton shirt and attached with a small paper clip.

Survival Use #5: Clean Your Gun

A firearm is only good if you keep it in reliable working condition. You might be faced with doing a little field maintenance if you're far from civilization, whether on a camping trip, or a hunting trip, or while bugging out from a crisis.

Task 1: Use the small knife blade or scissors of your Swiss Army knife to cut cleaning patches from a cotton shirt.

Task 2: Use the toothpick and tweezers to reach into tight places to remove debris.

Task 3: Use the small screwdriver to punch pins.

Task 4: Use the parcel hook with a length of paracord to make a pull-through bore cleaner.

Task 5: Use the screwdrivers to adjust the sights or remove grip panels.

The Army Advantage

A Swiss Army knife makes an excellent everyday-carry tool. It can often be carried when it's not practical or legal to carry a larger knife. They're more socially acceptable too, as they're not apt to be seen as a threat when in civilized company.

So, tap into your inner MacGyver, no matter if your travels take you to wild forests, tall peaks, or urban jungles. With a Swiss Army knife and a little imagination, you have one of the best problem-solving gadgets ever created.

And yes, in case you're wondering, we've saved the day many a time by actually using the corkscrew to open a bottle of wine. ⁙

Whether in the open spaces of Mother Nature or the confines of an overcrowded city, a Swiss Army knife can help you solve most problems. These days there are plenty of models available that'll suit your needs and preferences.

Sources:
Swiss Army Knives: A Collector's Companion, Compendium Publishing Ltd.
www.amazon.com

Victorinox Swiss Army
www.swissarmy.com

6 › Survival At Home

Household Survival

Commonplace Items that Can Help in Survival Situations

By Tim MacWelch
Photography by Michael Grey

Don't let the hyped-up doomsday television shows fool you. You don't need to have a bunker full of olive drab-colored gear crates and radiation-proof water barrels to consider yourself wealthy in the realm of survival gear. To a creative and resourceful survivor, the average broom closet, kitchen pantry, and bathroom cabinets are already loaded with useful items. Many of these everyday household supplies can be repurposed into vital survival gear, home remedies, and emergency equipment, should you ever find yourself in a disaster setting or be faced with an urban survival scenario. Get ready to look at the ordinary things around you in a whole new way.

Source Supplies in Your Closet

Linen closets, broom closets and hall closets can all contain a treasure trove of good stuff. From towels and bedding, to cleaning chemicals and tools, closets are always a grab bag of the random items that are so handy in everyday life — and even handier in an emergency.

Bleach

Common, unscented bleach is about 5-percent sodium hypochlorite. This powerful disinfectant can be used for a number of tasks that involve dangerous germs. The same bleach that you pour into your laundry can also make a disinfecting solution to use on people, pets, surfaces, and supplies in the event of a pandemic or biological terrorist attack. Use 1 tablespoon of bleach added to 1 quart of water to make a wipe or spray for intense disinfection.

Disinfecting drinking water can also be achieved with bleach. Add two drops of bleach to 1 quart of water, if the water is warm and clear. As the water gets colder and/or dirtier, you could increase the bleach from two drops to three or four drops per quart. Shake the water to disperse the bleach and allow it to sit for one hour prior to consumption. By no means will you confuse the concoction with Evian, but it's better than the alternative.

Pull-Tab Top Canned Food

When shopping for canned food, you might have noticed that some cans are equipped with easy-to-open, pull-tab tops. These types of cans have the advantage of being opened without any tools, which is an obvious advantage. While these types of cans seal and protect the contents just as well as standard cans, they are more susceptible to damage from being dropped. If damaged, the tops have a chance of opening or buckling. So, which type is best? The tradeoff between convenience and sturdiness is something that you'll have to decide.

Towels and Linens

Hand towels, bath towels, beach towels, and bed linens represent an almost unlimited resource to crafty and creative people. This kind of absorbent fabric can be used for wound dressings, insulation, baby blankets, fire starter, and hundreds of other applications. For someone who can sew by hand, the fabric can be cut into pieces and stitched into an infinite number of handy items.

Tools

Even if your home is small, you probably still have a basic tool kit for simple repairs. If not, then you now have a homework assignment to complete after reading this article. The average toolbox should contain things like hammers, nails, screws, screwdrivers, pliers, and other handtools, which can be important for their intended uses, but they can also be repurposed.

To help with cooking tasks, you can use the pliers to pick up hot metal food containers (like the food cans) by the rim. For defensive applications, use your nails and hammer to nail windows and unnecessary doors shut. And for offensive applications, hammers make serviceable weapons, as do utility knives, screwdrivers, and larger wrenches. Again, sheaths and holsters for these makeshift weapons can be made out of cardboard and duct tape in a pinch.

Get Geared Up in the Kitchen

Water and food are critical priorities in an emergency setting. And while you may logically turn to your kitchen for these life-sustaining commodities, there are plenty of other supplies in the average kitchen just waiting to be reimagined and used.

Oil

With so much emphasis these days on healthy lifestyles, many people focus on low-calorie and low-fat foods in their daily life. But in a survival situation, it's all about high calories. Cooking oil from your kitchen can be used as intended for cooking and baking, but it can also serve as a high-calorie food supplement. One tablespoon of any food-grade oil contains approximately 120 calories. As your metabolism and workload go up due to the strain of an emergency, your calorie intake should also increase. Add a spoonful or two of oil to any foods to spike up the calories.

Food-grade oils are also useful as a lotion or balm for dry, cracked skin and lips. And that same oil can be used for lighting as the fuel in oil lamps. You can pour liquid forms of oil into traditional kerosene lanterns.

Knives

The jangling drawer full of kitchen knives can be easily be used as tools and weapons, should the need arise. Twist a knife, and it becomes a drill. Chop with a cleaver, and it performs like a hatchet. Steak knives and paring knives can be a passable replacement for a pocket knife, after you fit them with an improvised sheath. Use two strips of cardboard or plastic, and a generous amount of duct tape, to put these quick and dirty sheaths together. As anyone who's seen Psycho would know, the bigger knives in your culinary collection could pass for weapons, but they will need to be outfitted with sheaths, similar to the smaller knives.

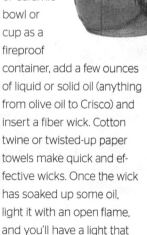

You can also create your own oil lamps from scratch. Using a glass, metal, or ceramic bowl or cup as a fireproof container, add a few ounces of liquid or solid oil (anything from olive oil to Crisco) and insert a fiber wick. Cotton twine or twisted-up paper towels make quick and effective wicks. Once the wick has soaked up some oil, light it with an open flame, and you'll have a light that performs just like a candle.

Canned Food

While MREs may seem to be the survival food of choice (see OFFGRID Issue 1), don't ignore their forerunner, canned foods. Besides being a bug- and rodent-proof source of nourishment, canned food will also give you a reusable container once the can is empty. These metal containers can be used to serve food and drink. They can also be safely used over a fire or stove, allowing you to boil water and cook other foods.

An empty food can easily converts to a small cook stove, too. Pack a cotton rag or insert a partial roll of toilet paper into the can. Pour in melted wax or high-proof alcohol and then light up your new emergency stove.

Once you have an abundance of cans, you can use a few to create a low-tech alarm system. Tie several cans at the end of a length of fishing line or a dark-colored thread. Use two pieces of duct tape to stretch this line across your walkway, hall, or driveway, leaving the cans stacked or piled off to the side. When someone hits this homemade tripwire, you'll hear the cans clanging together and know that company is coming.

Snack Chips

Sure, they're tasty and provide a lot of caloric energy — bet you can't just eat one. But they also make a tempting trap bait and burn like hellfire. To use chips as fire starters, make your selection by looking at the labels. The chips with the highest calories per serving  are your top choice to burn. This is due to the insane amount of fat that each oh-so-tasty crunchy chip holds. Fat equals fuel value in the world of fire making, and Fritos are my fire-building favorite. Just place a few of these precious snacks underneath some twigs or tiny pieces of split wood. Apply an open flame to the chips, and you'll have your grill, stove, fireplace, or backyard bonfire started in no time.

Fire Extinguisher

Aside from the intended use of a fire extinguisher, these pressurized vessels of powder and air can be a startling defense against an assailant. Aim for the face, spray them liberally, immediately follow up with a strike (or more) to the head using the butt-end of the extinguisher. Then make a hasty retreat. Unorthodox tactics like these might just buy you enough time to escape from looters and home invaders.

Tea Bags

A cup of tea may not seem like a survival item, unless you're being blinded by a caffeine withdrawal headache. But a wet tea bag is another story. A regular black tea bag contains tea leaves that are full of valuable tannic acid. This acid shrinks inflammation when used topically as a wet compress. In the event you cannot get to a dentist or doctor, you can use the wet tea bag on boils, ingrown toenails, hemorrhoids, and other inflamed skin maladies. You can even get toothache relief by placing the wet tea bag against a painful tooth in your mouth (but please don't use the same one that you previously used for a hemorrhoid). This dental remedy can be boosted by adding whole or powdered cloves (the spice) to the wet tea bag. Cloves contain an anesthetic oil that works well for temporary relief of dental pain.

Find Some Useful Stuff in the Bathroom

Most bathrooms contain a very diverse assortment of goods. After analyzing your needs, and all of the random stuff in the cabinets, you might just find some items in the bathroom that will help you out of a jam.

Dental Floss

Need some strong string? Or something to actually floss with? Dental floss is made from amazingly strong fibers, allowing floss to be used for emergency cordage, fishing line, trap components, suture material, sewing thread, and a host of other purposes (perhaps a Borat "man-kini" if you wish to frighten women and young children).

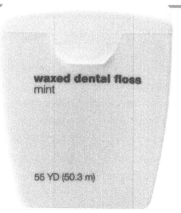

Toilet Paper

This ubiquitous stuff serves its everyday task very well, yet most people don't give it proper recognition for its versatility. Toilet paper can be used as wick material for the oil lamps and alcohol cooking stoves already mentioned in this article.

It can be an insulating material for bedding and clothing, providing it stays dry. Toilet paper also helps with fire building, applying medicines, and signaling for help in a dry climate (toilet paper a prominent tree, as you would for a prank). TP also makes a great trade good — since anyone that has run out will really want to get some.

Hygiene Supplies

Many feminine hygiene items like pads and tampons have alternate uses for first-aid. Pads make a fine dressing for wounds and tampons can be opened up to act as a replacement for gauze and sponges to stop bleeding. Guys, no longer will you feel embarrassed at the drug store when purchasing feminine hygiene products. Cotton balls, makeup pads, and similar bath and beauty supplies can also serve medical and fire-building functions.

Alcohol-based mouthwash, hydrogen peroxide, and other related products can be used as improvised disinfectants.

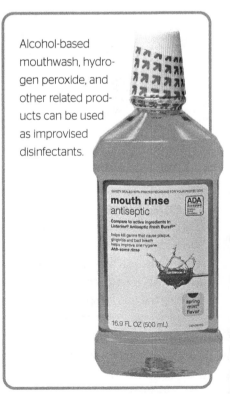

Stock Up On These Three Things

It's not necessary to be a hoarder of survival gear to feel more confident about your ability to fend for yourself. Since planning ahead is one of the most important aspects of a survivor mentality, you should seize the opportunity to plan ahead by picking up some multi-use supplies on your next trip to the store.

Duct Tape

This modern wonder can repair, replace, and revitalize almost anything. Duct tape can mend your clothing, your cracked water bottle, and your footwear. Duct tape can be used as tinder to start fires, a binding to attach items together, and it can be twisted into strong rope. A few rolls of duct tape are a great addition to any home survival stash. And don't forget to add some tape to your vehicle emergency kit and bug-out bag.

High-Proof Alcohol

If you're at the drug store, you can pick up high-percentage rubbing alcohol. And if your shopping trip takes you to the hardware store, you may be able to find a can of very high-proof denatured alcohol (ethanol). These can be used as stove fuel, fire starter, and disinfectant for surfaces. The rubbing alcohol can even be used to (painfully) disinfect wounds. Just make sure you read the labels before performing medical tasks with alcohol. Denatured alcohol and anything containing methanol should not be used on the skin or imbibed due to their poisonous nature.

Batteries

Your flashlights, radios, and many other useful items will be in heavy use during an emergency situation. Make sure you have dozens of spare batteries of each size that your equipment requires. Sure, you could steal some out of the TV remote, but it's better to have fully charged batteries that are ready to use. If you have high-intensity flashlights or other gear that requires odd batteries, stock up on a few packs of those while you're at it. Your $200 tactical flashlight isn't much good without the special batteries.

Grid-Down Gardening

The Intersection Where Sustainability and Survivalism Meet

By Tim MacWelch

When's the last time you got your hands dirty? Really dirty? Like, stuck-them-in-the-dirt-on-purpose dirty? It's OK if the answer is never. You can still grow your own food, with very little in the way of experience or materials. And this home gardening can happen if your home has a backyard, or just a balcony, or even just a sunny window. You just have to pay attention to the details in gardening.

There are lots of reasons to take up this skill set, beside the taste and enjoyment of growing your own food. A significant crisis could cut off our current food supply, and a widespread grid-down scenario could mean that food would be at a premium. Even a job loss could be the culprit behind your hunger.

One of the best ways to inoculate yourself against starvation regardless of the cause is to have your own sustainable garden. But how can a city dweller get started?

So many of our ancestors were once gardeners, farmers, foragers, and capable agrarian types. They had to be. The food-packed grocery store is a luxury that is only a few decades old. Our hardy progenitors successfully built and maintained sustainable gardens that weren't dependent on modern conveniences. They did it because they had to.

But waiting until you "have to" is not the right approach for the modern, would-be gardener. There's a learning curve you can't afford in a contemporary crisis scenario. Get started now, before trouble arises. You eat every day — why not tend some plants every day (within the growing season)?

5 Critical Things

If you want to succeed, you'll need to pay attention to five vital areas: light, soil, water, plant selection, and damage control. When these five issues are in balance, plants can thrive. When even one of these areas has a problem, your plants have a problem.

Light: The area where you grow your vegetables will need *at least* eight hours of direct and uninterrupted sunlight each day. Less than eight hours of direct light means that their growth will be severely stunted, and interrupted light signals to the plants that night is coming, which also disturbs their growth. In a standalone house, duplex, or townhome, try to find a south-facing patch of yard where no trees, structures, or buildings block the sun. For apartments or condos, the south side of the building may offer you all the light you need. You may be able to set up on your balcony or fire escape. Better yet,

High-Calorie Crops

Calories are the whole point behind a survival garden. Sure, salad plants look nice and grow fast, but you couldn't eat enough lettuce to sustain you. Leafy greens like lettuce can have as few as 10 calories per cup. It's a smarter path to focus on high-calorie crops. Here are some survival garden veggies to consider, and their calories per 8-ounce cup (seeds and beans counted dried, roots and fruits counted cooked).

- **Peanuts** (a massive calorie payout at 1,200 calories per cup)
- **Sunflower seeds** (800 calories)
- **Soybeans** (775 calories)
- **Chickpeas, kidney, lima, and fava beans** (about 600 calories)
- **Sweet potato** (180 calories)
- **Potatoes** (140 calories)
- **Carrots** (80 calories)
- **Tomatoes** (50 calories)
- **Turnips** (35 calories)

get permission to place containers on the roof. Failing that, purchase a few sturdy window boxes to hang on sunny windows. Finding light is often the *biggest* hurdle for backyard and urban gardeners.

Soil: Unless you're working on a hydroponic system, you'll need some dirt. Potting soil can be purchased as your soil medium, and it is usually weed-free. Bagged topsoil is cheaper, but may be full of weed seeds. In a yard, just use the dirt that's already there.

Water: If your plants are in the ground, in a backyard for example, they can draw some of their own water from the soil. Container plants, however, are very dependent on your regular and thorough watering. If using tap water, fill a bucket (or several) and let the chlorine evaporate away for two to three days before watering the plants. A better way to water is by collecting as much rain water as possible for your plants (if it's legal in your area).

Plant Selection: Each species of vegetable plant usually has several "varieties" for you to choose from. For plants in containers, it's best to select plants that are meant to stay small. Look for words like "patio" or "miniature" in the description. These don't need as much space to grow, or such a big container of soil. Also pay attention to the calories the veggie would provide. A post-apocalyptic salad might be nice, but salad leaves are painfully low in calories. Focus on higher calorie vegetables (see sidebar below).

Damage Control: You aren't the only thing that wants to eat your vegetables. Insects smell the plants you are growing and come to wreak havoc on your unsuspecting crops. Diseases can also affect your plants. Many vegetables are susceptible to viral and fungal ailments, which could kill them quickly. Be vigilant for signs of pests and disease to maintain the health of your plants. Frost will also damage or kill plants. Find out the date of the last expected frost in your area. Don't plant frost-susceptible plants till the danger of frost has passed for the season.

Now Get to Work

As soon as you have your game plan in mind, it's time to get busy. Follow these steps to vegetable glory.

STEP 1: GO SHOPPING

Once you've found your sunny spot, it's time to buy some basic supplies. For backyard gardens, you'll need:

Shovel: A round-point full-length shovel, to dig your garden bed and harvest root crops like potatoes and carrots.

Fertilizer: There is a dizzying number of fertilizer types and numbers on the bags. Those numbers are the NPK numbers. This stands for nitrogen, phosphorus, and potassium. It's always in that order. Nitrogen is needed for leaves, stems, and green growth. Phosphorus helps flowers and fruit. Potassium is needed for root growth. The average organic fertilizer has about a 3-3-3 rating and a good conventional fertilizer has a 10-10-10 rating. Follow the instructions for application rates.

Plants or seeds: If you have time to wait for seeds to sprout, this is a cheaper way to get your veggies. If time (or patience) is short, buy seedling plants that are already several inches tall and growing strong.

For container gardens, you'll need:

Containers: These can be pots, buckets, even small garbage cans. If there are no holes for water drainage, you'll need to punch some in the bottom. You may also purchase (or build) self-watering contain-

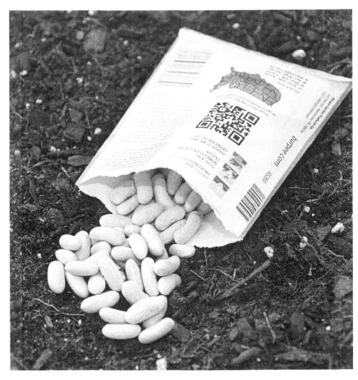

ers. These are filled up with water every few days, and they water the plants slowly and automatically. Window boxes are also an option if you truly have no space to use.

Soil: Potting soil is a great choice, and it can be purchased with fertilizer already included.

Fertilizer: If not included in the soil mix.

Plants or Seeds
STEP 2: PREP YOUR SOIL

You can't just throw out some seeds and hope for the best. Contemporary vegetables are not as hardy as their wild edible forebears. To perform well, your plants will need loose, rich soil and no other plant competition. Get out your shovel and dig up the grass sod from new backyard garden spots. Then dig deeply and chop the dirt clods with the shovel until they are loose soil. Dig down at least 1 foot if you can, but 2-feet deep is even more productive.

While this is backbreaking work for most people, it's worth the effort. Deeply prepared soil allows deep root growth, more nutrient and water uptake, and happier earthworms and other beneficial organisms. For container gardens, the work is much easier. Open a bag of potting soil, fill the container, and move to step three. Although potting soil lacks many nutrients and helpful soil creatures, it's easy to work with and reusable for several years.

STEP 3: PLANT YOUR VEGGIES

If you're sowing seeds, study the package info on the depth and spacing requirements for each plant. You can use your fingers to poke holes in the loose dirt, and a tape measure or ruler to get the spacing right. Cover the seeds with soil, unless the package says differently. Water the soil gently and wait for the seedlings to emerge. Large seeds grow quickly, since they contain more fuel for growth. Expect beans and squash to pop up in days.

Small seeds are generally slow to sprout, tomatoes taking several weeks to rise from the soil, while peppers and eggplants take more than a month to emerge. Live seedling plants give you a major head start. Bury each root ball in your prepared

soil and water deeply. Again, pay attention to spacing. Overcrowding stunts all of the plants that are in competition with each other. As a final option, you could plant living shoots. Cut sprouting white potatoes and sweet potatoes into chunks. Plant each one a few inches deep, and 1 foot apart.

STEP 4: MAINTAIN YOUR GARDEN

Once the seeds or seedlings are in, water them gently each morning until they are established. You may be able to back off to watering every other day once their roots are deep and the plants are healthy. You may also want to mulch the bed or container to maintain moisture in dry climates. In the beginning of the growing season, you'll still need to be alert to frost and freeze warnings in your area. Cover plants with a light plastic or bed sheet, and anchor it in place if frost is expected. Remove the plastic as soon as the sun rises to prevent the combination of light and condensation from burning the leaves.

With container plants, if frost or freeze is predicted, just bring the whole container inside. Not all plants are this sensitive to the cold, just plants of tropical descent like tomatoes, peppers, eggplants, and a few others. Later in the season, heat can also be an issue. For urban gardeners, be careful that summer sun and heat aren't reflected off walls, fences, and other structures. This extra heat can actually cook them. If plants are well watered, but still become "droopy" in mid-afternoon, move them to a cooler spot.

STEP 5: BE PATIENT TILL HARVEST TIME

Gardening isn't like the push-button activities of the modern world. Plants grow at their own pace. Some are faster than others, but they are never fast enough to suit an impatient person. Consider the length of time until harvest as you plan your vegetable selection. Radishes offer you the quickest turnaround, growing from seed to harvestable root in about one month. The bad news is that they only have 19 calories per cup. High-calorie plants like peanuts can take four months or more for the edible part to reach maturity. Be patient and be realistic, as you wait for your food to

How to Cultivate Your Own Seeds

It's surprisingly easy to save seeds from year to year, and continue your own gardening traditions (and genetics). This isn't legal when dealing with modern protected plant varieties. Heirlooms, on the other hand, still exist because of home gardeners saving their seeds. Here's how you can carry on the heritage of seed saving in your own family.

Plan ahead for seed saving by growing single varieties of each vegetable species. This will help you avoid unpredictable results from crosspollination and mutant vegetables next year. Let the fruiting part of your plants mature fully. This will mean mushy tomatoes, dry crusty bean pods, and rock-hard squash. This also means that the seeds are fully formed.

Next, cut or tear open the fruiting body and pick out the seeds. Large seeds are easy to pick from the flesh, smaller ones take a little time. Place them on newspaper to dry in the shade. Once they are thoroughly dry, pick off any dried flesh and place the seeds in a jar with a small desiccant pack. Store these seeds in a cool, dry, dark place until next spring. A few odd seeds require a fermentation process or scratching with sandpaper for best results, but generally, it's that easy.

Common Mistakes to Avoid

There are a few areas where new gardeners often screw things up. Avoid these likely pitfalls and blunders, and your plants will thank you for it – by feeding you.

Using Too Much Water: The western ideal that "if some is good, more is better" doesn't apply to watering. Overwatering can cause the soil to remain too damp for too long, leading to fungal diseases which can kill otherwise healthy plants. Too little water is a mistake also, leaving the soil dry and stunting plant growth. Water deeply and regularly, preferably in the morning. Nighttime watering can breed fungus as well.

Ignoring Pests: You never know when an insect invasion will arrive. Frequently inspect the plants for bugs and bug eggs (underneath the leaves). A few bugs are helpful, like pollinators, but the rest are enemy combatants. Crush them with extreme prejudice.

Using Too Much Fertilizer: You may be head over heels for your new vegetable plants and want them to do well. But don't overdo it on fertilizer. The overuse of conventional fertilizer can cause harm to your plants. Follow the package instructions for directions on the use of the product.

Foregoing Regular Checkups: Plants can pick up diseases from insects, fungal spores on the wind, and even from you! If you smoke around your tomatoes, for example, they can pick up a nasty virus from the tobacco. At the first signs of sickly leaves or messed up vegetables, prowl the Internet or good gardening books to find out the cause. Many diseases can be remedied – *if* caught early.

reach maturity and ripen; and be watchful for pests and disease.

Conclusion

Like all living things, plants want to grow. Their roots dig deep, and their leaves reach toward the sun. If we provide the right plants with the light, fertile soil, water, and protection mentioned throughout this article, chances are that you will have some success. But like most endeavors, there'll be some missteps too. Learn from your mistakes, do some research and find out what went wrong. Use that information the next time, and your results should speak for themselves. There's no such thing as a green thumb, just dirty thumbs with calluses.

Backyard Survival Training

Practice for Worst-Case Scenarios in the Comfort of Your Own Home Before They Happen

By Jim Cobb

Many of us would love to be able to take a few weeks off and travel to a remote, privately owned forest where we can practice wilderness survival skills without fear of violating a city ordinance or, perhaps worse, incurring the wrath of our homeowners association. The reality, though, is that unless we're somehow picked for the next round of contestants on some goofy reality show, we're not going to be doing a lot of primitive camping any time soon. We simply don't have the time for an extended trip. And if we did, most of us can't afford it (not all of us have the scratch to fly to Jasper National Park in Canada or the rain forests of Costa Rica).

Fortunately, these skill sets don't require a background of towering pines and the gurgle of a babbling brook to be successfully learned. Many of them can be practiced right in your own backyard. Doing so has a milder impact on your wallet — plus, if things go awry, help is likely just a scream away.

Fire-Making

The ability to reliably make fire under both ideal and adverse conditions is one of the most important survival skills to master. Plus, you earn massive field cred when you're able to get a fire going where others have failed.

Backyard Bonfire: Even if there are city restrictions on what you're allowed to burn and when, I doubt there are any rules at all dictating how the fire is started. Many homeowners have invested in some sort of patio fire pit in recent years, whether it is a permanent brick structure or just a metal bowl that gets moved off to the side when the kids are playing basketball. Either way, they work great for practicing your pyrotechnic talents.

Spark Selection: Try using a variety of different fire-starting tools and techniques, from the reliable butane lighters and strike-anywhere matches to ferrocerium rods and perhaps even the bow drill. Don't overlook the magnifying glass or the fire piston, either. Practicing these techniques in the backyard is a great way to learn which are easiest for you to use and under what conditions each seems to work the best.

Tinder Finder: If you lack natural materials to use as tinder, mimicking what you'd find out in the field, search for "Michigan Wildfire" on Facebook. Their fire kit consists of about a dozen different types of natural tinder, a full pound of it total, along with a custom-handled ferrocerium rod. The materials, such as birch bark and chaga fungus, are all separated and labeled, making it a great tool for learning how to use varied materials in fire-making.

Fuel Placement: Try out different fire lays, too. Most of us are familiar with the teepee fire lay, where you build a cone of sorts out of kindling over the tinder bundle. How about the Dakota fire hole? You won't be able to use your patio fire pit for it, but it can be very useful out in the field. Dig a hole about 10 inches deep and maybe a foot in diameter. Dig another hole the same depth but half the diameter, about 18 inches from the first one. Then, dig a tunnel to connect the two holes.

Sounds like a lot of work, I know, but it's worth it in the end. Build your fire in the larger hole. Once it starts burning well, it will draw air through the second

Off-Grid Cooking

Make no mistake, cooking over an open flame outdoors is as much art as it is science. While campfire cooking traditionally means impaling something on a stick and holding it over the fire until it burns, with the right tools and some practice you can cook just about anything. The following are some considerations.

Coal Cooking: First things first, though. You don't cook over the actual flames, you cook over the coals. Those provide a much more consistent temperature. Flames will reach up and scorch the food, leaving the outside burnt to a crisp and the inside cold and raw. What experienced camp cooks will do is get a good fire going, then once it dies down, scrape the coals to the side for cooking.

Side Burner: Another thing to keep in mind is that most grills, unless they have a side burner, are horrible when it comes to boiling water. They are very inefficient because the heat kind of goes everywhere rather than focusing on the bottom of

hole, causing the fire to burn hotter and consume the fuel more efficiently. This results in far less smoke being generated, making the Dakota fire hole a great option for keeping things on the down low. Plus, it is quite easy to lay a few green branches across the fire hole, on which you can place your pot or pan for cooking.

the pot. You folks who sprung for the side burner feature, though, are good to go.

In theory at least, anyone can heat up a can of soup over a campfire. But, if your outdoor cooking experience tops out at turning hot dogs into briquettes, you have some practice ahead of you.

Cookware: For potentially long-term situations, consider investing in at least a couple of cast-iron pots, such as a deep skillet and a small Dutch oven. While you can sometimes get by with using your normal kitchen pots and pans, they typically aren't made to withstand the higher heat generated by a campfire. They may warp or bend, and plastic handles will almost certainly melt. Good cast iron isn't cheap but, if cared for properly, it will last several lifetimes.

Wild Edibles

I will readily admit that I am a die-hard carnivore. A meal just isn't a meal unless something had to bleed before it hit my plate. That said, if I'm hungry and the only food available has leaves on it, I'll be filling my plate with greens and possibly coming back for seconds.

Being able to not only recognize wild edibles in your area, but knowing how to properly use them can be a crucial life-saving skill. Rather than trying to properly identify a whole ton of plants most of the time, concentrate on being able to identify a short list of plants all of the time. The goal here is to learn what you can put into your belly to stop the missed meal cramps, not give a botany lecture.

Edible Education: Start by visiting your local library for a few books on wild edibles in your area. Two references I highly recommend are the *Peterson Guide to Edible Wild Plants* by Lee Allen Peterson and *The Forager's Harvest* by Samuel Thayer. See also "Urban Foraging" in Issue 8. An important thing to remember is you'll need to be able to identify the plants at various stages of their development. Many guides only show what the plant looks like when it

You'd be surprised at what you'll find in your backyard once you know what to look for.

Learning how to use a knife effectively is a survival requisite.

A Simple Recipe

An easy dish to make while you're camping — whether off the grid or in your backyard — is something this author likes to call "campfire potatoes." Here's the recipe:

- Tear off a sheet of aluminum foil about 18 inches long. Spray the inside with nonstick spray.
- Wash a few red potatoes, then leave the skins on, and dice them into roughly 1-inch cubes or so. Lay those in the center of the foil.
- Add a couple of pats of butter and sprinkle with salt, pepper, and garlic powder to taste.
- Bring up the long sides of the foil roll them together down to the potatoes. Roll up the ends to make a nice, tight little package of goodies.
- Toss this on hot coals for about 10 minutes, then flip for another 10.
- Remove from the coals and carefully unwrap the foil. If the potatoes aren't tender, wrap it back up and put it back on the coals for a bit longer.

Add some hamburger, peppers, and other goodies before tossing it on the coals, and you have a meal fit for a grid-down king.

is ready for harvest. By knowing what the plant looks like as it grows, you can spot it earlier and note the location for later.

Plant Compatibility: Another important aspect of wild edible gathering and use is that just because the plant is edible doesn't mean it will necessarily agree with you. We all have certain foods that just don't get along with our digestive systems. I'm not talking about being lactose intolerant or having issues with gluten. I'm referring to the fact that many of us are no longer able to wolf down Taco Bell at 3 a.m. without some serious repercussions. The same basic principle applies with wild edibles. Each person's body is different, and the body changes over time. Learn what you can eat safely now, when medical help, as well as working indoor plumbing, aren't issues.

Continuing Education: Another possible learning resource is your local county extension office. They are the folks who manage the Master Gardener programs. Reach out to them and find out if they have someone who is well versed in wild edible identification who could work with you for an afternoon or two. You might be surprised — there could be existing classes you could join.

Tracking

Animal Analysis: Identifying animal tracks is a great way to learn what animals are living in your area and thus would be available as a potential food source, should the need arise. Back to the library you go, this time for a couple of books on animal tracks. *The Peterson Field Guide to Animal Tracks* is a good place to start, but don't overlook the children's section

Grid-Down Grub

If it's truly a long-term grid-down situation, you're going to want to try to salvage the refrigerated and frozen foods as best you can. It might turn out that the best thing to do is to cook as much of it as possible and have a little feast. That's preferable over letting it all just go to waste, right?

Meat can be cooked on the grill, of course. Invite the neighbors over and have a cookout. Hopefully they'll have buns that match what you're serving. Hot dogs can be sliced for hamburger buns, but burgers on hot dog buns is troublesome.

Frozen Fries: Many of us have one or more bags of frozen French fries in our freezers. Here is one way to make use of those fries before they defrost: Take a sheet of foil, lay it on a counter, and spray one side with nonstick cooking oil. Toss a few handfuls of fries on the foil, then wrap them up. Cook this over hot coals for about 20 minutes or so, moving it around every now and again to shake up the fries so they don't get burnt. Once the fries are about done, open the foil and pour a can of your favorite chili over the fries, then sprinkle with cheese. We always have a bag of cheddar or Colby mix on hand for quesadillas and such. Wrap the foil closed again and put back over the coals for five to seven minutes. When the cheese is melted and the chili is warmed through, unwrap the foil and grab a fork.

Frozen Veggies: Of course, you can always make vegetable soup with all of your frozen beans, peas, and such. Add some pasta noodles to boiling water, toss in chicken bouillon and veggies, then simmer until the pasta is tender. If you cook up a chicken breast and dice it for the soup, so much the better.

Premade Dough: Refrigerated dough, such as the kind that scares your mother-in-law when you pop it open, can be cooked over the fire, too. Take the dough and roll it into a snake, then wrap said snake around the end of a stick that is roughly an inch thick. Hold it over the coals and turn it slowly to avoid burning.

Dairy: Milk should be consumed before it goes bad. Eggs will last a fair length of time without refrigeration so put those toward the bottom of the "Need to cook before it might kill you" list.

Take a peek in your freezer and refrigerator today. What foods do you routinely have on hand that you'd want to cook up before they go bad? How would you prepare them?

of the library, too. Many of the advanced guides have so much information it can be overwhelming. You probably aren't interested in the mating habits of the Eastern Humped Whatsit; you just want to know what made the tracks that lead to and away from your upended garbage cans.

Get Outside: One great thing about winter is that snow allows for easier tracking. Rather than just staying bundled up by

a fiend about lifting weights and running laps until you are in such good shape that you cause professional wrestlers to stop in their tracks. But, if you can't walk from the kitchen to the upstairs bathroom without getting winded and there's no underlying health issue at work, you need to get your heart rate up a bit every now and again.

Get a Checkup: Before embarking on any sort of exercise routine, you should probably get the all-clear from your physician. The last thing you want to do is end up hurt or worse when you've finally decided that while a sphere is indeed a shape, it isn't the shape you want to be in any longer.

Move Your Butt: If it's been years since you put on gym shorts, start small by walking the perimeter of your yard. Or, do a few jumping jacks on your back patio — anything that will get you up off your butt and working up a little sweat. (Check out the *Health* column in this and every issue of *OG* for more fitness ideas.) You don't need

the fireplace, only venturing outside when your paycheck is threatened, take some time to get out there and practice tracking. Learning to identify prints is just the first step — you need to practice following the trail as far as you can. This is something you can read about, sure, but you'll never be any good at it unless you spend some time outside.

Physical Fitness

As he recalled later, this is right where he lost most of his readers. I know, exercise isn't all that high on the fun list for most people. But, the fact is, poor physical conditioning will be a hindrance in a true survival situation. I'm not saying you need to be

Dust off the weights and kettlebells: You can't survive a calamity if you can't climb the stairs without getting winded.

to invest in a fancy workout machine or even a set of free weights. Join your kids in a game of tag. Play catch with your family.

Grab a length of clothesline and start jumping rope. If your neighbors look at you funny, remind them that if the zombies do come, you don't need to outrun the brain-eaters, you just need to outrun the neighbors.

No matter what your living situation might be, you should be able to find some space for practicing some survival skills every now and again. It might require some creativity on your part, but being able to think outside the box is a survival skill in and of itself. Don't get wrapped up in finding reasons you can't do these things. A true survivor never gives up.

Common Backyard Edibles

Dandelions are universal. There just aren't too many places where dandelions don't grow, at least not in the United States. The entire plant is edible, despite the general "milky sap means bad" rule of thumb.

Garlic mustard is the bane of oh so many homeowners. It is extremely invasive and will take over a flower bed in no time at all. A great way to get rid of it is to eat it. All parts of the plant are edible. The leaves have something of a bitter taste so some folks like to cook them or at least mix them with other vegetables rather than just eating them raw and alone.

Clover can be eaten raw, though the taste is improved a bit by boiling. Up to you whether you want to check for any having four leaves before munching them.

Many plants tend to get bitter as they grow and plantain is no exception. The leaves are best when fairly young.

Wood sorrel grows almost everywhere. The roots make a good alternative to potatoes after boiling. The leaves are typically eaten raw.

As you research wild edibles in your area, don't be surprised if you find out a fair number of them are usually thought to just be invasive weeds. That works in our favor, though. The gardening rule of thumb has always been if it pulls up hard, it is a plant. If it pulls easy, you're holding a weed.

Hydroponics Basics

What is it and How Practical is it in a Survival Situation?

By Phillip Meeks

Rarely do we daydream of less-than-perfect soil. We fantasize about our rural retreat — a picturesque cabin equipped with solar panels. We own a well with pure water, a stocked trout stream just a few paces out the backdoor, and a mature woodland with excellent hunting. We have a milk cow and two stands of honeybees, and every plant in the vegetable garden is green and thriving.

In reality, few locations have garden soil that doesn't need some adjustment. We'd be lucky if the only requirement

is 100 pounds of lime to raise the pH or perhaps organic matter applied to the top. But it's not always so simple. What if the land on our dream acreage has thin (or nonexistent) topsoil? Maybe we're too far from a quarry to have reliable access to lime. Maybe the only affordable real estate on the market is reclaimed surface mined land. The land could be rocky, heavily compacted, and not likely to be tillable without a few years of prep work.

Hydroponic production may be the best (or only) solution for growing vegetables in scenarios like this.

According to the United Nations' Food and Agricultural Organization, global food production will need to increase by 70 percent by 2050 in order to provide for a projected 9.1 billion people. Plus this growth must happen as more and more cropland is lost to urbanization and as tighter regulations are placed on farmers in regards to emissions and environmental impacts.

Hydroponics represents one method by which food production can expand into regions not historically known for their suitability to agriculture. This science can be defined on the most basic level as soilless production. Plant nutrition is delivered via water, and the plants are held in place by inert materials, wire trellising, or other means.

Hydroponic growing has a place even if the soil is decent. It can extend the growing season and make protection from severe weather and wildlife more feasible. One of a gardener's worst enemies is weeds, so an avoidance of weed pressures may be another motivator toward hydroponic production.

What Plants Crave

No, it's not Brawndo. A plant requires 16 elements for optimal growth, which can be remembered with the jingle, "C. Hopkins Café Mighty Good, Managed by Cousin Como Clark" (C HOPKNS CaFe Mg Mn B CuZn CoMo Cl). Of these, carbon (C), hydrogen (H), and oxygen (O) are supplied by air and water. Nitrogen (N), phosphorus (P), potassium (K), calcium (Ca), sulfur (S), and magnesium (Mg) are *macronutrients* that the plants require in relatively larger amounts. The remainder — iron (Fe), manganese (Mn), boron (B), copper (Cu), zinc (Zn), cobalt (Co), molybdenum (Mo), and chlorine (Cl) — are *micronutrients*, which plants tend to access through naturally occurring organic matter or amended compost in garden soil.

Lettuce and tomatoes are two crops that do well in hydroponic culture.

An investment of less than $30 can provide enough pre-mixed fertilizer to create up to 200 gallons of nutrient solution.

A float system can work well in a home-scale operation.

A conventional grower usually doesn't have to think about all these elements. How many are represented in a bag of fertilizer? Only three: N, P, and K. Discolored leaves or other reactions will sometimes reveal a need to add some boron or magnesium, or blossom-end rot on tomatoes or peppers will signal a lack of calcium, but for the most part, a traditional gardener manages the pH, the N, P, and K, and lets nature do the rest.

A hydroponic gardener, in contrast, doesn't enjoy that luxury and must be mindful that every needed component is present in the water. Furthermore, in systems that recycle the nutrient solution, it's necessary to consistently monitor against salt buildup or drastic changes in pH.

The easiest way for beginners to address nutrition is through the purchase of products specifically formulated for hydroponics. These may be either dissolvable granules or liquids. Some are pre-mixed, and others will have components added in stages. Not just any liquid fertilizer will do, because fertilizers formulated for traditional gardening focus primarily on nitrogen, phosphorus, and potassium.

Of course, those who are preparedness-minded may eventually prefer to wean themselves from commercial nutrients in favor of "homebrewed" options. There are a lot of do-it-yourself resources online discussing the solutions that worked in various circumstances. With these as a starting point, you may want to find your own recipe through trial and error, experimenting with nutrient "teas." Compost, Epsom salts, and various organic fertilizers are examples of ingredients that can contribute the necessary elements to your hydroponic growing. Again, though, expect to do some close monitoring to fine-tune your formula. Be mindful, too, of sanitation and the possibility of splash on your fruits, and especially if you market your produce, adhere to proper Good Agricultural Practices regarding the use of certain organic fertilizers.

Hydroponic Myths

While this style of growing can fill a lot of gaps in home food production, it's not a magic pill. One of the greatest disadvantages is that it requires an initial investment in time and money to construct your system and then a considerable amount of homework and monitoring to keep it functioning properly.

Some mistakenly believe that yields are greater with hydroponic crops in comparison to their conventional, soil-based counterparts, but that's simply not true. With all things being equal, the plants in a hydroponic system will bear about the same as those in a traditional garden.

Because light requirements don't change, it's also untrue that you can space hydroponic vegetables closer than you can in a garden plot. (Spacing plants too closely in either scenario can be an invitation to not only poor production, but also to spread fungal diseases from plant to plant.)

Taste and nutrition of the final product will be similar between the two systems as well, provided that each plant has access to the required amounts of light, oxygen, nutrients, and water. For any who have been less than impressed by a hydroponic tomato or other vegetable, that could be blamed on a simple missing nutrient.

Growing hydroponically can be rewarding, but it doesn't require less work than conventional gardening — just different work. No, you won't have to hoe, plow, and dig, but you'll need some

The Kratky non-circulating method doesn't require a lot of equipment.

Nutrient Deficiencies
If plants are deficient in ...
... then the symptoms are:

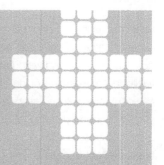

Nitrogen: Lower leaves are yellow; rest of plant is light green; leaves small
Phosphorus: Lower leaves yellow between veins; red or purplish color on leaves
Potassium: Papery and mottled leaves; dead areas on leaf edges and tips
Calcium: Newer growth (shoots and leaves) dies; hooked leaf tips
Magnesium: Lower leaves with green veins, but yellow elsewhere; puckered leaves
Zinc: Papery leaves; leaf veins darker than surrounding tissue
Sulfur: Stunted and spindly plant; young leaves pale green
Iron: Veins darker than surrounding tissue; edges and tips of leaves die
Copper: Leaf edges dark green or blue; leaf edges curl upward
Manganese: Dead spots on newer leaves; leaf has "netted" appearance
Boron: Stems brittle; young leaves scorched at edges
Molybdenum: Leaves deformed and stunted
Cobalt: Reddening of leaves and stems; stunted growth
Chlorine: Leaf wilt; leaf mottling

basic plumbing knowhow, and you may become more of a chemist than you planned to be.

Furthermore, while the commercial hydroponic operations you may have seen are constructed in greenhouses and under artificial light, this doesn't have to be the case. It's possible to have a system on your patio or in a south-facing window, where growing can take advantage of natural light and temperatures, following roughly the same growing season as a conventional garden.

You can spend as much money as you want on hydroponic gardening (as with most hobbies), but it doesn't have to be expensive. It's possible to buy enough equipment for 25 to 30 plants (nutrients included) for under $50, provided you use recycled buckets or containers, and quite a few complete kits can be found online in the $100 range.

Which Crops?

Almost any crop can be grown hydroponically, in theory, although maturity days and plant size can make some more challenging than others. For this reason, crops most often seen in hydroponic production systems include herbs, tomatoes, peppers, cucumbers, celery, watercress, and leaf lettuce. A brand-new hydroponic grower would do well to start with one or two of these.

Strawberries can also do very well hydroponically. The advantages include removal of the crop from exposure to soil-borne pests and the labor benefits of picking berries that are elevated above the ground. Hydroponic strawberry production has proven to be a viable method in some arid parts of the world, including desert regions of Israel.

The Simplest Method

A technique developed by Dr. B.A. Kratky of the University of Hawaii makes hydroponic growing accessible to more people by removing pumps and electricity from the equation. The "Kratky Method" is a non-circulating system that can be housed in a plastic bucket or tote.

"The suspended pot, non-circulating hydroponic method is a convenient way to grow short-term vegetables like lettuce and pak-choi," Dr. Kratky explains, "because a small tank containing 1 to 2 gallons per plant only needs to be filled with nutrient solution (water plus fertilizer) at transplanting time and no additional effort is needed until harvest."

Crops grown in a suspended pot, non-circulating system can be quite portable.

Net pots are useful in several different hydroponic methods.

Compost provides many micronutrients to gardens and can contribute to the richness of homemade hydroponic nutrients, too.

With this method, plants are placed in a "net pot" and then suspended above the nutrient solution. As the liquid is used up, the roots reach further. The humid air between the water and the pot provides for oxygen exchange in the roots. For fast-maturing crops, the water and nutrients initially loaded will be sufficient to carry the crop through to harvest.

The first step to employing non-circulating hydroponics is to collect containers with lids — 5-gallon buckets and storage totes are fine. Delis and bakeries often have used plastic buckets they're willing to part with.

Net pots and some type of sterile medium will be needed to keep the plants upright and suspended in the solution. Clay pellets, gravel, rockwool, vermiculite, perlite, sand, or packing peanuts are some commonly used growing media. I recently ordered 50 2-inch net pots and a bag of clay pellets for just over $20.

Use a hole saw of the same diameter as your net pots to make one to four holes in the lid of your bucket.

Next, add water and nutrient to make a solution for your crop, but take care to leave an air gap between the water level and the bottom of the lid where your pots are placed.

The crop should have a short enough maturity that it's ready for harvest by the time the solution is 10 percent of its starting level. Lettuce and bok choy, for instance, should do well in 5-gallon containers. Longer-term vegetables should be grown in larger containers, or a secondary tank can keep levels topped off with the use of a float valve.

A Kratky system can also be quite portable, allowing growers to set their buckets into a garage if a late frost is forecast, or to move them into and out of direct sunlight as needed.

Other Methods

Another growing method common in both commercial- and home-scale hydroponic production is the nutrient film technique (NFT). Here, a constant flow of nutrient solution is circulated through a plastic-lined trough or enclosed channel via a pump and reservoir. The plant roots remain in the flow. The plants themselves may be supported via an overhead trellising system, or they may be held in place by net pots, rockwool, or other media. PVC pipe or guttering can work in a home system, with an ideal slope of a half-inch drop every 15 feet.

Because the nutrient is recirculated, water quality can become a concern, and it's usually necessary to completely change the solution periodically.

Float systems are another type of hydroponics that are relatively simple for a home grower to grasp. In these, rafts made of

Crops grown hydroponically are physiologically no different than crops grown in soil.

Tobacco transplants begun in float beds.

The nutrient film technique recirculates the nutrient solution so that roots sit in a constant flow.

Styrofoam hold the plants and float directly on the nutrient solution. Since there's no air space between the solution and the raft, some type of bubbler is needed in the reservoir to supply oxygen to the roots.

This system is often used by tobacco farmers to start their transplants, and many of these systems have been adapted over the past decade to start other transplants, such as tomatoes, pepper, and even corn. The transplants that are started hydroponically are then grown in natural soil.

In the aeration method, the nutrient solution is misted onto the roots, often from within an A-framed Styrofoam structure into which the plants are placed. Excess solution runs back into a reservoir and is recycled.

Yet another style of hydroponics is bag culture, where plants are grown in polyethylene bags filled with a medium-like vermiculite or peat. Capillary tubes that run from a main nutrient supply line are inserted into each bag, delivering the nutrients. (In one university demonstration, bag culture tomato plants grew so heavy that they damaged the steel frame of the greenhouse to which they were trellised!)

What About Aquaponics?

The concept behind aquaponics is that edible tilapia (or other fish species) are grown in large tanks, and their waste water is cycled through the hydroponic vegetables. The nutrient film technique is often used in these systems. In theory, the fish waste supplies the nutrient needs of the plants, while the plants themselves filter the water before it's recirculated back into the fish tanks. The reality is that both plants and fish will require closer monitoring than in standalone aquaculture or hydroponic systems. Root diseases can be exacerbated due to an overabundance of organic matter in the water, and plants don't actually "clean" out all elements that can harm the fish.

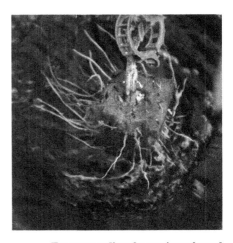

Tomato seedings begun in rockwool cubes quickly extend their feeder roots into the solution when placed in a nutrient film technique system.

Aquaponics will require a lot of inputs to keep both plants and fish healthy.

However, people have merged the two systems, and enterprising homesteaders who want a challenge may consider taking on an aquaponics project as a means to provide both vegetables and protein. Just keep in mind that a lot more management (and patience) will be needed.

Conclusion

Hydroponic growing isn't for everyone. It can be tricky to master the chemistry of nutrition and the nuances of plumbing for plants. But for those with poor soil, or who live in places where the deer and rabbits eat better than the people, it can be a via-

Aquaponics is an interesting concept, but one that can be very challenging to master.

Lettuce in an NFT system.

ble option. Furthermore, employing both conventional and hydroponic growing can make a lot of sense, with your corn, beans, and potatoes in the earth, but bok choy and celery in Kratky buckets beside the garage, where you can watch them develop beyond the groundhogs' comfort zones.

If this is a method that captures your imagination, you can start on the most basic level now to add some variety to your gardening. By next season, who knows? Perhaps a full-blown nutrient film technique system will become part of your daydreams. 😊

About the Author

Phillip Meeks is an agriculture and natural resources educator originally from Tennessee, but now based in the mountains of Southwest Virginia. He likes to spend his weekends hiking, gardening, beekeeping, fishing, and mushroom hunting.

Well Informed

Thinking of Building a Well? Here's What You Should Know

By Phillip Meeks

A fitness guru once said, "If you're craving something and you don't know what, it's water. It's *always* water."

Indeed, water is our most basic human need, a resource that we'd only survive for three days without, so water availability naturally ranks high on wish lists of the self-reliant. Local governments have lobbied hard over the last decades to carry public water to even the most rural areas. As a result, 87 percent of the U.S. population has access to a public water supply, which explains why we never hear home seekers on those real estate-themed reality shows ask, "Does this place have water?"

A forgotten well can be both a safety hazard and a source of groundwater contamination.

If your chosen dwelling has access to a municipal water supply, an argument can be made for embracing that. The federal government regulates public water to ensure its quality against bacteria, heavy metals, and other contaminants, but when it comes to the purity of well water, the property owner is essentially on his or her own.

But 13-million homes in the U.S. still rely on wells, whether by necessity or choice. If you aren't blessed with a spring or an idyllic mountain stream in your backyard and you desire to meet or supplement your family's water needs without "city water," then a well could be a viable option. Furthermore, with proper construction and regular monitoring of water quality, it's entirely possible to have well water that's as safe and reliable as your neighbors' public supply.

"In some regions, there may be a large cost barrier for drilling a well, maintaining it, and treating the water," explains Ryan Bushong, president and owner of Bushong Drilling LLC in Marysville, Ohio, and a fourth-generation driller. "For the most part, however, a complete private water well system will cost less to install than a private septic system, and the toughest barrier to overcome is the age-old stigma that well water is stinky, stains everything it contacts, tastes bad, and is unsafe."

How Wells Work

A portion of surface water will make its way deeper and deeper into the ground, eventually accumulating in the pores and fractures of a layer of soil and rock. This accumulated water is known as an aquifer, and aquifers can be classified as either confined — bound both above and below by impermeable layers — or unconfined.

Confined aquifers tend to be deeper than unconfined, and because the water can't move directly down into them, it may enter from a considerable distance away.

Specific Contamination Issues

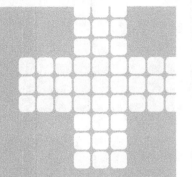

Lead: Likely due to older plumbing; there's no acceptable level.
Arsenic: Naturally occurring in some types of rock; linked to cancer, stomach pain, paralysis, blindness.
Copper: Blue-green staining; nausea, vomiting, stomach cramps; children and infants most susceptible.
Iron and manganese: Often occur together; reddish-brown staining; metallic taste; not usually a health concern.
Sodium: Salty taste; corrosion of plumbing.
Nitrate: Could indicate contamination by sewage, livestock manure, fertilizers; serious health threat to infants.
Hydrogen sulfide: Rotten egg smell; naturally present near coal or oil fields.
Fluoride: Naturally occurring, as well as added to public water supplies; long-term exposure linked to bone cancer.
Total dissolved solids: General indicator of water quality; sources may be either natural or man-made.
Hardness: High levels of calcium and magnesium; not a health risk; shortens lifespan of plumbing and fixtures.
pH: Mainly associated with the geology of site; general indicator of water quality.

The water contained in a confined aquifer may be thousands of years old.

A well is simply a drilled or dug hole that intersects that aquifer, allowing the water to accumulate in the bottom of the hole to be carried to the surface as needed by a well bucket or a pumping system.

Depending on the depth of the well and the hydrogeology of the site, it may take hours or years for water to move from the surface into the aquifer. Therefore, a seasonal drought won't necessarily impact the availability of water in the well, at least not immediately.

Generally, the closer to the surface the aquifer, the more the water will be influenced by surface conditions, such as pollution or climate. Unconfined aquifers are more prone to contamination from the surface, due to the limited buffer between what goes on above and what makes its way below.

Types of Wells

There are three types of wells that may be used in supplying water to a home: bored, driven, and drilled.

Bored or dug wells are what most of us past a certain age may remember from our childhoods. Imagine the picturesque, stone-lined wells with a bucket on a rope dangling at the top. These are typically only 10 to 30 feet deep, with a relatively large diameter. Again, because they tend to be accessing aquifers that are relatively close to the surface, this type of well is most directly impacted by surface activity.

Driven wells are the result of a pipe being driven 30 to 50 feet into the ground. This is usually done in areas with large deposits of sand or gravel, where the depth to the groundwater table is only 15 feet or less. As with bored wells, contamination from the surface is a moderate to high risk.

"Most people want a drilled well, so it's drilled into bedrock with casing at the top," explains John Jemison, an extension professor for soil and water quality at the University of Maine. "The well head sits up above the ground, and it has to be separated from the septic system."

Drilled wells typically extend 500 feet or less, but modern drilling technology makes it possible to drill in excess of 1,000 feet.

Preliminary Steps

Bushong suggests a bit of homework for anyone contemplating a well, including requesting a database of historic well records for your area from your state's department of natural resources. This will provide an idea of the quantity and quality of water, as well as average

Not all wells will require a storage tank, but it is an option.

depth. This is also a good time to talk with neighbors, as their experiences with the process and with certain contractors can be invaluable.

"Be careful to ask others in the area how productive their wells are," advises Jemison. "If your well recharge is less than a gallon a minute, you may need to install a cistern to hold water in times of greater use."

In determining the placement of the well, the contractor's expertise in the local hydrogeology will guide you toward the most reliable water. Beyond that, the goal is to avoid anything that could contaminate your water supply.

"Well placement is usually done based on access, distance from septic systems, and drainage," says Jemison. "You would not want to drill where water might sit around the well head."

Distances can vary from region to region, but as an example, Texas law requires wells to be at least 50 feet from septic tanks, cisterns, non-potable water, and property lines; 100 feet from septic leach lines and drain fields; 150 feet from where fertilizer, pesticides, and animal feeds are stored and from pet and livestock yards; and 250 feet from any liquid waste disposal area.

During this fact-finding phase, consider any old wells on the property, which can provide a direct link from the surface to the aquifer, in addition to being hazardous to people, pets, and livestock. If old, unused wells are present, it would be wise to factor their decommissioning into the overall project cost.

Finally, a phone call to the local courthouse or reputable contractor can help

A hand-cranked well is simple, but can be susceptible to contamination. Photo by Elizabeth Farris.

Vet any contractors and speak to any of their previous clients to determine the quality of their work before hiring them.

determine what permits and other paperwork, such as a well completion report, may be applicable. The red tape can be confusing. Legal requirements vary from state to state and even across counties, so enlist someone in the know to help navigate. If a permit is needed in your situation, that's likely to cost a few hundred dollars.

Construction

The website of the National Groundwater Association (NGWA), wellowner.org, has a contractor lookup feature, allowing users to pinpoint professionals based on location and certification.

"Contractors who are actively involved in their industry — and who undergo continuing education — are more likely to construct a well in compliance with industry standards and governmental regulations," explains Bushong, "and more likely to construct for you a water well that can last a lifetime."

He furthermore suggests that potential well owners seek a contractor who's certified by NGWA and who's licensed and/or registered and bonded through the appropriate state. Don't be afraid to ask for references when seeking a contractor and speak with two or three customers about their experiences.

The process of constructing a well will include the actual drilling, followed by the installation of the casing, a steel or plastic tube that protects the borehole from contamination.

"In most areas with abundant water from precipitation," says Jemison, "the key is getting a good seal — getting the casing fitted into the bedrock so that water can't run right down the well head and drip into the well without getting adequately filtered. That's the biggest issue I have found over time with new wells."

The space between the casing and the sides of the drilled hole will be "grouted" with cement or bentonite. The depth of the casing and grouting will be determined by the geology of the site and/or by local or state law.

Finally, a watertight well cap can prevent contamination. Older types of well caps allowed insects to move inside, thereby transferring any bacteria or chemicals to which those bugs had been exposed. Modern well caps exclude that type of exposure and may be required by local ordinances.

In some instances, water flowing downward into a confined aquifer will create enough pressure to push water to the surface without the aid of a pump. This is known as a flowing artesian well. However, most water wells will require some type of pump, be it electric, solar, manual, or wind-powered.

Says Bushong, "Pump technology has come quite a long way in the last hundred years — from hand pumps to jet pumps to submersible pumps to variable frequency drive (VFD) pumps. The conventional pump systems of yesteryear could provide pressure varying between 30 and 50 psi, and later, between 40 and 60 psi. Today's VFDs are constant pressure systems that can provide a constant 70 psi at every tap."

Is Dowsing a Real Thing?

Dowsing or "water witching" is the process by which an individual walks across a parcel of land with a forked stick or bent wires in search of water. The claim is that, once the person walks over top of water, some form of subtle energy causes the stick to bend downward or the wires to cross.

The scientifically minded will argue that the practice is based on the outdated belief in underground rivers. The fact is that, in an area that receives sufficient rainfall, water will be encountered practically anywhere you dig, so the spot signaled by the water witch is no better or worse than a spot 100 feet away.

On the other hand, believers share stories of the almost supernatural success that their own dowsers had in finding just the right spot. See "Debunked" in RECOIL OFFGRID Issue 28 for more on this topic.

When the well is up and running, a minimum flow rate of 6 gallons per hour (gpm) should be sufficient to meet the demands of most households. However, even with lower gpm, a plastic or concrete storage tank or cistern can ensure that water is available during peak demand.

Well construction costs alone will range from $2,500 to $8,000, not counting the pumping system and water treatment. According to Bushong, expect to invest an additional $2,500 to $4,500 on a pumping system and $1,800 to $4,900 on water treatment.

Keeping it Clean

The quality of well water isn't static, but can be influenced by a number of factors. The hydrogeology of the area can certainly influence water quality, as can construction, agricultural, mining, and other surface activities near the well. The integrity of the well itself, as well as the condition of household plumbing can have negative impacts on water quality.

Yet, with all these variables that can lower drinking water purity, it's estimated that 80 percent of wells have never had a maintenance inspection. Most well owners tend to fall into the rut of being reactive, addressing maintenance only when a problem is noted.

The U.S. Environmental Protection Agency monitors the public drinking water supply via the 1974 Safe Drinking Water Act, setting standards for biological and inorganic contaminants, but private wells are unregulated at the federal level. That means the well owner is solely responsible for ensuring the quality of his or her drinking water.

It's important to handle samples according to the lab's instructions.

Testing for coliform bacteria should be conducted annually. Coliform bacteria isn't harmful in and of itself, but it's an indicator organism that can signal that surface water is moving into the well, and more serious bacteria such as *E. coli* could be present.

Every three years, the pH of the water should be checked, and a sample should be tested for total dissolved solids (TDS). Depending on observed water issues or surrounding land use, other testing may focus on lead, arsenic, copper, iron, manganese, nitrates, water hardness, sulfates, fluoride, iron, and sodium.

Some land-grant universities offer formal well-owner education through their Cooperative Extension program. Texas A&M University, Pennsylvania State University, Montana State University, and Virginia Tech all offer programs that include classroom training on well construction

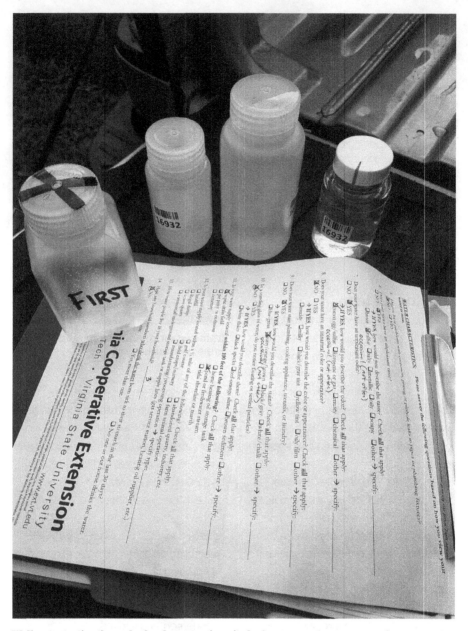

Well water testing through a land-grant university looks at several parameters of water quality.

and maintenance, as well as water testing. Water sampling may cost in the neighborhood of $300 through a private lab, but can run considerably less than $100 through one of these programs.

To find out if this type of outreach is available near you, do an internet search for "[your state] extension well water program," or ask Cooperative Extension personnel who serve your county.

Conclusion

Constructing a water well is within the realm of possibility for most folks in the U.S., but it isn't a do-it-yourself project, nor is it a crill-it-and-forget-it endeavor. It will take an investment and ongoing commitment, but the prize is the one thing that life on this planet needs the most.

Says Bushong, "Please understand, especially if you are a self-reliant type, you can own your own personal low-maintenance water plant on your own property for a reasonable cost that provides you and your family with water pressure and quality that meets or exceeds municipal water pressure and quality. Knowing this, why would anyone want to rely on a public water system when you can tap into Earth's most precious resource right beneath you?"

Winning the Germ War

Improvised Disaster Sanitation and Hygiene

By Morgan Atwood

Pick your favorite (or least favorite) disaster scenario and ask what your top priorities following that disaster will be. Are a clean body and living space on your list? They should be.

Sanitation and hygiene are fundamental forms of preventative medicine to block disease transmission. Human waste and household garbage harbor numerous infectious diseases. Properly disposing of these items and maintaining clean bodies are staples of the modern running-water world. With a flush of the toilet, taking a can to the curb, the turn of a knob, a little soap, and a few seconds, most of our sanitation and hygiene is handled effortlessly — so much so that very few of us ever consider life without these conveniences.

The household cleaners and soaps you already have can work with improvised hygiene and sanitation methods. Separate into smaller containers for rationing to group members.

History shows that in disasters, one of the first things to become compromised is the infrastructure we rely on for hygiene and sanitation. The power goes out, and pumps shut down. Water lines are broken or compromised. Essential personnel to maintain infrastructure services fall ill or are unable to reach their workplaces. No matter the scenario, one of the greatest disaster challenges is maintaining clean and healthy living conditions. Meeting needs for clean water, sanitary waste disposal, and individual hygiene tops the list of priorities for every disaster response organization. Many tasks come later, or simultaneously, but without these fundamentals, the spread of disease runs unchecked.

Sanitation means keeping environments clean and healthy. Hygiene means keeping the body clean and healthy. Disease risk from unsanitary conditions and poor hygiene can be extreme, as bacteria, viruses, and other pathogens not only thrive in dirty environments but can be spread more easily.

Of primary concern is the transmission of diseases via the fecal-oral route, where pathogens in human waste pass from one person to another and are ingested. Diseases and pathogens that can be found in human solid waste include cholera, shigella, e. coli, hepatitis, giardia, cryptosporidium, tapeworms, amoebas, and even the SARS-CoV-2 virus. Fecal-oral transmission occurs most readily in environments where human waste cannot be dealt with appropriately. Pathogen-containing particles can be carried by unwashed hands and insects like flies to other people, uncovered food, shared water, and other items. Human waste above ground can be carried by run-off to contaminate

Wash bowls filled with 1 tablespoon of bleach to 1 gallon of water can be reused repeatedly for washing your hands.

waterways. Buried human waste can soak into the ground and contaminate below-ground water.

Trash is also a concern, as many of the items we throw away can rot, grow bacteria, and attract insects. Food wastes are a particular concern. Food itself can also be a culprit for disease spread, as without ready means of preservation, food can spoil and host a cornucopia of nastiness, including toxic spoilage-produced waste products, such as botulinum toxin.

To manage these concerns, we must plan for providing sanitation and hygiene in a disaster.

Clean Water

Nearly everything in this article requires having clean water. Without clean water we are lost, regardless of the other severity of our situation. Entire books can be written on this subject, and to cover sanitation and hygiene we don't have room to take a deep dive into water. If you take nothing else away from this, take away a desire to research water storage, emergency water access, transport, filtration, and purification.

For the majority of Americans, water comes from the tap. Some of us may buy purified water to drink, or have filters in our kitchen, but most of our water comes out of the faucet without thought. Implicit in this arrangement is that we have very little water storage. The toilet tank, the hot water heater, and maybe a rain barrel or two if we have a yard — that's it. If the municipal water systems are disrupted, accessing more water will become a challenge. The World Health Organization recommends access to 2 to 4 gallons of water per person, per day, for disaster response provisioning. Those "native" storage resources in the home will supply that only briefly. You need to identify water sources in your area now, before something happens, and think of ways to transport, purify, and store that water.

Fundamental to our discussion of hygiene and sanitation is using bleach (sodium hypochlorite) to disinfect water.

Although bleach cannot remove particulate contaminants, it can render water safe for use. Only a few drops are required for *potable* water, around eight drops per gallon. To make a cleaning solution of water and bleach, use 1 tablespoon per gallon. Only use regular sodium hypochlorite bleach; avoid scented, additive-containing, or color-safe bleaches.

Personal Hygiene

History has shown time and time again that good personal hygiene helps to prevent disease and maintain health. Though the disaster environment may make it difficult, your immediate survival and long-term success are affected by your hygiene.

Critical among personal hygiene tasks is hand washing. Pathogens from anything we touch can linger on hands and be transferred to mouths, eyes, food, and water. The barrier to this is hand washing with soap and water. We've all heard it a lot recently: Thoroughly lather palms, backs of hands, and fingers and scrub for at least 20 seconds under running water. Complication? You have to have running water.

Buckets and jugs with a spigot attached are the most apparent solution to creating a faucet. Turn the spigot and wash as normal. A towel can be used to turn the spigot off, or it can be washed as you wash. A larger vessel underneath can capture gray-water. Simpler systems can be created using plastic jugs filled with water and rigged up to tip slightly, running out water without spilling and returning upright by gravity. You can also create a reusable hand-washing basin with a large bowl filled with a solution of water and bleach. The aforementioned 1 tablespoon of bleach to 1 gallon of water is the right ratio. Refresh the bleach when you can no longer smell

A gallon jug with the lid drilled or perforated in multiple spots can be mounted on a rod to tip, by hand or with an attached cord pull, to wash hands or even shower under.

chlorine in the water and refresh the whole thing after several uses.

You must wash your hands after going to the bathroom, disposing of waste or trash, manual labor, or changing a diaper, and before providing medical care, preparing food, or eating, touching another person intimately, and any other time your hands might be contaminated. These common-sense rules are even more important to remember during a disaster.

The next step is keeping your body clean. Sweat attracts dirt, and unwashed bodies are ready hosts for various infections. The easiest, and least water-consumptive method is to take a "bird bath" using a bowl of water, soap, and a washcloth. Wash with the soap and cloth, and lave clean water with a dipper to rinse. While far from the most effective, this will meet the basic requirements of washing the face, armpits, crotch, and feet.

More proper bathing can be performed using portable camp showers. A heavy-duty water bladder that hangs above head height with a gravity-fed tube and shower head, these are designed to hang in the sun for heat. Hanging on a balcony or in a window, rather than fully outdoors, may only get partial sun, but will at least take the chill off. Improvised showers can be made using the same idea. Insert a spigot or tap in the bottom of any water container, with a hose running to a shower-head type fixture, be it a garden sprinkler or something improvised (a water bottle with holes in it, capped and drilled PVC pipe, or a cannibalized shower head). Use caution hanging heavy containers and make sure whatever you use can bear the weight of several gallons of water.

Another means of improvising a shower is to use a garden pump-sprayer. You *must* use a clean sprayer and not one that has ever had herbicides or pesticides in it. Just fill with water, pump, and spray. You can even set your sprayer in the sun for several hours to warm the water first. Baths should be avoided as they use excessive amounts of water. Wet wipes can be used for quick and minimally effective hygiene of critical areas, but are

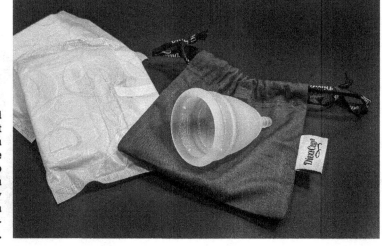

Menstrual cups present a long-term reusable alternative to pads that can be extremely valuable in disaster environments.

A receiving blanket can be folded and used as a diaper.

less effective and more wasteful than soap and water.

Routine hygiene must be maintained too. A disaster is no excuse to stop brushing your teeth. Toothbrushes are cheap, especially bulk disposables such as those used in hospitals. Toothpaste too, though in an emergency baking soda can be used in place of toothpaste. Extra or worn out toothbrushes can be sterilized and reused to clean hands and cuticles. Fingernails should be trimmed to avoid breaking and injury, as small wounds on the hands are very susceptible to infection.

The next point of hygiene to take care of is bodily functions. As with different washing strategies, we must be willing to adapt. Realize that while none of these measures are convenient or comfortable, done right they achieve the goal.

Since a post-disaster run to the store is an unlikely hope, you'll need to be stocked up on reusable hygiene supplies, or prepared to improvise them. Washable cloth menstrual pads, and reusable menstrual cups, are a long-term replacement for unavailable disposables. If caught unprepared, cloth pads can be easily sewn from absorbent materials with a nonabsorbent backer. Improvised pads can be made from household materials. Rectangles of cotton wool or similar can be wrapped in a layer of soft cotton, or a thin rectangular fold made of absorbent fabric. A thin plastic liner, between pad and underwear, can prevent leakage. Ensure you have or make enough to change frequently.

If you have young children, you may already be cloth diapering, which puts you ahead of the curve in a disaster. If not, now would be a good time to begin. Receiving blankets, which most parents have, make an excellent improvised diaper. Soft cottons, like T-shirt material, also work.

Maintain good hygiene for your little one and clean them gently but well when changing. Baby wipes would be ideal, but soft washcloths dampened with warm water work, and go right to the laundry with cloth diapers. For diaper rash, you can use coconut oil or petroleum jelly as a barrier paste.

Hand bidets and squeeze-bottles can be kept near, or brought to, bathroom facilities.

Keeping yourself clean after going to the bathroom is as important as keeping your kiddo clean. Again, you'll have to improvise. Frequent campers know the natural materials that can stand in for TP, but good leaves and dry grass bundles may be in short supply in urban environments. Newsprint and similar paper can be crumpled and flattened repeatedly to soften it, for a less unpleasant experience. Rags can be used too.

Your hand is an option, along with a stream of water, followed by a thorough washing. If you have the water, a bidet can be improvised from a pump sprayer, as discussed for showering. Travel bidets, basically a squeeze bottle with a spray nozzle, can be purchased now and cached. Squeezable sports bottles with push-caps make a solid improvised bidet.

Sanitation

All the good hygiene in the world won't help if your environment lacks sanitation. Just because you cannot flush or take the trash to the curb every Thursday doesn't mean waste production stops. Human waste, food waste, and trash will continue to be produced. If these outputs aren't dealt with, they pollute and lead to the spread of disease.

Top priority is dealing with human waste, as it is the most likely to spread disease. Our goals should be to remove all wastes from the household/living quarters as soon as possible. An indoor bathroom is hard to beat for comfort and morale, but making this work requires some adjustment. If the sewer lines are unbroken, you can activate most flush toilets by pouring water into the bowl. Urine can be left in the bowl, to reduce water use, until solid waste needs to be flushed. A large jug or pitcher can be staged in the bathroom, pre-filled with water, for this purpose. This is an excellent use of gray-water captured elsewhere.

If the sewer lines are compromised, or water availability low, the home toilet can still be used. Line the toilet with garbage bags, ideally doubled, and secure them under the lid. This may be used as normal, and when full, the entire bag simply lifted out and tied closed. Unpleasant odors and

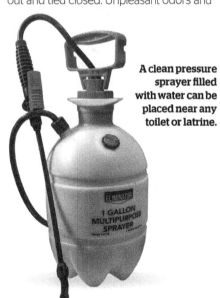

A clean pressure sprayer filled with water can be placed near any toilet or latrine.

flies can be managed by topping each deposit with RV toilet sanitizing chemicals, wood ash, sawdust, cut grass, hay, or alfalfa.

The next option, which can still be in the existing bathroom, is to use a portable camp toilet. A five-gallon bucket with an improvised toilet seat frame is almost the same thing. Bucket toilets should be lined with a garbage bag, and material spread over deposits. Empty bucket toilets when they are half-full to avoid a mess.

With any container toilet, effort should be made to deposit only solid waste. Liquids fill bags faster, add weight, and can leak. Urination outside, or even in open drains, can provide an alternative to filling the toilet with liquids. In the long term, areas used for urination should be sprinkled with disinfectant to keep down odors.

You can also set up an outdoor toilet area in many ways, some better than others. An immediate first choice is to use a bucket system. For many caught in a disaster, however, the only choice ends up being various forms of trench or pit latrine. These systems are holes in the ground, dug deep enough and long enough to accommodate days' or weeks' worth of deposits from the entire group. Outdoor latrines create significant health hazards unless built properly, as there's more to them than simply digging a hole and using it.

Latrines can leach into the ground, eventually contaminating ground water, as well as attracting insects that can carry pathogens out of the waste. To mitigate this, latrines must be away from any water sources, open water, dwellings, food prep areas, and showers. The minimum safe distance is 100 feet; 200 to 300 feet would be even better, but even in larger suburbs that distance may not be available in the backyard. In dense urban settings, this may require cooperation to utilize a local open space for community latrines.

You can dig a single deep hole, or a long deep trench, for a latrine. Trench latrines serve more people, or serve fewer people for a longer duration as you move from one end of the trench to the other. Latrines should be deep enough to have 18 inches of soil above the waste when filled back in.

A clean household plunger, perforated to allow water passage, makes an effective manual agitator for doing laundry in buckets and tubs.

Fitting a garbage bag into the emptied toilet bowl, with the seat closed over the opening, makes for a comfortable, easily maintained, toilet solution.

They can be equipped with a pair of boards across the pit for squatting over the hole, or made more comfortable with a seat frame, toilet seat, and privacy screens. Each person should cover their deposit with appropriate materials. When the latrine is filled to 18 to 20 inches below the ground level it should be buried and a new one dug.

If you use bucket toilets, or bags lining your indoor toilet, disposal of each full bag becomes the next priority. For a short duration, a tightly sealed garbage can works for a disposal station. It should be lined with heavy garbage bags, with shredded or crumpled paper between bags to absorb moisture and reduce odor. Bags of waste can be added to the can, and the lid tightly sealed each time. A locking lid, or other means of animal proofing the container, is a must. This must be kept a safe distance from water and living areas, and should be fastened tightly to a post or tree to prevent knocking over. In the longer term, disposal pits can be used with depth and placement constraints similar to a latrine. Waste bags should be buried immediately to prevent insect or animal access, reduce smells, and prevent infection.

Food waste and other trash is the next sanitation issue. Trash attracts bugs and animals and can be a festering ground for bacteria and disease, just like human waste. Separate your trash by wet and dry. Wet trash includes food waste, containers with food remnants, and so on; it should be handled similar to human waste. Dry trash is paper, clean containers, and the like; it can be contained with somewhat less concerns.

Liquid trash, excluding grease, can be dumped in soakage pits. To build a soakage pit, you dig a hole or trench similar to a latrine, but then fill it with rocks. Start with large stones in the bottom, and reduce to medium rocks in the middle, reducing size until the top layer is gravel. This graded fill allows the liquid waste to settle to the bottom without creating a nasty, disease-promoting, trash swamp. The concept of a soakage pit also works for building a urinal.

Reducing your trash output during a disaster can help too. Consider alternate or more complete use of everything. Evaluate all your trash for reuse — containers for water transport, washing stations, and other purposes. Clean paper trash for fire starting, lining waste containers, even improvised toilet paper. Food waste can be reduced by better use and preparing only the amount that'll be eaten. Get creative with leftovers and use all the parts of plants and animals. This will provide more nutrition out of a given item, make food stocks last longer, and reduce the amount of waste. Dehydrating, canning, and other shelf-stable preservation methods will help to reduce spoilage.

Food prep and eating areas should be kept clean by removing large physical remnants of meals and wiping down all surfaces with soap and water or a bleach solution. Dishes should be washed thoroughly, though every effort to conserve water should be taken. Laving water over dishes, rather than filling an entire sink or basin, can reduce water use.

The final point is laundry. We've talked about keeping the body clean, and clean bodies require clean (or at least sanitized) clothes. We've also talked about numerous uses for fabric in waste management and cleanup. This means laundry must be done. The same clothes can be worn repeatedly, but for no more than 1 week. Items soiled with waste will need to be washed almost immediately, however. You can wash clothes entirely by hand in a bucket or tub. A few clothes at a time go into the bucket with water and detergent, and you agitate and scrub them one at a time by hand until the dirt and grime come out. Then, you repeat the process with clean water to get a thorough rinse. Devices like washboards can reduce fatigue while improving results.

One of the most effective labor savers for bucket or tub washing clothes is a plunger. There are several designs for laundry agitating plungers popular with homesteaders, but a new household toilet plunger works too. Insert the plunger into the bucket and plunge, making sure to fully agitate and compress all of the clothes within. Cutting or drilling some holes into the plunger can reduce resistance and increase the cleaning agitation. Clothes and fabric can also be disinfected, but not cleaned, by a 1- to 2-minute pass through boiling water. Leaving cloth items in direct sunlight for several days, turning them over halfway through, can also disinfect them.

Disaster survival means adaptation to the unfamiliar and the uncomfortable. For many of us, these methods will seem primitive and unattractive. The reality, however, is that they're adequate to meet the needs of surviving until you can begin thriving, either through your own long-term solutions or the return of infrastructure and services. Non-flush toilets, wash basins and buckets, trash burial, and other improvised methods are the norm for millions of people worldwide. You can do this, maybe not with a smile, but you can do it and you will prevail.

About the Author

Morgan Atwood is the founder of No One Coming, a firm providing services, tools, and education for survival environments. A dedicated wilderness professional, Atwood has been an EMT and wildland firefighter, provided risk management and anti-poaching services for remote ranches, and lived off grid on a historic cattle ranch most of his life. **www.noonecoming.com**

7 › Survival Outdoors

MacGyver-Level Pyro

10 Ways to Start a Fire Without Matches

By Ryan Lee Price

Warning! This article is meant to be a quick overview and not a detailed guide. There are inherent risks when starting a fire — especially when doing so unconventionally. We encourage you to enroll in a course from a reputable instructor or agency and adhere to wildfire-prevention techniques at all times.

A small collection of common items one could employ to help start a fire.

Fire — it can be both our salvation and our destroyer. As humans, we share a primal link with fire. Perhaps early man looked upon the smoldering aftermath of a lightning strike with rousing curiosity or ran away in sheer panic as a towering wall of flames swept across a forest. How many generations did it take for them to be able to replicate fire and then learn to control it, respect it, and finally benefit from its many qualities?

Half a million years or so later (depending on your math), the ability to start and maintain a fire, like our ancestors, is mostly lost on modern man — what with matches, lighters, flares, and ignition stoves. However, somewhere deep in the recesses of our brains remains our attraction to the magnetic powers of a campfire. Its flames can evoke haunting stories, deep discussions, and jocular camaraderie. Sitting around the fire, we get back to basics. No jobs, no smartphones, no office commute — just homo sapiens harkening back to a time when fear, hunger, and pain guided us to our most essential needs. That time could return more easily than you think. A massive solar flare, an electromagnetic pulse attack, or a nuclear holocaust could easily destroy our way of life and force us to live like cavemen.

Fortunately, there's a big handful of ways to start a fire without matches, a lighter...or even a magnesium stick. Some methods described here are easy, while others take practice, patience, and perseverance. The materials used in these examples are not ideal, but instead are used to show how you'll have to do your best MacGyver impersonation to adapt in a given survival situation. Because, after all, you'll have to make do with what you packed in your go-bag or can scavenge around you, which is reason enough to learn more than one way to start a fire.

In general, fire needs air, fuel, and heat to start. However, since air and fuel are abundant in most situations, finding something that can translate a source of energy into roughly 450 degrees of heat can be a challenge. Fire-starters like these come in three basic categories: reflection/convection, combustion, and friction.

The Reflectors

Most of the easy ways to start a fire merely use the energy of the sun by focusing its light into a small pinpoint. If 4 or 5 square inches of the sun's rays can be focused down to about an 1/8-inch diameter of white hot light, most anything will burn.

Magnifying Glass

The convex lens has been used as a magnifier since at least the era of Aristophanes. And as any sociopathic delinquent knows, a magnifying glass is an easy way to roast ants on a hot summer's day. Similar to the survivor's friend, the Fresnel lens (originally designed to increase lighthouse efficiency), a magnifying glass concentrates light from the sun on a compact point, which easily ignites. Using a convex lens of any kind will start a fire with dry tinder in seconds. Simply point and light.

Only You Can Prevent Wildfires

Just because you're lost and in a survival situation doesn't mean you can accidentally burn down the whole forest. No, the authorities won't understand, you will not pass Go, you will not collect $200, but you'll go directly to jail. Don't be that guy; listen to what Smokey the Bear always says.

› Pick a good spot to build your fire, clear of any dried leaves or dead trees. If it's windy, build your fire in a protected place (between boulders or in an arroyo).
› Build your fire downwind of your campsite and at least 15 feet away.
› Build a fire ring of rocks to contain the coals.
› This is probably the most important tip: When you're done with the fire, put it out.

Water Balloon/ Water Bottle

METHOD 2 — DIFFICULTY LEVEL: ADVANCED

In about 60 A.D., Pliny the Elder described how glass balls filled with water could set clothes on fire when placed in line with the sun. The concept of filling a water balloon or condom (finally you'll have a use for one, right?) with water and holding it in the proper position to focus the sun's beams onto some dry leaves is a skill reserved for the utterly patient. It took four days' worth of attempts to get small wisps of smoke from either the bag of water or the water bottle, but fire was still illusive. Also consider using discarded beer bottles — the clearer and cleaner the glass and water, the better the results.

Reading Glasses

METHOD 3 — DIFFICULTY LEVEL: NOVICE

Are you farsighted? If so, you're in luck, as your glasses can be used to start a fire; however, ironically, you'll need some water to do so. The difference between a magnifying glass and your reading glasses is that the converging lenses of glasses for farsightedness bend the light toward a focal point — but only in one direction. A magnifying glass is biconvex, meaning it bends the light once it enters the lens and again when it leaves. Regular glasses aren't powerful enough to start a fire on their own, so to increase the power of your glasses, add a drop of water to the inside of the lens. This will turn your regular glasses into a biconvex lens. Find the focal point similar to how you would with a magnifying glass. If your glasses are expendable, put both lenses together to create a compound lens — for twice the power!

METHOD 4

DIFFICULTY LEVEL: MACGYVER

Soda Can and Chocolate Bar

The worst thing about people is that they throw trash everywhere, but the best thing about people when you're looking to make something out of nothing is that they throw trash everywhere. In this case, hopefully, you'll come across an old soda can and some chocolate (even some melted to the wrapper will do), and you're desperate enough to give it a try. It takes about an hour, but rub some chocolate on the bottom of the can (toothpaste works great, too, as does steel wool — see method 6) and use a rag or the candy wrapper to polish the can bottom to a mirror shine. You know you're done when you can clearly see your face in the can. Aim the "bowl" toward the sun so that the focal point is directly on the tinder and after a few moments, you'll have fire.

METHOD 5

DIFFICULTY LEVEL: MACGYVER

Ice Disc

The last thing you think you're going to find in a frozen wasteland is something that can help start a fire, and in the middle of a summer Californian drought, a frozen wasteland is difficult to replicate on camera (as awesome as the editorial staff is). But if you happen to be in subzero conditions this fall or winter, look for a disc of ice approximately 3 or 4 inches in diameter and about 2 inches thick at the center — but it has to be crystal-clear ice, the kind of ice made from pure water, not fancy bottled water, not tap water, and not boiled water. You need frozen natural spring water. Despite our efforts, we could not replicate clear ice without contaminants frozen inside, which is why our ice discs were better sunglasses than convex lenses. That said, if you're able to carve a suitable disc of clear ice into a convex shape (think flying saucer), you just might be able to use it to make fire. Many winter survival experts have.

The Combustors

Sometimes sunlight is a difficult thing to obtain, and you can't very well sit around on a cloudy or rainy day and wait for the sun to show up. You'll have to find another way to start a fire (after all, on cloudy and rainy days, you'll need fire the most).

Battery and Steel Wool

METHOD 6 | DIFFICULTY LEVEL: NOVICE

The principle applied here is electrical, as the energy stored in the battery (in this case, a 9-volt battery) is more than enough to start a fire when short circuited by the steel wool. The great thing about a 9-volt battery is that it's compact, fairly powerful, and has adjacent terminals. Use fine steel wool, as the coarser wool requires more energy to get hot. Merely touch the steel wool to the battery terminals and it will spark immediately as the battery overloads the strands of wool. Have a bundle of tinder available to transfer that spark.

Gun Powder

METHOD 7 | DIFFICULTY LEVEL: ADVANCED

You're never really without a way to start a fire if you have a live round in your pack. The ubiquitous Winchester .30-30, in this case, holds 1.9 grams of gun powder, which is easy to get to in a pinch (of course, you can use any unexpended cartridge). With a couple of pliers, pulling off the bullet is done easily, exposing a case full of combustible propellant. (Despite the popular misuse of the term, a "bullet" is just the projectile component of a round and not the entire round itself.) Pour out the powder and ignite it using almost all of the methods presented in this story. Make sure to bed your propellant in a pile of tinder, as it flares up quickly once ignited.

The Rubbers

The old adage is true: If you want to start a fire, just rub two sticks together. Heat leads to fire, and a great source of heat is friction, as first explained by Leonardo da Vinci. Of course, it's more efficient to use more advanced methods if you have the means, but sometimes branches might be all you have access to.

Rope Rubbing

If you're feeling limber and you frequent the rowing machine at the gym, then getting over the painful awkwardness of this method will be easy for you. To add suspense in a pirate movie, there's always a shot of a capstan where a length of smoking rope is frantically being pulled through. Aiming for similar results, wrap a piece of rope around a stick sitting in tinder and pull the rope back and forth like you're trying to saw the stick in half. Use your feet as leverage and give yourself a solid 30 minutes to get enough heat built up to start to see some smoke. Soon enough you'll have fire and a Hugh Jackman-like physique.

Fire Plough

The concept of the fire plough is that by rubbing a stick back and forth along a cut grove in a piece of wood, small pieces of tinder are produced at the opposite end, which will help ignite a tinder bundle as the temperature increases. If you can't find an ideal piece of wood as a base, use a knife and cut a groove wide enough to allow the point of your stick to slide back and forth. Start "plowing" by rubbing the tip of the stick up and down the grove. Once you see some embers, cultivate them with light blowing until they produce a flame.

Bow Drill/ Hand Drill

METHOD 10 — **DIFFICULTY LEVEL: ADVANCED**

When one pictures a backwoods survivalist starting a fire without tools, this is the go-to method they think of. There are five parts to the bow-drill set, and each must be made carefully if you want a successful experience: The bow, string, drill, board, and handhold. The drill spins via the bow and string against the board on one end and is supported by the handhold at the other end. We notched out a space large enough for the drill's end to fit snugly, and toward the end of the base we created a small triangular space to collect the embers we hoped to create. From there, it's just a matter of sawing back and forth, keeping the drill squarely in the hole, watching for the slight embers to flame up.

Conventional Fire Starting

Flint and Steel: This tried-and-true method dates back thousands of years, and if you know a little bit about geology, you might be able to find a piece of chert (AKA "flint") in nature to use. Striking it with high-carbon steel (such as a bushcraft knife) onto a char cloth will provide the best and quickest results.

Magnesium Stick: A mag stick with a ferro rod (which is just synthetic flint) fits easily into your pocket and is cheap and long lasting. Scrape some magnesium into a dime-sized pile, hold the ferro rod over the pile, and strike it with something steel.

Flares: An unconventional way using a conventional tool. As a multitasker, a road flare is great for signaling. But since it can be used in inclement weather (rain, snow, wind) and is self-lighting, it's a great tool to ignite a fire with.

Matches/Lighter: Just pack these in waterproof containers and store them everywhere. Of course, matches are vulnerable to being damaged or dampened (especially in wet conditions), while lighters can break or run out of lighter fluid. But for the most part quality matches or lighters hold up, and they're cheap, lightweight, and easy to carry. Snap, presto, flame on!

DIY Improvised Bucksaw

All You Need is a Few Parts and Some Ingenuity to Fashion a Practical Cutting Implement

By Ryan Houtekamer

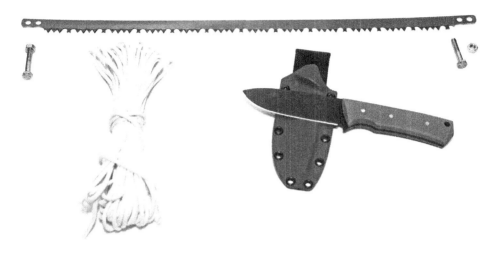

Why build it when you can buy it? It seems that we've become a nation of consumption, more likely to spend our money than our time or effort. We solve our problems by buying things — and when they break, we just purchase new ones instead of repairing what we have. Due to this trend of disposable products, the ability to fix, build, or create seems to be becoming a lost art. Since this publication is all about self-sufficiency and using what you have around you, we wanted to provide you with a couple of ways to think outside the box.

Knowing how to MacGyver things in a pinch can go a long way in a desperate situation. If all you have at your disposal is a long saw blade, paracord, and some nuts and bolts, you might think you're SOL in terms of any serious cutting or sawing. Don't lose hope though — it just takes a little ingenuity. With the items listed and some pieces of wood, we can create a frame to improvise a practical cutting instrument that'll make it a heck of a lot easier to cut some firewood or tree trunks for an improvised shelter.

First of all, what exactly is a bucksaw? For our purposes, it's a wooden frame that has a blade held in place using tension, some branches or pieces of tree trunk, and some nuts and bolts. Twine, paracord, or other heavy string provides the tension, created when the vertical arms pivot on the crossbar, and pull outward on the ends of the saw blade. Bucksaws allow for a more natural handle position compared to trying to grab the end of a flimsy saw blade to move it back and forth. This frame will give you better leverage and grip, allowing more control of the cuts you make. This is beneficial for processing a lot of wood or building your survival palace.

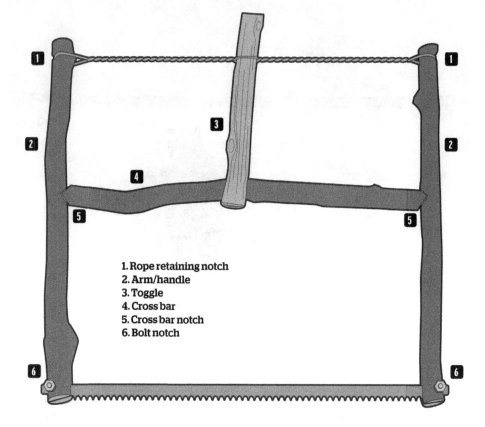

1. Rope retaining notch
2. Arm/handle
3. Toggle
4. Cross bar
5. Cross bar notch
6. Bolt notch

First, examine the saw diagram above. We'll describe its various parts and how to fashion them in further detail as you read on. The parts you'll need to purchase, if you don't already have them, are the saw blade, bolts, nuts, and paracord. We prefer replacement bucksaw or bowsaw blades with four to six teeth per inch. Hacksaw blades tend to be shorter than we'd like, plus the size and number of teeth are more geared toward cutting metal or plastic. They can work, but it's really a matter of preference. The blade on our example is 21 inches.

After you've acquired a blade, the next step is finding a couple nuts and bolts. It's important that this hardware fit through the existing holes on the ends of the blade that are usually used to mount it to a standard plastic and metal frame. Ideally, you want the two bolts to be long enough to have around 1 inch of thread showing through the nut at the end, as this will give you some extra room when you mount the blade to your homemade frame. The longer the bolts, the bigger the branches or pieces of wood you can work with.

You'll also need to find or purchase some paracord. Typically it comes in lengths of 50 feet, but if you have a survival bracelet with paracord, it should provide enough length to complete the project. The paracord, or acceptable substitute cordage, creates the pulling force on the handles or arms to keep the blade taut.

Next, you need a nice straight tree or two that are close to the handle diameter you want. Look for branches that are around ¾ to 1 inch in diameter. The actual length depends on how long your blade is and how long you want your handles to be. Typically they'll be around 12 to 15 inches long. A good rule of thumb is to select three pieces that are as long as, or slightly longer than, the blade being used.

In procuring the wood needed to build the bucksaw frame, you'll quickly see the disadvantages of working with a bare saw blade. First, insert the nuts and bolts into the ends of the blade and get ready to look like a terrible accordion player as you painstakingly cut some appropriate lengths of wood.

Hold the blade in between your fingers and curl your fingers around the bolts. This will give you something to hold on to as you sway your arms back and forth to hack some lengths of tree branch or trunk. If you have gloves, wear them — they'll help you hold the blade more securely and reduce the risk of accidental cuts if your hands slip on the blade. Good news: You'll have a handle soon, so this should be the last time you'll need to use the blade in this frustrating manner.

Now it's time to assemble the pieces. The first is the crossbar. This piece will likely require a bit of fine-tuning to achieve the appropriate length. You should aim to cut this a bit shorter than the distance between the screw holes in the chosen blade. This is because the screws will be on the outside of the saw's arms.

Once you have the crossbar cut to size, its ends must be finished in a way to help secure them to the vertical arms. In our case we fashioned triangular ends, as they're fairly easy to make. You can do this with your knife, or if you have to use your crude bolt-handled saw blade. Try to create two symmetrical cuts, so that each end of the crossbar resembles a wedge. You might need to adjust the angle on these for fitment and to remove any twist your blade has once it's all assembled.

The arms or handles are your next task, which you can adjust based on your preferences. The crossbar will be held in place about halfway up the arms. The distance from the teeth of the saw to this crossbar is known as the throat, determining the thickest object you can cut through without making multiple cuts. So if all the trees in your area are half a foot in diameter, it's best to make the arms a bit longer than a foot in length.

Each arm needs three cuts, the first one being a V-shaped notch for the crossbar. Start approximately halfway up from where the teeth will be, or a bit higher, and mark a line on both arms in the same spot. Make a corresponding notch that the ends of the crossbar will fit into. This will allow them to lock in and provide the pivot point. You'll need a small amount of slop in this so that the arms can move when tightened. If necessary, you can start with a small notch and gradually widen it. Remember, you can't remove too little from the wood, but you *can* remove too much. If your notch is too wide or deep, you may have to start over on that particular piece.

Next you'll need to cut a slot in one end of each arm to accommodate the saw blade. You can use the blade itself or a

278 | OFFGRIDWEB.COM

sharp knife to whittle these openings. The width of the slots should only be as thick as the saw blade so the ends of the arms will securely hold it in place. Make the slots just slightly deeper than the height of the blade so the ends fit snugly into the wood when you fasten them with the bolts. It's also helpful to add small notches for the bolts on the outside of the arms.

The last cuts are the rope-retaining notches at the ends of the arm opposite the blade. Similar to the bolt notches, just cut small V shapes on the outside near the top of each arm. Your paracord will attach here, and the notch will prevent it from sliding off. Now that you can see how much distance you're playing with, cut enough paracord to wrap around each end of the arms. Tie the ends together as tightly as possible.

To tighten the cord and create the leverage to hold everything else in place, you need to make a toggle that goes from the crossbrace to just above the paracord. You can see on the diagram that the toggle should be a little more than half the length of the arms. It's held in place by the tension of the cord and will be spun around the paracord to twist it. Thread it through the paracord and twist it as if it's the windlass in a tourniquet. One end of the toggle will eventually rest loosely on the crossbar when you've tightened it appropriately. Some people make a slight indentation on the crossbar for the toggle to sit in. It's up to

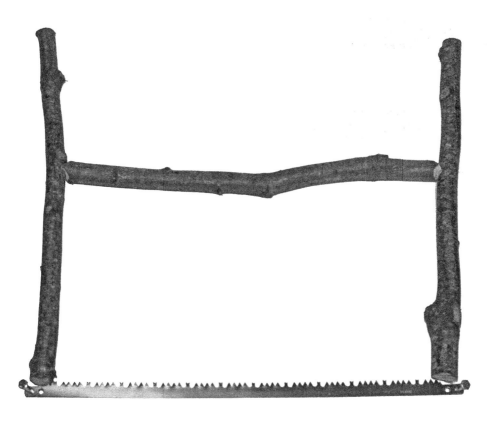

In order to make the toggle as light as possible, one could theoretically split a long branch in half lengthwise to help reduce weight.

you how (or if) you want to add this notch to secure it.

Finally, it's time to tighten it all up and get to cutting. Once you've constructed this frame, you can smooth out handle surfaces or make aesthetic improvements. You now have a functional tool that'll help you build a solid structure or break down wood to build a fire.

With this improvised bucksaw, if anything other than the blade breaks, you can simply make new parts for the frame. If you're venturing out into the woods, you can always carry spare blades and create the other components when needed. We'd also advise you to practice building a few versions to get the hang of it. The last thing you want is to need to figure out how to build one when you're in dire need of a saw. Eventually you'll get the hang of it, and it'll be that much easier to build one in a hurry so long as you have the requisite hardware. You can devise other ways to use branches to create a slightly different style of saw; the point is to get you thinking about how you can still function with only limited resources on hand.

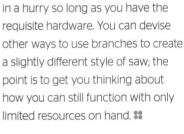

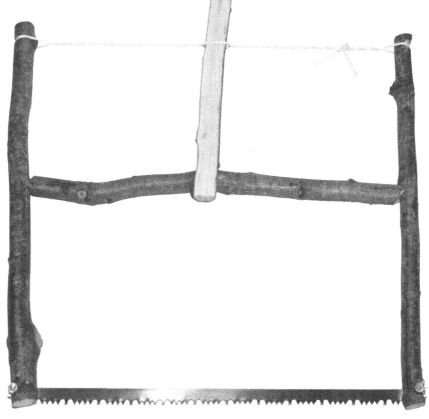

Eat This, Not That

Edible Plants and Their Dangerous Doppelgängers

By Andrew Schrader

Most of our readers already know that our preference is for fresh meat in the wild during a bug-out or backcountry hiking scenario. And as Green Beret Mykel Hawke noted in Issue 23 of RECOIL OFFGRID, it's much easier to get life-saving nutrients and energy from animals than it is from plants.

That being said, animals aren't always available to us. And in a true survival situ-

Warning! This article is meant to be an overview and not a detailed guide on identifying and consuming edible plants. Seek guidance from a trained botanist before attempting to eat any plants. Any attempt to consume plants shall solely be at the reader's risk.

ation we may need to end up foraging for plants in order to scrape by. The problem is that foraging for plants, although easier because they can't run away from you, is complicated by the fact that some plants can harm you and others can kill you. The second issue is that some plants that resemble edible options and look familiar to us can actually be quite harmful if ingested. If you've ever seen the movie *Into the Wild*, this situation was depicted to reflect one of the theories about how Christopher McCandless died.

To help us sort things out, we tracked down professional backpacking and climbing guide Lee Vartanian. These days, besides guiding in his "spare time," he works as the founder and head of Modern Icon, which handcrafts K9 leashes and harnesses for high-end law enforcement and military applications. He also helps train U.S. Department of Defense (DOD) agencies in "the art of vertical access in nonpermissive environments." In other words, using ropes and climbing skills to gain passage to areas that bad guys don't want you to access.

Lee earned his bachelor's degree in outdoor education, with a minor in environmental science, and has been guiding professionally for 18 years. As a kid, he practiced by foraging for food in his neighborhood and constructing homemade snares. Besides reading every book on edible plants he could find, he also hoarded magazine clippings from survivalists, including wild food proponent Euell Gibbons, author of *Stalking the Wild Asparagus*, who some readers may recognize from circa-1970s Grape Nuts commercials.

"Everyone thinks about clubbing a wild rabbit and cooking it over a fire when they think of survival experiences," Lee told us. "But they forget the importance of being able to eat on the move. Killing and prepping wild game with primitive tools is a challenge even on a good day. Doing that while you're malnourished, cold, and sleep deprived can be close to impossible and potentially hazardous to your physical safety."

If unexpectedly stranded in the backcountry, Lee's recommendation for most people, most of the time, is to shelter in place and wait for rescue. Hiking out, however, may sometimes be necessary. "In either scenario," Lee said, "you may have to rely on both hunting and gathering depending on how long you are lost. So don't miss out on the benefits of gathering plants that are plentiful and won't run away when you're on the move."

TESTING PLANTS

First of all, don't just randomly chow down on the first thing that looks like a tomato or a berry. Follow a series of protocols to help make eating in the wild less hazardous (note that we never used the word "safe.")

Crush the plant's leaves and take a whiff. If it smells unpleasant, or like almonds, discard it.

Rub the juice of the crushed leaf on the inside of your arm, and wait for 15 minutes. If no irritation develops, place a small piece on your lips, then in the corner of your mouth, then the tip of your tongue, and finally under your tongue, holding each for three minutes before moving.

If the plant irritates your skin or mouth, treat it as you would an acid. Pour water

over your skin to remove toxins, and use alcohol or dish soap to clean off the residue. Contaminated clothing must be washed or thoroughly discarded.

If no negative side effects are observed, swallow a small amount and wait for five hours, consuming nothing else in the meantime. Assuming nothing bad happens, the plant can be considered less hazardous to eat.

"The part a lot of people miss," Lee said, "is ensuring that whatever they're testing is plentiful. Don't let your curiosity override your logic, and always consider boiling the plant to make it more easily digestible."

ACCIDENTAL INGESTION

If the sample you ate starts to give you a bad ride, or if you or someone else inadvertently ate something that's turning out to be toxic, there aren't a lot of great options. An unpleasant reaction can turn deadly in a short amount of time. The best thing to do is to make a note (or take a sample) of the plant or plants ingested, then evacuate immediately to a hospital. However, if you're in such a bad situation that you're forced to eat plants in the first place, it's likely that immediate evacuation isn't feasible.

If you can't get your victim to a hospital, place them into the recovery position (¾ prone) and prepare to wait it out. Rest will give their body the best chance at fighting the toxins in the event you've exhausted all other options.

Many people assume that the easy solution at this point is to induce vomiting, but that's really not the answer. First, a toxic plant may cause vomiting on its own, so if it's going to happen, it's probably already happening. Second, induced vomiting can cause caustic substances to create more damage on the way up, especially if the vomiting is projectile and goes through the nose. Last, there's also a chance to inadvertently inhale the vomit accidentally, further complicating an already bad situation.

Because your self-treatment options are so limited, it's critical to avoid eating anything that you can't 100-percent positively identify in the first place. The mess you don't make is the mess you don't need to clean up.

So now that you know how to test items, and just how dangerous it can be to accidentally eat the wrong thing, watch out for the following deadly doppelgängers — though keep in mind that this is just a small sampling of harmful plants. Our hope is that this listing will help you more safely stalk your own wild asparagus and get more nutrition with less nausea. Good luck out there, and happy "hunting!"

Wild Grapes
(Vitis riparia)
vs.
Poisonous Virginia Creeper
(Parthenocissus quinquefolia)

"This is my favorite deadly doppelgänger comparison because everyone seems to want to eat anything that resembles a grape or berry," Lee said. "When in season, wild grapes provide a tremendous amount of nutrition with their fruit, leaves, and even new shoots being edible, but keep in mind that the roots are poisonous. Wild grapes also provide a great source of potable water through cutting their vines. Cut high first, then low, to maximize the amount of water yielded per vine."

Tell Them Apart: Wild grape tendrils are more conspicuous and grow in branches, as opposed to Virginia Creeper, which adhere using terminal pads. Also, Virginia Creeper leaves are compound leaves, meaning that they consist of several leaflets joined to a single stem. Wild grape leaves just have one leaf attached to each stem.

Wild Grapes Range: Eastern Half of Canada and throughout the United States, excluding the far Southwest and Southeast U.S.

Virginia Creeper Range: Eastern half of United States and Canada

Black Nightshade Range: Southern and Western United States, British Columbia

Photo by Richard A. Howard, hosted by the USDA-NRCS PLANTS Database

Photo by Larry Allain, hosted by theUSDA-NRCS PLANTS Database

Deadly Nightshade Range: Central United States, Saskatchewan

Black Nightshade
(Solanum americanum)
vs.
Deadly Nightshade
(Atropa belladonna)

American Black Nightshade berries and leaves are traditionally eaten by Native Americans as well as modern cultures in Central American communities. Black Nightshade also has more protein, calories, fiber, calcium, iron, B vitamins, and vitamin C than spinach.

Deadly Nightshade, on the other hand, can cause delirium, hallucinations, and death when eaten in large quantities. "This is the most likely deadly doppelgänger to get you into trouble," Lee said. "Avoiding both varieties, if you're unsure, would be your best bet."

Tell Them Apart: "The most obvious way to differentiate between them is that the edible Black Nightshade berries grow in bunches, as opposed to Deadly Nightshade berries which grow individually. Remember that only the ripe berries can be eaten safely, and the leaves still need to be boiled before consumption."

Virginia Ground Cherry
(Physalis virginiana)

vs.

Horse Nettles
(Solanum carolinense)

The Virginia Ground Cherry is edible when ripe, resembling a small tomato. However, more often than not, any "wild tomatoes" stumbled upon in the wild should be regarded with suspicion due to their similarity to Horse Nettles.

Though they look quite similar to cherry tomatoes, all parts of the horse nettle are poisonous and can cause abdominal pain, nausea, vomiting, and death.

Tell Them Apart: Horse Nettle has large spiky prickles on its stems, while the Ground Cherry only has thick, stiff hairs. Additionally, the fruits of the Ground Cherry are enclosed in a papery husk while those of the Horse Nettle are bare.

Horse Nettles Range: Throughout the United States, Parts of Eastern Canada

Virginia Ground Cherry Range: Central and Eastern United States, Eastern half of Canada

Photo by Katy Chayka

Photo by Ted Bodner, hosted by the USDA-NRCS PLANTS Database

Photo by Jennifer Anderson, hosted by the USDA-NRCS PLANTS Database

Wild Garlic Range: Eastern half of United States and Canada

Photo by Thomas G. Barnes, hosted by the USDA-NRCS PLANTS Database

Death Camas Range: Throughout the United States and Canada

Photo by Al Schneider, hosted by the USDA-NRCS PLANTS Database

Wild Garlic
(Allium canadense)
vs.
Death Camas
(Toxicoscordion venenosum and others)

Wild garlic should smell strongly of onions or garlic, and is generally edible without issues. Use the chopped green leaves as chives to make any food more palatable and eat the onion-like bulb. Be aware, though, that Death Camas also looks a lot like an onion. It can cause loss of voluntary muscle movement, diarrhea, vomiting, among other unpleasantries.

Tell Them Apart: Take a whiff. Although the Death Camas bulb looks like an onion, it won't have the smell of garlic or onion like its edible cousin.

Wild Carrot aka Queen Anne's Lace
(Daucus carota)
vs.
Poisonous Hemlock
(Conium maculatum)

The roots of young carrots are very edible, although as they age they become more woody and inedible.

Tell Them Apart: Look for purple blotches or spots on the smooth (hairless) stems of Poison Hemlock. Wild carrot stems are usually covered in hairs, while hemlock is bare.

Wild Carrot Range: Throughout the United States and Canada

Photo by Joaquim Alves Gaspar

Photo by Gary A. Monroe

Poisonous Hemlock Range: Throughout the United States and Canada

Photo by Doug Goldman, hosted by the USDA-NRCS PLANTS Database

ADDITIONAL SOURCES
> Florida Native Plant Society
> Ohio State University Perennial and Biennial Weed Guide
> Purdue University Department of Agriculture
> University of Texas, Lady Bird Johnson Wildflower Center
> U.S. National Library of Medicine at the National Institute of Health
> U.S. Department of Agriculture, Natural Resources Conservation Service

Lee's Recommendations for
Where to Learn More

Books by Tom Brown Jr. and Courses at his Tracker School in New Jersey
"Tom Brown is one of my literary mentors," Lee says. "Anything written by Tom is a sure bet, and any survival courses at his school come highly recommended, even though people think he is a little 'out there' with the spiritual side of things."
www.trackerschool.com

Courses at the Nantahala Outdoor Center in Western North Carolina
Look for courses titled Wilderness Survival 1 and Wilderness Survival 2. The first course teaches you how to survive the first 72 hours in the wild, when most rescues typically happen. In the second course, you learn what to do after the first three days have passed, addressing the need to survive on the move while self-rescuing.
www.noc.com

Survival Courses from 88 Tactical at their Tekamah Training Facility in Nebraska
With introductory to advanced courses ranging from 8 hours to 48 hours, 88 Tactical offers skillset training you can benefit from regardless of skill level.
www.88tactical.com

Delicious or Deadly?
Wild Mushroom Foraging 101

By Phillip Meeks

When you mention harvesting — and eating — wild mushrooms, though, especially in a room full of people who've never experienced more than the store-bought variety, get ready to see expressions of admiration shift to skepticism.

That's for good reason, perhaps. According to the National Poison Data Center, there are over 7,000 exposures to toxic mushrooms in the U.S. annually. Of these, 39 per year result in major harm, and statistically, 2.9 per year prove fatal.

For those who make it a point to learn

Warning! This article is meant to be an overview and not a detailed guide on identifying and consuming edible mushrooms. Seek guidance from a trained mycologist before attempting to eat any mushrooms. Any attempt to consume mushrooms shall solely be at the reader's risk.

A good knife and a couple of mesh bags should be in the forager's tool kit.

a few wild mushrooms, though, nutritional rewards await. Mushrooms have more protein than most vegetables. They hold high levels of riboflavin and niacin and trace amounts of vitamin C, B1, B12, D, and E, according to the *International Journal of Microbiology*. Vegetarians, especially, can benefit from adding mushrooms to their diet, not only because of the protein levels, but also because mushrooms are the only nonanimal food source of vitamin D.

Medicinally, species of fungi have been shown to have antioxidant, anticancer, antiallergic, antiviral, and antibacterial characteristics, again according to the *International Journal of Microbiology*.

Knowing What's Out There

Foraging for mushrooms isn't a leap one should make without being anchored to knowledgeable allies. Between 5,000 and 10,000 species of mushrooms are native to North America. Of these, about 100 are considered edible and roughly the same number are counted as toxic.

The old saying that "all mushrooms are edible once" shouldn't be put to the test. You should be certain of the identification beyond the shadow of a doubt before ingesting any wild mushroom. In fact, learning just one or two edible species each year and then expanding your repertoire slowly is advisable to ensure that you know your chosen fungi well.

Tools for mushroom hunting will include a sharp knife, a good camera, and a few mesh bags to allow spores to be dispersed as you walk. Field guides for your location are good to include — not just identification books for mushrooms, but also for associated trees if you aren't already familiar with common species.

If you have a reliable cell signal, iNaturalist is a beneficial app. You can post pictures and location data that other enthusiasts can view, and multiple experts can offer input on the taxonomy of your discoveries. The Mushroom Identification Forum on Facebook is another social media tool. With 170,000 members, there's a good chance someone has seen the mushroom in question before.

Whenever you're relying on photos for identification, take detailed pictures of both the upper and underneath portions of the cap, as well as the stalk. Note whether it arises from the ground, from dead wood or a living tree. Species may be distinguished by the presence of gills, pores, or other spore structures.

Spore prints can also be useful. Put the mushroom cap — spore structure down — on a sheet of paper, hydrate the cap with a few drops of water, and cover it with a cup or glass for a few hours. The color and arrangement of the resulting print can aid in identification.

Help in the Flesh

As valuable as books or online resources may be, these methods aren't nearly as beneficial as seeing mushrooms in their natural habitat alongside someone who knows.

"The best advice I can give for people wanting to forage for edible mushrooms is to join a local mushroom club," says Dr. Jean Williams-Woodward, University of Georgia Extension plant pathologist. "Here, we have the Mushroom Club of Georgia. The clubs often conduct forays where people can learn to identify and locate edible mushrooms in person."

If you can't stand shoulder-to-shoulder with an expert in the mushroom's habitat, bring the mushroom to the expert. Don't sweat about picking a mushroom for identification later. It's not the same thing as yanking up a wildflower. What we call mushrooms are the fruiting bodies of a complex network of vegetative fibers we can't see beneath the soil surface or under the bark of a tree. The mushrooms are analogous to the apples on an apple tree, springing forth from an extensive hidden organism that has successfully colonized a fallen log, a standing tree, or a patch of soil.

Raw or Cooked?

Most of us have eaten raw mushrooms from salad bars, but cooking any mushroom is a good idea for a couple of reasons. First of all, the cell walls of fungi contain chitin, a fibrous substance. Breaking down the chitin via cooking will make the mushrooms easier to digest, as well as making the nutrients within more accessible.

Connoisseurs often opt against washing their mushrooms, citing the fungi's ability to soak up water like a sponge. Given that characteristic, brushing off the visible dirt and then cooking the mushrooms is a means of "cleaning" your harvest. If that leaves you squeamish, a quick rinse is acceptable, but definitely refrain from soaking them.

Finding that first morel in the spring can be a thrill for a forager.

Size, color, and shape of morels can vary considerably.

Some You'd Want to Eat

Morels (*Morchella* species)

It's fair to say that many mushroom hunters get their start with the elusive morels. I decided to seek them out one Easter in Kentucky, adhering to the local lore of waiting until "the poplar leaves are as big as a mouse ear." I walked a hundred yards along a skid trail beneath a tulip-poplar forest without finding a single "dry-land fish" (as they're known in some locales). When I did an about face to return to my starting point, I collected a pound along that same trail I had failed to see earlier.

Mushrooms in the genus *Morchella* are considered the true morels, and several species are indigenous to North America. (There's some debate on exactly how many species there are, as these mushrooms have been classified and reclassified over the years.) Foragers may distinguish them as black, white, gray, or yellow or identify them based on the trees they're typically found beneath.

Morchella species grow throughout the U.S. In my part of the world, I find black morels in tulip-poplar woods first and larger white morels in old orchards or beneath sycamores. Certain morels can be found under elms and sugar maples. Forest fire sites can be good locations as well.

The false morel is a toxic look-alike for which distinguishing characteristics are described later.

Chanterelles (*Cantharellus* species)

As with morels, there are multiple species within the *Cantharellus* genus commonly referred to as chanterelles, and these are distributed throughout North America. However, species within the same family, but within different genera are also called chanterelles, such as the prized black trumpet or black chanterelle (*Craterellus cornucopioides*). And as with morels, there's debate about the classification.

Chanterelles grow from the ground and not attached to trees or logs, and they can

Chanterelles emerge individually from the soil — not in clumps from wood like some look-alikes.

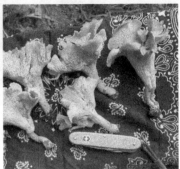

A feature of chanterelles is the presence of false gills.

be found in both hardwood and coniferous forests in the summer and fall. The golden chanterelle (*Cantharellus cibarius*) is perhaps one of the most easily recognized species in the genus, with a yellow to yellow-orange color and, some say, a fruity aroma.

Chicken of the woods (*Laetiporus sulphureus*)

Some consider this firm, orange and yellow fungus to be a good choice for beginning foragers, as it stands out like a neon sign. You'll find chicken of the woods

It's not unheard of to harvest 50 pounds of chicken of the woods from a single tree.

The pheasant back or dryad's saddle is said to have a lemony flavor that goes well with chicken or fish.

Two experts correctly identified this eastern cauliflower mushroom within an hour of posting it on the iNaturalist app.

A translucent ghost fungus (nonedible) — an interest in edible mushrooms will spark a broader interest in fungi in general.

in the summer and fall growing on logs or standing trees (living or dead). In addition to the bright colors that catch your eye, the underside will be marked by pores rather than gills.

This colorful mushroom has a texture that allows it to be used as a substitute for chicken — coated in batter and fried or added to pasta or soup.

Note that there are *Laetiporus* species in the western U.S. and Great Lakes region that are considered mildly toxic. Until recently, these were believed to be *Laetiporus sulphureus*, but they tend to grow on conifers (and on eucalyptus in the case of one). Just to be safe, only harvest chicken of the woods from hardwoods.

Hen of the woods (*Grifola frondosa*)

While the name will make you believe it's a close relative of *Laetiporus* species, hen of the woods (also known as maitake) isn't even in the same family. This species is a large mushroom, comprised of lobes that fan out from a central core.

More often than not, hen of the woods is found attached to the base of living oaks in late summer through fall. Just like *Laetiporus*, it has pores underneath rather than gills, and the upper portions are wavy and brown, bringing to mind the tailfeathers of a hen.

Hen of the woods is found in the northeastern and mid-Atlantic United States and Canada. Once you find an oak that hosts this species, you can return to the same tree again and again to harvest the fruiting bodies.

Some You Don't Want to Eat

Death caps and death angels (*Amanita* species)

An estimated 90 to 95 percent of mushroom-related deaths in North American are due to ingestion of the *Amanita* genus, according to the *Journal of Forensic Science*. Of those deaths, *Amanita phalloides*

Galerina marginata

Death caps and death angels

False morel

Jack-o-lantern mushrooms

(the death cap mushroom) is responsible for more than 90 percent, and while this species isn't native to North America, it has been introduced and is quite common along the West Coast of our continent.

Other species of *Amanita* are native to North America and widely distributed. Multiple species share the common name of death angel. One cap from an *Amanita* mushroom can contain a lethal dose of toxin.

Amanitas can be recognized by volvas (veils at the base through which the stalk protrudes) and white spore prints. They'll sometimes (but not always) have warts and stem rings.

Galerina marginata

A little brown mushroom that contains amanitin, the same toxin as that in death caps and death angels, *Galerina marginata* can be found year-round in both coniferous and hardwood forests all across North America.

This species is typically attached to wood and sometimes grows in clusters, and while it's relatively nondescript, it can be distinguished from look-alikes by its spore print, which will appear rusty brown in color.

It's estimated that 15 to 20 caps of this species will provide a lethal dose to adults.

False morels (*Gyromitra* species)

Only 20 cases of false morel poisoning have been reported in the United States since 1900, but half of those proved fatal, according to the *Journal of the American Board of Family Medicine*.

Gyromitra species are distributed widely across the United States and typically emerge in the spring.

Rather than the pitted caps seen on true morels, this toxic look-alike will have a cap that more closely resembles a smashed and wrinkled brain on a stalk. Slicing the mushrooms open lengthwise, the true morels are hollow, but the insides of the false can be somewhat cottony in texture.

Jack-o-lanterns (*Omphalotus illudens*)

Jack-o-lantern mushrooms are often found growing in the same habitats and at the same time as chanterelles, so the two can be easily mistaken.

While you may see several chanterelles together, they'll be separated on different stalks that emerge from the soil, while jack-o-lanterns will grow from wood in clumps. Furthermore, the stalk of chanterelles will have a texture reminiscent of string cheese.

Jack-o-lantern mushrooms have blade-like gills beneath the cap, whereas chanterelles have false gills more akin to wrinkles. Right in line with its Halloween-inspired common name, the jack-o-lantern has the characteristic of being bioluminescent.

If you suspect that you or someone you know has eaten a toxic mushroom, get medical attention immediately. Contact the Poison Control Center at (800) 222-1222, and the call will be routed to a nurse or pharmacist near you. If it's possible to take a sample of the ingested mushroom to the emergency room with the patient, do so.

The Legalities of the Hunt

A limited number of mushrooms for personal use may be harvested from U.S. Forest Service lands. The limit is one gallon per day or five gallons per season. If the harvest exceeds this, or if the mushrooms are to be marketed, a permit will be required.

This can vary if the species of interest is listed as threatened or endangered in the area or in regards to harvesting in designated special biological areas. The rules are more variable in regards to National Park Service property as well as state forests and state parks. If you intend to forage on public lands, it's wise to check with a manager first to avoid legal woes in the long run.

Labeling requirements and other regulations that relate to selling wild-harvested mushrooms at farmers markets or other outlets will be location-specific. Check with the market manager or your county's Cooperative Extension office for the most reliable information.

Foraging for wild mushrooms can be a rewarding proposition, with nutritional, gourmet products to be found from spring through fall. For those new to the game, there's a lot of homework to do. Guidebooks, online communities, face-to-face time with experts, or, preferably, all of the above can help you gain the knowledge to feast safely. And if there's ever any doubt as to a collected mushroom's identity, it's best to just walk away.

About the Author

Phillip Meeks is an agriculture and natural resources educator originally from Tennessee, but now based in the mountains of Southwest Virginia. He likes to spend his weekends hiking, gardening, beekeeping, fishing, and mushroom hunting.

Golden chanterelles sautéed in butter on the top; strips of chicken of the woods grilled with peppers and onions on the bottom.

72-Hour Ziploc Bag Challenge

Lessons Learned from Three Days Surviving in the Desert with a Quart-Sized Plastic Bug-Out Bag

By Kevin Estela

Warning! This 72-hour survival challenge was performed by a professional survival instructor under close supervision by rescue personnel. Do not attempt any potentially dangerous survival challenge without prior training, and always establish contingency plans in case something goes wrong.

The gear the author was allowed to carry needed to fit inside a closed 1-quart plastic bag.

Working for Fieldcraft Survival, I've learned to expect each day to be filled with the unexpected. We have a highly dynamic work environment with new projects and tasks on a regular basis. One day, we're scouting land for upcoming courses, the next we're flying to another state to teach a defensive handgun class, the next we're filming online content in the mountains — you get the idea. In June 2021, my boss Mike Glover challenged me to survive for 72 hours in the desert with nothing more than the contents of a quart-sized Ziploc bag. Since I was hired to be the lead survival subject matter expert, I wasn't going to pass up this opportunity.

Statistically speaking, most emergencies last no more than 72 hours. Within those 72 hours, a person can self-rescue, problem solve, and affect their situation to prevent the emergency from becoming a survival scenario. There's no doubt anyone can be thrust into an emergency bivouac or short-term emergency in their day-to-day travels. In an unfortunate circumstance like that, the contents of one's pockets or a small emergency kit may be the only gear available. Pocket gear will generally not take up more space than what can fit into a quart-sized Ziploc bag. Hypothetically, a person should be able to survive 72 hours in a given environment with a quart-sized kit designed to address basic survival needs. Hypotheticals are good for debate, but practical exercises are better for proof. I recently took a single Ziploc to the high desert and survived triple-digit heat and gained many teachable points to share here.

Kevin Estela is the Director of Training for Fieldcraft Survival, with over two decades of outdoor skill teaching experience. He drew upon his edible plant knowledge to sustain himself for the 72-hour challenge.

Planning

Mission always dictates gear. Surviving 72 hours in the high desert of Utah during the hottest month of the year meant shifting survival priorities around. Deciding whether shelter or water is priority number one is conditional on clothing and existing makeshift structures like a broken-down vehicle. Since this challenge required using the contents of the Ziploc, I carried a North American Rescue Emergency Wrap blanket to sleep under and an Adventure Medical Kits 1-Person Bivy to sleep inside of. In terms of water, I premeasured and marked 24 ounces on a collapsible bladder for easy use with Aquatabs. Aquatabs call for 1/10 gallons or 25 ounces and even if I were off by 1 ounce on my water collection, the tabs would work as expected.

Given the fire restrictions in the area, I packed some basics just for proof of concept including a Mini-BIC, Exotac nanoSTRIKER ferro rod, and some premade tinder. Cordage was carefully chosen with emphasis on smaller "disposable" cordage as a space-saver. Duct tape and superglue rounded out the kit for multipurpose use in binding and first-aid. Nutrition was a serious consideration in this challenge. Since most people carry plenty of food stores on their body in the form of fat, I knew I could go longer than 72 without food. That said, I didn't want to compromise my health. I packed a sleep aid, multi-vitamins, and rehydration tablets. Part of the challenge was an allowance of reasonable clothing. I couldn't pack a puffy jacket just for sleeping at night if I wouldn't normally wear it. This meant a pair of pants, boxers, a long-sleeve T-shirt, button-up shirt, wide-brim hat, sunglasses, neckerchief/scarf, and boots. I didn't carry a spare set of socks, and I didn't have gloves for hand protection with me.

Another thing worth noting is the large safety net the Fieldcraft Team cast for this challenge. I was monitored by our medic Austin Lester and I carried a small Kifaru Escape and Evasion Pack filled with an emergency medical kit, short-wave radio, electrolyte drink, Kestrel device for taking weather readings, and battery packs to recharge my electronics used to up-

These wild rose hips were dry but still edible. Collecting and processing them helped pass the time.

An emergency blanket was used, reflective side out, to create a shade structure for protection from the sun and 110-degree temperatures.

The author constructed a funnel fish trap out of narrow-leaf willow on day one. Unfortunately, the trap did not yield any fish.

The author used the stripped willow saplings to construct a bird trap. The trap was triggered by a field mouse.

date social media. I had an emergency trailer about a quarter mile from my location I wasn't allowed to enter, as well as my vehicle nearby. I had to remain in the environment on 2,500 acres of private land and not use the emergency provisions unless they were absolutely necessary.

This type of challenge is very rewarding to the participant, but it can be dangerous if precautions aren't in place.

Practice

Starting at 7 a.m. on Tuesday, I immediately went to work creating a shade structure before the temperatures rose too high. I pinned down one long side of my emergency blanket with rocks and propped up the other side with two sticks and some tarred twine with pebbles acting as "buttons" rolled up inside the corners. With a basic sun structure set up, I moved to the river about a quarter mile away. I used my marked bladder to measure out approximately 2 gallons of water and carried it in the Reynolds Oven Bags doubled up for strength. My button-up shirt was used as a makeshift backpack with the sleeves tied up around the waist as well as the collar. I carried my water higher off the ground from thistle and spiky plants that could have torn my bag. Instead of risking popping my emergency water bladder by lifting and moving it, I used the small length of tubing to create a flexible straw to drink from. After establishing the essentials, I built up my bedding with local vegetation before taking the first of three daily siestas from 10:30 to 2:30 each day when the sun was hottest.

Over the next three days, I kept a busy schedule to prevent boredom. This meant building projects like a single-funnel fish trap, Lincoln-log bird trap, chopsticks, and a slingshot (even though I didn't plan on hunting anything due to local hunting restrictions). Some of these items served to demonstrate concepts rather than generate immediate results. While my fish trap didn't yield anything edible, my makeshift fishing rod made from a 7-foot length of narrow-leaf willow did. I caught two small trout that I later cooked with fire extinguishers and safety officers on standby to prevent any risk of wildfire. Fishing helped keep me sane, so it was part of the daily routine along with gathering water. During one trip to the creek, I spotted two beavers, making the decision to pack and use purification tabs extremely justified. As one day carried into the next, the temperature continued to climb from 99 to 104 degrees F. On the final day, I decided to jump in the creek with all my clothes on, only to find they'd dry off in under an hour in the hot and dry air.

There's an old Spanish proverb that "the belly rules the mind." Even though I could survive on my body's fat stores, there'd definitely be associated hunger pains from not eating frequently. My first real meal was on day two — roughly 30 hours into the event — and it consisted of broad-leaf plantain, dandelion, clover, and a couple flexible stems of mullein spiced up with a single-serve packet of Cholula. I snacked when I could and found golden currants on the verge of ripeness with a bit of astringence to be regular trail nibbles. I carried single-serving ghee/coconut

The author dunked his Tilley hat in the water to cool off.

Fishing resulted in catching two small trout.

oil packets I planned on using every six hours on the final day; this nominal source of calories and energy from fat was a welcomed treat. I was used to a schedule of intermittent fasting with an eight-hour-per-day eating window already. This helped prepare me for ignoring the pain of hunger experienced on this challenge. Even though I found food to eat from the land, I definitely experienced fatigue from a lack of calories.

Each night, I used the Wolf21 sleep supplement and was able to get between seven and eight hours of sleep easily. Sleep is highly underrated, and it provides the body with time to recover both mentally and physically. Temps dropped to about 60 degrees at night, and I found I climbed into my emergency bivy only when the wind picked up. Sleeping out in the open, I was exposed to some insects and occasionally felt them crawling on my face and neck. It's an inconvenient reality of roughing it that interrupts an otherwise peaceful night's sleep.

I wrapped up the 72-hour challenge with great energy. I made a single cup of cold coffee and smoked a celebratory cigar. Over three days, I dropped from a pre-challenge carb-loading weight of 207 to 199 with my usual weight around 202.5. I used most of the kit with the exception of the superglue, compass, and zip ties. Other than that, all the items I carried found their

Small fish can be eaten whole. Cook until their eyes turn white.

Hot sauce can be used to spice up locally harvested greens like clover, dandelion, and plantain. The inner pith of flexible mullein stalks can also be eaten.

way into my solution to spending time in an incredibly inhospitable environment.

Post-Action

After a few sleep cycles, it was easy for me to begin assessing what worked and what didn't. As always, the devil is in the details, and it's only by testing gear in realistic scenarios that we can learn and modify our preparedness. There really isn't any gear I would've swapped out of my kit given the size constraints of the package it had to be carried in. Of course, there were many times I wished I had a more substantial knife, a larger tarp, a metal container to make hot drinks, a closed-foam sleeping pad, a mosquito head net, and a better fishing setup. That said, these items couldn't fit in the Ziploc and were just wishful thinking.

If there were any items I wished I had that did fit, they were simply more of what was already in the bag. On the third day, my slingshot band snapped. I wished I had brought a spare. I wished I doubled my electrolyte tablets. I wished I had drink mixes and small packets of salt, as I began craving it more with more of my body's salt escaping through sweat. Even something as simple as chewing gum could've been useful to take the taste of bitter plants out of my mouth. As I used my knives to carve and build, I noticed the edges getting dull. I picked up some smooth stones to sharpen the blades, but a simple diamond hone would've worked quicker and with less effort. Looking back at the experience, even something as simple as barbed hooks instead of barbless flies could've been beneficial when the trout bit but weren't landed because of this easy oversight.

In terms of clothing, everything I wore worked as planned. My scarf was wet each day and worn around my neck to cool off. My boots were breathable enough to prevent my feet from suffering the effects of poor hygiene. My pants were durable enough to endure walking through brush and slipping down hillsides as I navigated the scree. Something noteworthy is the eye protection I wore. My shooting glasses have a wraparound lens providing better protection from the light stimulus that works underneath and around standard "flat" sunglasses. That saved me literal headaches from the brightness.

While I had a medic on hand for major injuries and illnesses, I could've probably had a more substantial med kit with me in my bag. While I planned to pull the plug on the experience in the event of a major issue, minor issues were going to be treated with makeshift med gear, which is simply never as good as proper medical supplies. Next time, I'll stash some triple antibiotic ointment, some finger bandages, and maybe some pills for common issues.

To keep the fish fresh, the author kept them alive on a micro-cord stringer until they were ready to be eaten.

Kit Breakdown

SHELTER:
- North American Rescue Rescue Wrap
- Stay Outside Longer (SOL) Emergency Bivy Sack

WATER:
- Fieldcraft Survival Collapsible Bladder
- Reynolds Oven Bags
- 3-Foot Vinyl Tubing
- 30 Aquatabs

FIRE:
- Mini BIC lighter
- Exotac nanoSTRIKER
- 4x Procamptek Tinder Plugs

KNIVES:
- Victorinox Farmer
- ESEE Knives S35VN Izula With Duct-Tape Edge Guard

CORDAGE AND UTILITY:
- 6-Foot Duct Tape
- 12.6 Feet 550 Paracord
- 25-Foot Braided Tarred Catahoula Line
- 3-Foot Stainless Steel Wire
- 1x Single Use Superglue
- 2x Small Cable Ties
- 1x Button Compass
- 1x Quart-Size Ziploc

FISHING AND "HUNTING":
- Assorted Dry Flies
- 6-Foot 4x Fly-Fishing Tippet
- 25-Foot 50-Pound Test Spiderwire
- Assorted Hooks, Split Shot, Snap Swivels
- 2x Sheffield Floats
- 1x Theraband Slingshot Band

NUTRITION:
- 6x Wolf21 Sleep Supplements
- 3x Nuun Hydration Tablets
- 3x Kifaru Revival Packets
- 3x Ghee/Coconut Oil Packs
- 3x Black Rifle Coffee Instant Coffee Packs
- 1x Cholula Hot Sauce Packet

Closing Thoughts

Overall, this experience was a testament to proper prior planning and a firm understanding of survival fundamentals. It wasn't comfortable, but it was educational and a deed that'll hopefully help fellow readers recognize ways to improve their own preparedness. We intend to continue pushing the limits of this 72-hour challenge with different players and kit limitations. Just as the challenge continues to evolve, we hope the collective understanding of what's needed to survive 72 hours in an emergency evolves too. For more information, please follow Fieldcraft Survival **@fieldcraftsurvival** and **fieldcraftsurvival.com**.

8 › Weapons

Hunger Games

Build Your Own Survival Stick Bow

Story and Photos by Tim MacWelch

Cool leaves of yellow and red pelted my face and hands in the autumn breeze. The wind was in my face, blowing from my quarry toward me. Good, I thought, one more advantage. He wouldn't be able to smell me. I waited for my prey to move clear of the vegetation, as one stray vine or branch could send my arrow careening off target. The shot was lining up perfectly. It was as if I were watching this happen to someone else. I was detached, emotionless, and simply allowing things to happen.

Age-old instincts took hold, and I began to draw the bow. My camouflage was perfect, right down to the bark still clinging to the back of my field-built bow. I drew the nock of the arrow to the right corner of my mouth. Then, to my dismay, the wooden bow made a sound like the "tick" of some large clock. My prey, a fat gray squirrel, looked right at me and bolted faster than my arrow could follow. I muttered a curse under my breath, and then fixed myself on the same thought that my ancestors must have thought on 10,000 failed hunts before me: next time ...

It's entirely true that a field-built bow has a lot of quirks, ticks, and actual ticking sounds as you break-in the wood fibers (or actually break them). But if you don't have access to a bow after wolfing down the last of your emergency food supplies and firing your last round, it's nice to know that you can build your own bow just as our forebears once did. The natural materials for the archery tackle haven't changed at all in 10 millennia — all you need is wood, fiber, glue, feathers, and a sharp point for each arrow.

So maybe you're a hunter, looking to take things to the next level by building your own equipment. Or perhaps you're a serious prepper, interested in yet another backup method of food procurement. Or maybe you just watched the movie *Predator* one too many times as a kid and want to build an alien-slaying primitive bow, worthy of Arnold himself. Whatever the motivation, we're glad you're here. Bow making is an ancestral art form dating back thousands of years and appears in almost every traditional culture on earth. It's a means of hunting for food and fighting back against predatory animals and similarly motivated humans.

Making your own bows, arrows, and archery tackle are also a confidence builder and quite a bit of fun. Read along, and we'll give you the beginner's guide to the tools, materials, and techniques for survival bow making.

The Setup

You may imagine that you'd need an entire woodworking shop to build a wooden bow, and certainly, that wouldn't hurt. But you can also do all of the important work with a fixed-blade knife, a multitool, and a billet to strike the spine of the fixed-blade knife that will baton your way through the wood (see "Firewood Fundamentals" in Issue 10 of OG). The knife and multitool could be part of your normal everyday carry gear, and to finish off your bow-making toolkit, carry a few bow strings, some thread, a few fletchings, and some arrowheads.

Modern "glue-on" broad heads or "trade blank" points can be bought from specialty catalogs and websites, and are similar to the ones that were once traded to native cultures by Europeans. If you're particularly handy, you could chip arrowheads from

Making Bows = Breaking Bows

It's been said by wiser bowyers than me, that a fully drawn bow is a stick that's almost broken. This is an unpleasant thing to imagine, especially when you have to invest so much time and labor into the process of bow-making. Yes, the lovely bow that you have carefully crafted could break at any time. It could be a hidden flaw in the wood, or more likely, an error in craftsmanship. But there are a few ways to prevent untimely breaks and cracks in your finished stick bow:

› Never over-draw your bow (bending it farther than it was meant to bend).
› Don't cut through the growth rings on the back of the bow.
› Taper the belly of the bow smoothly. Abrupt changes in the bow's thickness create "hinges." These are spots where the bow limb literally folds and creases, leading to breakage.
› Protect the finished bow from dings, cuts, scrapes, and scratches. Don't use the bow as a tool, pry bar, walking stick, digging stick, etc. Damage to the bow's surface creates weak points, and weak points lead to breakage.

Oil the bow with grease from your first kill. Wipe some warm animal fat into the bow limbs to keep them supple, prevent cracking and prevent moisture from soaking into the bow. A dry bow is a snappier bow, while a damp bow is more sluggish.

stone or glass. You could also improvise your own bow strings from 550 cord, but a word of caution: 550 cord is a bit too elastic for the job of bowstring, even after stretching and twisting.

Finally, you'll need the bow stick (also called a stave or billet, respectively). This can be a recently deceased sapling or branch from a larger tree. You'll want it dead and dry (but not rotten) for same-day use. If you can wait a few weeks, you could also cut a live sapling and allow it to dry in the shade, ideally with any cut ends sealed with paint or glue to prevent cracking. Do a bit of research to find out about the favored bow woods used by the native peoples of your area. Chances are good that those are your top choices.

In the East, I go out of my way to get hickory and black locust. I've also used ash, oak, maple, and other local hardwoods with good results. For those in the Midwest, look for osage orange, which is excellent. Midwesterners can also try more flexible species of juniper. And for the West Coast, try your hand with yew and cedar.

And while you're assembling your supplies, treat yourself to a strip of leather for an armguard. This may save you from a nasty bruise or large blister if you are shooting with bare forearms. A pencil is handy too, though a chunk of charcoal will suffice. A piece of 100-grit sandpaper and a tape measure will finish out your supplies for your first bow.

The How-To:
Step 1: Pick your Stave

This is where you begin striding down the golden path to glory, or the nature trail to hell. You need to select a suitable bow wood species, and it needs to be a good specimen. Start with one of the woods listed above, such as hickory or black locust. Osage orange is a little finicky for beginners. The bow we are creating here is a "quickie" stick bow. It will be more forgiving if the finished bow is longer, rather than shorter.

Start with a dead branch or sapling that shows no sign of rotting (no fungus, and the bark is tightly attached). It could be 6 or 7 feet long when cut in the field, and worked down to 5 or 6 feet long for the finished bow. Pick a stave that's relatively straight and free of knots, side branches, and twists. It should also be about 2 inches in diameter at the thicker end.

Again, if you plan to work the wood later, cut a live sapling and dry it for a few weeks, preferably a few months.

Step 2: Plan Your Bow's Shape

This means that you'll need to find the bow's belly, back, grip, and lay out the limbs. Start by figuring out which way the stick "wants" to bend. Hold the bow stave upright, with one end on the ground. Generally, this is the thicker end on the ground, in the orientation that the sapling once grew. Grab the top of the stave loosely with one hand and push on the middle of the stave. The stick should naturally swivel to indicate its tendency to bend. The outside of the bend is known as the "back" of the bow, and it is the side of the bow that faces your target. The inside of the curve is called the "belly," and it faces the archer.

Be careful not to mix up these terms (or sides) as you work. Since the back receives the tension when the bow is drawn, damage to the outer growth ring on the back can cause the bow to break.

Don't carve, hack, or saw into the back of the bow.

Finally, figure out where your grip will be. Find the middle point of the stave and mark out a 6-inch grip area in the middle. The belly area of the grip will remain unworked (for now). The wood above the grip is called the upper limb, the wood below is the lower limb.

Step 3: Shape the Belly

Bend your prospective bow again, pushing on the grip area from the belly side of the bow. Do this repeatedly and study the way that the upper and lower limbs bend. Generally speaking, the thicker limbs don't bend as much and will require more carving than the thinner limb. Look for areas that bend and spots that don't. Mark the areas that don't bend. Rest the bow stave against a tree, ideally in the fork of a tree. Use your fixed-blade knife and a baton to begin removing wood from the belly of the bow where you have marked them as stiff. Thin down the areas that don't bend, and for now, leave alone the sections that do bend.

Your goal for this rough shaping process is to leave the back of the bow untouched,

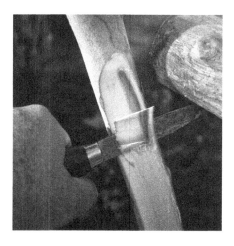

and to get the limbs to bend equally by thinning down the belly of the bow. Go slowly and bend the bow often to check your progress. The grip and limb tips (ears) shouldn't bend at this point. Once the stave is bending equally and looking a bit like a bow, you're ready to put a string on it to more accurately see its action. Remember that thick staves require a significant amount of carving, but they typically yield stronger bows. And conversely, slender staves may only need a little belly shaping, but they're often weak bows.

Step 4: Cut Your Notches (Carefully!)

This can be the part were neophyte bowyers destroy all of their hard work. Notch cutting on the bow ears must be done carefully. Use the saw on your multitool to cut small matching notches on the both sides of each bow ear. Cut them on an angle, thinking about the direction the string will pull from each ear toward the grip. Do NOT saw into the back of the bow, just cut into the sides. These cuts should be shallow, just enough to seat the bow string. Attach your string to both ears. It doesn't need to be tight yet; this is simply for testing. Don't be tempted to do your best *Hunger Games* pose yet either, drawing a rough-shaped bow is a great way to shatter it!

Step 5: What the Hell Is Tillering?

Chances are good that you've never heard the word "tillering" before. It's simply a word that means thinning and shaping, usually in the context of woodworking. And that's what we are doing next.

Cut off a nearby tree branch, about head height, leaving a stub. You could also use some similar way to affix the bow grip. Pull downward on the bow string, gently at first. Carefully study how the limbs bend. You want to see each limb bending equally across its full length. You also want to make sure that the limbs bend equally — compared to each other. The two limbs should look like a mirror image of each other when bent. Use your pencil again to mark areas that are not bending enough. I like to shade them in aggressively, then carve away the marks completely, yet cautiously. It's best to take your string off when carving, so you don't accidentally nick it or cut it.

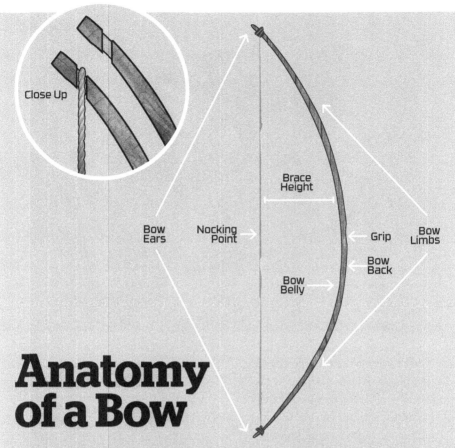

Anatomy of a Bow

Back: This is the side of the bow that faces away from you as you pull on the bow string. The back of the bow is toward the target. If a bow breaks, the back will often produce splinters of wood, as the back is under tension due to the wood fibers pulling away from each other.

Belly: The belly of the bow is on the inside of the bow, facing you as you pull the bow string. If a bow breaks, the belly may hinge or fold while breaking due to the fibers being compacted in the belly. In modern archery, the belly is now called the "face."

Bowyer: A person who makes bows.

Brace height: The distance from the grip to the string when the bow is strung. The Old English term is "Fistmele," which is the length of your hand when giving a "thumb's up."

Ears: Each end of each limb is referred to as an ear, basically the last couple of inches on each end of the bow.

Grip: The grip is the middle of the bow where you actually grip it.

Limb: Each end of the bow is considered a limb, so every bow has two limbs, even though it may be made from one limb of a tree.

Stave: A solid stick of wood that will be made into a bow, also referred to as a "bow stave."

Arrowheads are modern glue-on broad-head, trade blank metal point, a stone point, and a beer bottle point.

Tillering may take a while, perhaps hours, but this is how you make a bow. Recheck your strung bow frequently, and continue tillering until you feel you are pulling the string nearly to your draw length. Draw length is measured by holding a bow and pull the string back as if to fire and arrow. Measure the length between the grip and your jaw. Most draw lengths are around 28 to 30 inches for adults. Shorter folks and kids have shorter draw lengths, taller folks have longer ones.

Step 6: Finishing

Continue tillering, checking your limb bend and checking your draw length until you are feeling confident that your bow feels like a real bow. Sand down or carefully carve the belly of the bow to smooth it and remove any "chop marks" from your baton work. This is critical to eliminate weak points. Chop marks tend to create hinge points in the belly, which lead to breaks in the bow back. If you're curious about the poundage of the bow, you can test it now by getting a 5-foot piece of 2x4 lumber.

Use a tape measure and pencil to mark the inches on the lumber, up to 30 inches. Stand the lumber vertically on a standard bathroom scale. Set the bow grip on top of the lumber and pull the string down across the numbers you've marked. When you've pulled down on the string to a full draw length, check the scale reading for a good estimate of your draw weight. You can use a 25- to 35-pound draw weight bow for small-game hunting and target practice. You'll need a 40- to 60-pound draw weight for bigger game animals.

Conclusion

Bow-making and arrow-making are some of the most challenging feats of

Take Aim and Fire!

We could write a whole book on traditional bow marksmanship and aiming ... and still not cover it all. But if you can stay alive long enough to get in lots of practice, you can learn a lot through observation and experience. So, to keep you alive that long (hopefully), here are the bare-bones basics.

First, you'll need to figure out your dominant eye. You can use the same trick that many early shooters use. Outstretch your arms, make a triangle or circle with both hands, and pick a distant object to look at through your hand opening (both eyes open). Take turns closing your right eye and left eye, to see which one is still looking at the distant object. The eye that's still on target (or sort-of on target) is your dominant eye. If you are right-eye dominant, hold the bow grip in your left fist and shoot across your left knuckles. If you are left-eye dominant, hold the bow grip in your right hand and shoot across your right knuckles. This puts your dominant eye looking right down the shaft. I'm right handled, but left-eye dominant. As such, I've been working on my "southpaw" shooting. Let me tell you without hesitation, eye dominance matters more than hand dominance.

Next, eliminate the variables. Make a mark on your bow grip so your hand always grasps the exact same spot. Then tie a wad of thread around your bow string to create a nocking point that matches the top of your grip. Don't tie your bowstring itself into a knot to create this lump in the string. That's too much stress on the bow string. Use a separate string tied in place.

Then start shooting the bow at a soft target, like a decaying stump. See whether you are more accurate with your arrow nock over or under the nocking point on the string, and try different finger placements. And for safety, wear a glove on the hand that is holding the bow, so that rough fletchings don't scratch up your hand.

Finally – practice, practice, and practice. Make certain that you draw the bow to the same spot for each shot. Try to keep your back "flat" when you are at full draw, and parallel to the target and arrow's path. And then practice some more.

craftsmanship you can take on during a survival situation, but they are also proven and vetted game changers. The skills of bow and arrow making, and archery itself, could make you an invaluable member of your team or group. With a serviceable bow and a few well-built arrows, it's possible to take down a variety of game animals (some of which are almost impossible to take without projectile weapons).

After taking small game like rabbits, opossums, and raccoons, you can feed yourself for a day. By taking deer and large game, you can feed yourself for a month or provide for a whole camp of people for many days. In darker times, archery could even be used as a means of self-defense, but let's all hope it doesn't come to that.

Archery and bow-making, like many skills, carry a big learning curve, so it's best to start working on them now, rather than later. And despite all the blisters, splinters, and tears, this can be an immensely rewarding pursuit and quite possibly — your new favorite hobby! ❖

Build Your Own Arrows

As you've seen, there's quite a bit of detail involved in the construction of seemingly simple survival stick bows. You'll have to pay close attention to craftsmanship if you're planning to build bows for the next Katniss Everdeen or some kind of dystopian Robin Hood. But now it's time for a bombshell. The bow isn't the hardest thing to make. At the end of the day (or the end of civilization), the bow is just a bendy stick with a string on it. That's all it is, a stick and a string.

The part that really takes some skill to create is the projectile, better known as the arrow. A great bow won't help us to survive without a proper set of arrows to fire from it. And if you thought bow making was hard, try crafting aerodynamic arrows from

Sources:

Hunting & Gathering Survival Manual
www.amazon.com

Three Rivers Achery Supply
www.3RiversArchery.com

Traditional Bowyer's Bibles
www.boisdarcpress.com

scratch – out in the woods. Arrow-making is where your biggest challenge lies. But don't let me scare you off. I'm just adjusting your expectations. Our ancestors built fine arrows from raw materials in the wild, and so can we. Here are the basic steps:

Step 1: Find slender and straight saplings, reeds, cane, or bamboo that are already arrow shaft diameter ($5/16$ inch underneath the bark for hardwood, a little thicker for hollow things like cane). Let nature do the work growing the perfect materials. Don't waste your time trying to whittle a log into an arrow shaft.

Step 2: Trim and straighten the arrow shafts. You'll need to trim, carve, or sand off anything that is not contributing to the perfect dowel shape. Cut the shafts a little longer than you think you'll need. Finished arrows should span from the nock to about 2 inches past your knuckles at full draw. The material should be dead, but not rotten. Straighten any curved or crooked spots by warming the spot over a fire, bending it a little beyond straight, and holding the spot in that position until cool. This heating (holding) cooling process helps the woody materials to retain a new shape, which could be "straight" if you do it right.

Step 3: Saw the notch and add the fletching. Carefully saw a notch (aka nock) about ½-inch deep into the end of the shaft (a multitool saw blade is usually the right size for this). It should match the width of your bow string. If using a hollow material, use a wooden plug and an insert and cut the notch in the solid wood – not the hollow shaft (unless you want to see the string cut the arrow in half). Then plan where your feathers will go in relation to the notch. Two feathers will need to line up with the notch, parallel to it.

With three feathers, the feathers will need to be equidistant from each other, with one feather perpendicular to the notch cut. These fletchings can be hard to accomplish without glue, even harder if you don't have a dead bird to provide a good assortment of feathers. Your feathers should match on each arrow. Use all right-wing feathers on one arrow, for example. Keep left wing and tail feathers together as well. Trim the fletching, apply glue if you have any, and tie them tightly in place with whatever string you can scrounge. Make sure the front edge of the fletching (toward the arrowhead) is smooth and well secured, or else it may scratch your hand as it glides across when fired.

Step 4: Attach your point. Small flat metal arrowheads would be a wonderful thing to add to your bug-out bag, along with a few proper bow strings. Saw a notch in the front of your arrow, then carve a slight tapering to the end of the shaft for better penetration. Glue the arrowhead in place, and bind it tightly with string. If you don't have metal points, try to make some or use stone or glass points you have chipped into a triangle shape. Failing all that, simply carve a point on the wooden shaft or leave it blunt to strike small game.

Improv Skills

Get Your Jason Bourne On By Turning These Five Common Items Into Self-Defense Weapons

Story by Jared Wihongi
Photos by Chris Vastardis

Warning! The content in this story is provided for illustrative purposes only and not meant to be construed as advice or instruction. Seek a reputable self-defense school first. Any use of the information contained in this article shall be solely at the reader's risk. This publication and its contributors are not responsible for any potential injuries.

The nature and history of combat is the utilization of weaponry, and victory most often goes to those who train with their weaponry. For an experienced prepper, this same philosophy can and should be applied to self-defense survival situations, so long as the weapon used is a legally appropriate response to the perceived threat.

Unfortunately, gone are the days when we can walk with a sword strapped to our side, and today's equivalent can't be carried legally in most parts of the world. Even in places where a firearm can be legally carried concealed or otherwise, many self-defense situations will not require the use of deadly force.

So, what are some of the best options for realistic everyday-carry (EDC) weaponry for when SHTF? There is a high likelihood that when you do need a self-defense tool, you'll be away from your at-home or in-car arsenal and be left with what you have on your person — or what's immediately in your surroundings. In an ideal world, you should always be carrying a variety of compact self-defense weapons on your person. Concealed-carry handgun, folding knife, and the like — the more options you have, the more prepared you'll be to deal with what may come. Unfortunately, many places in the United States and abroad don't allow for the carrying of guns, knives, or even common fist-loaded weapons like brass knuckles.

How can you convert everyday objects into improvised fist-loaded weapons that can be carried universally in even the most nonpermissive environments in the world? Following is a list of five common items that can be realistically carried in an EDC capacity, and some ideas on how they can be used as self-defense weapons.

Tactical Light

This item tops my list as one of the most useful and practical items that can be carried as a self-defense weapon. I've carried one on my person while traveling throughout many parts of the world. I've even kept one in my carry-on luggage for flights in multiple countries on five continents. As a common multi-function tool, I am yet to hear of a place where it's illegal. The only time mine was even scrutinized was at an airport in China, and they allowed it through because it didn't have the aggressive strike bezels found on many tactical lights. If you want a flashlight that does have strike bezels, look for one where they are removable. Take them off when going through a security check point, and put them back on afterward.

A handheld flashlight has practical functions in addition to being an ideal improvised self-defense weapon. The Stroboforce D-TAC 1000 (from www.theultimateknife.com) is one example of a tactical flashlight that doesn't look extra overly tactical.

Jared Wihongi, right, parries the punch, then "checks" the attacking arm so he can flank and gain control. From there he can counterstrike.

A tactical light can double as a temporary distraction device in low-light conditions when shone directly in the eyes. Something that cycles straight into a high-strobe mode is ideal, but even a constant beam can momentarily blind or distract an assailant. The window of opportunity gained should be utilized to make an escape, or to counterattack with "hammer fist" strikes.

Tactical Pen

Another item that I always have on my person is a tactical pen. Like the tactical light, it's a tool that has common everyday function. Defensively it can be used much like the tactical light, e.g. hammer-fist strikes to limbs, the torso, or the head/neck as necessary. It has a more focused point and as such can do more damage than a tactical light. Because I train often in double-wielded weapon combinations, in sticky situations I'll often carry my tactical light in my support hand as my distraction and secondary impact weapon, and my pen in my dominant hand as my primary

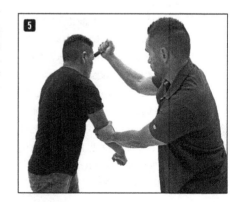

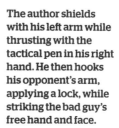

The author shields with his left arm while thrusting with the tactical pen in his right hand. He then hooks his opponent's arm, applying a lock, while striking the bad guy's free hand and face.

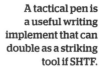

A tactical pen is a useful writing implement that can double as a striking tool if SHTF.

impact weapon. To avoid unnecessary attention, find a tactical pen that is strong enough to take a pounding, but discrete and "non-aggressive" in appearance.

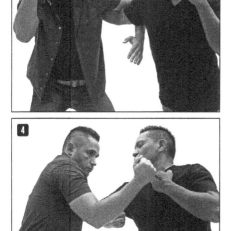

Rolled-Up Magazine

Another item I'll always have on my person while traveling: the most recent editions of RECOIL OFFGRID and RECOIL magazines. If you're into e-readers, this won't help much, but for those who like a good-old hardcopy of their favorite publication, a solid magazine rolled up tight can be become a short blunt weapon capable of delivering effective defensive and counteroffensive strikes.

Using a magazine as an improvised baton, Jared Wihongi stops the haymaker with a strike to the inside of the arm. He quickly traps the offending arm and follows up with several counters to the face.

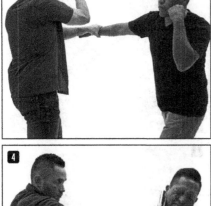

It offers more reach than a short fist-loaded weapon, and affords more protection of the hands by virtue of the strike surface being further away from the fingers. This might seem like a shameless plug, but the added length and weight of a RECOIL OFFGRID issue make it perfect for this application.

Don't believe me? Roll up the bad boy in your hands and imagine jabbing one end of this magazine into your throat or eye.

Carabiner

A common tool that can be attached to a backpack, day bag, or keychain, a carabiner of the right size and material can be used much like brass knuckles. Throwing common boxing punches can be harmful to your unprotected hand, especially hook and uppercut angles that sometimes make contact with the sides or corners of your fist.

A carabiner can not only protect the hand from injury when performing such strikes, but also makes them more effective by concentrating the impact into a smaller contact surface. Look for something with a locking collar to prevent opening and causing injury to the hand while striking.

This fist-load weapon called the JW.Vulcan is a collaboration between the author and RAIDOPS (www.raidops.com), a South Korean company that specializes in tactical and survival gear.

Improvised Fist-Load Weapons

There are companies that specialize in producing discrete (and sometimes not-so-discrete) fist-load weapons that are keychains, paperweights, and bottle openers. Regardless of how obvious their true nature is, these weapons will follow three general methods of application.

The first works on the same principle as brass knuckles, designed to protect the front of the fists while delivering standard punching techniques. The second kind is designed to protrude from the top and bottom of the closed fist, where it can be used much like a knife in forward or reverse grip. Others will combine the first two, having protrusions from the top and/or bottom of the fist and something protecting one or more of the knuckles, generally with a ring feature that one or more fingers will go into.

For those prepared to pay a little more for tools of this nature, there's my favorite

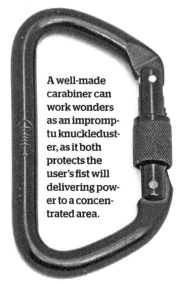

A well-made carabiner can work wonders as an impromptu knuckleduster, as it both protects the user's fist will delivering power to a concentrated area.

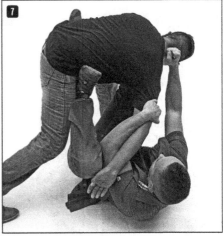

company, RAIDOPS of South Korea. It has a huge variety of tools and use titanium in almost all of them. You can expect to find several other companies with great products for considerably lower costs, depending on the materials they use.

Training to use these items for self-defense can be easier than one might think.

Focusing on the common principles utilized by each item rather than the differences between them will streamline the training process. In other words, use the principles of Kali, an umbrella term for the weapons-based combat systems of the Philippines. One of these principles is referred to as "transferrable methodology." This means using the same core set of movements, regardless of what weapon is in your hand.

Don't focus so much on the weapon, but rather the angles used to wield the weapon and the targets that should be addressed. All strikes will utilize either thrust or slashing motions. Think along the lines of a knife. When held in the hand with a forward (sabre) grip, you can use it to stab (thrust) or cut (slash). Using slashing angles, you can also strike with the pommel in a "hammer fist"-type attack. These same principles of angles and movement can be applied to any fist-load weapon.

The only difference to calculate for is the length of the weapon and whether it will cause puncturing wounds, lacerations, blunt trauma, or a combination.

An item like a carabiner used to protect the front of the knuckles will utilize the principles of a thrust, with the difference being the angle of the fist for a punch. Slashing angles can still be effective with a carabiner if it adequately protects the sides of the fist.

One of the things that often gets people hurt or killed in self-defense situations is hesitation. This often comes from not being able to make a decision based on a lack of understanding of self-defense laws. This lack of understanding can also result in using unlawful force against another person. So choose your weapons wisely, train with them often, and be sure to have a good understanding of local laws in the areas you plan to carry them.

About the Author

Jared Wihongi is founder and president of Survival Edge Tactical Systems Inc., a tactical training and consulting company. He is known to many as the face of Browning's Black Label tactical equipment line. Wihongi is one of a handful of *tuhon* (master-level) instructors in the Filipino combat art of Pekiti-Tirsia Kali and has 15 years of experience in law enforcement. Most of that was spent as a SWAT officer and instructor of firearms and defensive tactics. Plus, he's spent more than a decade teaching combatives and survival skills to police, military, and covert-operations units in Asia, Europe, North America, and South America.

www.facebook.com/jared.wihongi
www.jaredwihongi.com

Edge of Disaster

Improvised Knife Sharpening Methods

By Michael Janich

A knife is the most quintessential of all survival tools. Whether you're stranded in a desert, inundated by floods, caught in a snowstorm, or stuck in any other potentially life-threatening situation, having a reliable cutting tool is a must.

While opinions on what constitutes a proper "survival knife" will always vary greatly, the defining quality that makes a knife a knife remains the same: it must cut. It must also continue to cut until your emergency situation is over and life as you know it returns to normal. To make sure it does that, you need to know how to sharpen your knife, if necessary, with improvised means.

Cutting-Edge Basics

A knife essentially functions as a miniature saw or a miniature ax. When properly sharpened, its cutting edge terminates at an acute V-shaped angle. Depending upon the grit size of the abrasive used to finish the edge, the size of its microscopic teeth varies from relatively coarse (great for cutting rope and other fibrous materials) to extremely fine and polished (for scalpel-like cutting, usually in softer materials).

In its saw-like mode, the edge cuts when it's drawn longitudinally through the material while constant pressure is applied. This slicing style of cutting takes full advantage of the edge's tooth pattern and typically cuts with maximum efficiency.

As an ax, a knife's cutting edge works like a pure wedge. Rather than drawing the length of the edge through the material, it meets it at a right angle. The force of that contact — either ballistic (chopping or batoning) or sustained pressure (whit-

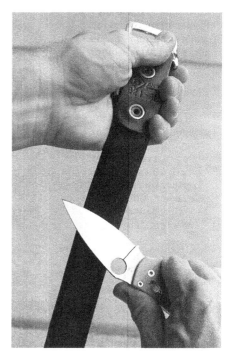

Like a barber's straight razor, knife edges can be touched up to cut more smoothly by stropping on a piece of leather — like this gun belt.

tling) — sinks the edge into the material to separate it.

Either way, the key to a knife edge's performance is the acute V shape at its terminus. The exact angle of the V depends upon the blade's grind (i.e. flat, hollow, saber, convex, Scandi), its thickness at the beginning of the terminal cutting edge, the steel the blade is made from, and the hardness of that steel at the edge.

When a knife gets dull, the tiny teeth at the edge become mangled and ultimately the acute point of the edge's V is worn away, broken off, or bent over. When this happens, the cross-section of the edge looks more like a U than a V and your knife's defining function — cutting — is compromised until you sharpen it again.

WEAPONS • EDGE OF DISASTER | **331**

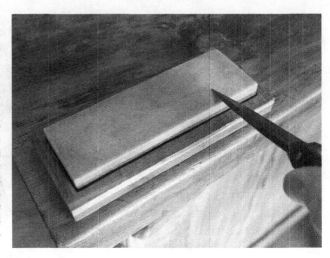

If you want to have any hope of sharpening a knife on an improvised abrasive, first learn how to do it with a traditional flat stone. After determining the proper angle, start with the heel of the edge closest to the handle and draw the entire edge across the stone as if trying to slice off a thin layer. Repeat on the other side and keep going until you've achieved the desired degree of sharpness.

Staying Sharp

In simplest terms, sharpening is the process of maintaining or, when necessary, recreating the V shape of your knife's edge. Since prevention is always better than a cure, let's start with keeping your knife sharp.

First of all, let's assume that when your specific balloon went up, you started the party with a sharp knife. *Sharp*, unlike *pregnant*, is a relative term, and some knife geeks have taken its meaning to crazy extremes. Assuming you have a life and don't spend all your time literally splitting hairs with your EDC folder, let's set a simple baseline. If you can cleanly slice a piece of typing paper with your knife, it's got a sharp, utilitarian edge suitable for most survival applications.

Based on that standard, let's say you've cut a few things and you notice that your knife's not as keen as it was when the emergency started. Rather than waiting for it to get duller, it's much easier to restore the edge by stropping it.

Have you ever seen an old-school barber run a straight razor against a piece of leather? That's stropping. It's basically the action of drawing your edge across a mildly abrasive surface to realign the terminal portion of the V.

To strop a knife, hold it in a normal grip and place the blade flat on the stropping medium. Ideally, do this with an overhead light source so you can clearly see the shadow under the edge. Now, raise the back of the blade until the shadow disappears and the bevel of the terminal cutting edge is flat on the strop. Maintaining that angle and moderate downward pressure, wipe the blade across the strop, leading with the spine of the blade so the edge trails behind (just like spreading butter on toast). Flip your hand over and repeat the process on the other side of the edge. Work from the "heel" of the edge (closest to the handle) to the tip so you strop its entire length.

Initially, maintaining the proper angle throughout each stroke will be tough, but with practice you'll get more consistent. That muscle memory and understanding of angles will also come in handy when learning other improvised sharpening methods.

Knife Sharpenability Factors

One aspect of knife selection that has a tremendous impact on sharpenability is blade steel. In recent years, the development of steels suitable for or specifically geared toward cutlery applications has exploded. The carbon steels and relatively simple stainless steels that used to dominate the production knife world have now been superseded by exotic, powder-metallurgy steels packed with ultrahigh levels of carbon, as well as vanadium, molybdenum, cobalt, niobium, and other elements. These alloys can greatly enhance the wear resistance and toughness of blade steels, allowing them to hold an edge better than ever.

Remember, though, that there are tradeoffs to everything. Blades that are resistant to dulling in use are also notoriously hard to grind and therefore more resistant to your efforts to sharpen them. Some high-performance alloys refuse to yield to anything less than diamond abrasives, so you'd be hard pressed to sharpen them with improvised means.

Simple, traditional blade shapes are also much easier to sharpen than blades with complex grinds and multiple bevels. In most cases, they cut better and offer greater versatility, too. Don't be fooled by hype or looks; focus on knives that look like knives, not something out of Star Wars.

Serrations are another controversial topic when it comes to survival knife selection. While well-designed serrations will hold an edge longer than a conventional plain edge and absolutely devour fibrous materials like rope and webbing, they are considerably more difficult to sharpen than straight edges and exceedingly difficult to sharpen with makeshift tools.

If you have to sharpen a serrated blade in the field, your best bet is to use a rock or other abrasive to work the edge on the side opposite the grind of the serration teeth (serrations are typically beveled only on one side of the blade). This method restores the sharpness of the serration points and edge without trying to reach down into the concave of every tooth. Depending upon the size of your blade's serrations, the rounded surface on the top of a car window may be able to fit the recesses, but it's still simpler and quicker to sharpen the non-beveled side.

Bushcrafters and other survivalists have always preferred simple carbon-steel blades with zero-ground "Scandi" (short for "Scandinavian") grinds that are easy to sharpen with any available abrasive. While modern steels, serrations, and other advanced features may offer improved performance in some circumstances, it often comes at the price of being high-maintenance — perhaps too high for SHTF-style sharpening.

Many old-school knife users sharpened their knives on the rims of crocks, bowls, mugs, or other ceramic vessels. The exposed rim of the bottom of a coffee cup, which isn't covered by smooth glaze, will easily sharpen knife edges. Note the darkened area, which displays steel that's been removed from the edge.

What materials make good improvised strops? The easiest and most practical is the stout leather belt that may already be part of your EDC kit. Take the belt off, hook the buckle to something or step on one end, hold the other end taut, and strop away. Purpose-designed leather strops are usually rubbed with jeweler's rouge or polishing compound before they're used. Doing the same with the inside surface of your leather belt ensures that you've always got a way to touch up your knife edge at all times. If you want to be an overachiever, you could even consider sticking a patch of fine (about 240-grit) adhesive-backed sandpaper to the inside of your belt for more serious improvised sharpening.

In addition to belts, heavy cardboard also makes a great improvised strop. Lay a piece of dry corrugated cardboard on a flat surface and use the same technique to touch up your edge. Ideally, it should be about twice the length of your blade to make it easy to hold as you sharpen. Sprinkling a little dry dirt or fine sand on it can replicate the abrasive quality of polishing compound and give even better results.

Stropping is very easy to learn, and keeping a knife sharp is simpler than making it sharp once it's dull.

Iron Sharpeneth Iron

If you watch a good butcher or chef in action, you'll notice that he regularly touches up the edge of his knife with a long, wand-like thing called a steel. Drawing the edge along the hard, grooved surface of a butcher's steel realigns its teeth and keeps it sharper longer. Like stropping, steeling is a maintenance strategy and won't restore a very dull edge, but it's still worth adding to your bag of tricks.

So where do you find a hard piece of steel with fine longitudinal grooves in it in the field? How about the spine of your other knife? In a survival situation, two is one and one is none. Carrying two or more knives allows you to have different tools for different jobs (i.e. one for tough jobs and one for fine work) and can allow you to use the back of one blade to steel the edge of the other. If your knives don't naturally have a longitudinal groove pattern in the spine, create that pattern before you go afield by draw-filing the blade spine with 150-grit sandpaper.

To steel your edge, use the same overhead light and shadow method described earlier to determine the sharpening angle of your knife. However, instead of wiping the edge as if spreading butter, lead with the edge — as if trying to slice a thin layer off the spine of the blade you're using as a steel. Use light pressure, work from the heel to the tip, and alternate sides with every stroke.

Back to the Grind

Sooner or later, your edge is going to get dull enough that stropping or steeling it won't be enough to keep it sharp. In simple terms, the acute V shape of your edge has been dulled to a rounded U shape. To restore its sharpness, you've got to grind away steel on both sides of the edge to turn the U back into a V. Doing that requires two things: 1) an abrasive hard enough to grind steel yet fine enough to leave an acute edge angle, and 2) a steady enough hand to maintain a consistent angle as you remove steel on both sides of the edge. Let's tackle the hard part first: skill.

Like using turn signals and saying *please* and *thank you*, knowing how to sharpen a knife on a flat stone used to be a common skill. However, as fewer people carry knives and old-school Arkansas stones are replaced by motors, angle jigs, and weird Rube Goldberg, crew-served sharpening contraptions, freehand sharpening is becoming a lost art. Well, if you have visions of yourself bringing your knife to hair-popping sharpness on a river rock, I strongly suggest you find that lost art. Invest in a good bench stone at least as long as your longest EDC blade, break

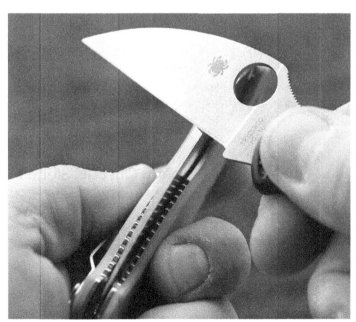

To steel one knife on the spine of another, draw the edge from heel to tip while maintaining the proper angle, then alternate sides.

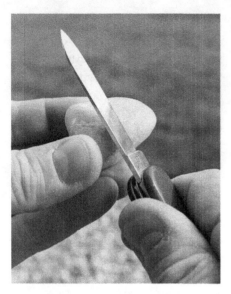

When all else fails, even a smooth, reasonably flat rock can be used to sharpen a knife. Light-colored rocks allow you to easily see when you're removing steel.

The rounded, frosted edge at the top of a car's side window is an excellent improvised abrasive for knife sharpening. If you learn proper technique on a traditional stone, translating it to the car window should be no problem.

out your knives, and spend some time learning how to sharpen.

The basic technique, as described previously, is to lay your blade flat on the stone. With a light source directly overhead, raise the spine of the blade until the shadow under the edge just disappears. For most knives, this happens when the blade-to-stone angle gets to about 20 degrees. Do this repeatedly until you start to get a tactile feel for the proper angle. Then, maintaining that angle and applying firm (but not hard) downward pressure, draw the edge across the stone from heel to tip. If your blade has belly (i.e. upward curvature) near the tip, you'll have to raise your hand a bit to maintain a constant edge angle.

To see if you're doing it right, get a Sharpie marker and a magnifying glass. Color both sides of the edge bevel with the marker and take a few passes on a dry stone. Then, examine your work with the magnifying glass. If your angle is correct, you should be removing steel right near the edge. If your angle is off or inconsistent, the shiny spots where the marker is scraped away will let you know and help you adjust your technique. Once you get the hang of it, follow the stone manufacturer's directions, using oil or water as necessary to keep the stone's pores clean.

When You Can't Get Stoned

Armed with the skill to sharpen on a proper stone, you can now apply that skill to less proper, field-expedient abrasives. The exact abrasives you choose will depend upon your environment, but anything that's hard enough to scratch your knife blade can work. In general, you want to look for relatively smooth materials that allow you to achieve finer teeth and a sharper edge. Light-colored materials are also preferred as they provide visible evidence that they're actually removing steel.

In an urban environment, one of the best expedient abrasives is the top edge of a car's side window. Glass is extremely hard and, when properly textured, will readily grind steel. The rounded, somewhat frosted surface at the top edge of a car window is just about perfect for this. Just roll the window down partway and use the same technique you use with a stone.

Many modern sharpening systems use ceramic abrasives. The very first modern sharpener of this type, the Crock Stick, got its name from the traditional method of honing knives on the rim or bottom of a ceramic crock. A modern expedient for this is the slightly rough bottom rim of a coffee cup or bowl. Use the same stone technique, pay attention to your angles, and you'll be cutting stuff in no time.

In wilderness environments, even ordinary stones can be used as improvised sharpeners. Smooth, flat, river rocks work very well, especially if they're lighter colored so you can see the steel coming off and confirm your progress. Larger stones are easier to hold or brace than smaller stones, and once your knife is reasonably sharp, you can always follow up by steeling and stropping the edge to refine it.

The only good knife is a sharp one. With the right skills and knowledge, you and your knife can stay sharp anywhere.

Sharp is a relative term, but in general, an edge that's keen enough to slice typing paper is sharp enough for most chores. The challenge is how to get it that way and keep it that way without purpose-designed sharpening tools.

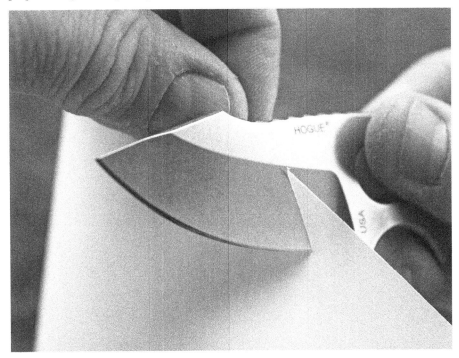

Pipe Dreams

The Pop-A 410 DIY Survival Shotgun

By Mike Searson

In the past few years, a "do-it-yourself shotgun" kit has become popular, billed as a "survival shotgun." It's made by Runway Sub-Cal, a manufacturer known for producing rifled flare gun inserts to allow shooters to fire pistol rounds through 26.5mm flare guns.

Essentially, they provide a barrel, firing pin, and an outer barrel sleeve; the rest of the shotgun is built from steel pipe fittings. I was a bit hesitant going into this assignment, but read on and see why it's important for a number of reasons.

Building a Shotgun

It's legal for you to build your own firearms. Convicted felons or other prohibited persons, however, cannot. There may also

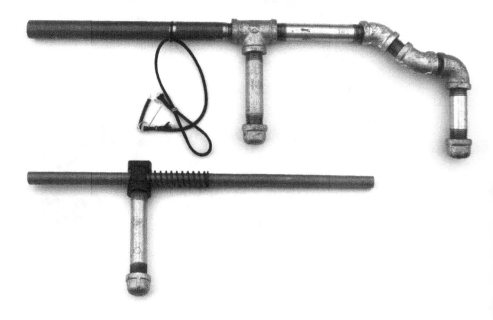

be other applicable laws where you live, so double check the regulations in your jurisdiction. Several retailers carry this kit. We ordered ours from Bud-K for $130 with free shipping.

The package arrived via FedEx Smart Solutions, meaning that FedEx did all the heavy lifting getting it to within 20 miles of me and transferring final delivery to my local post office. Bud-K packaged it well enough, but after opening it up I realized there was no instruction sheet.

This wasn't a big deal, as the kit is straightforward with a video on the company's website. When compiling the items needed to finish it up, I went to double check on the website what a "jam nipple" was and realized the firing pin wasn't included in the shipment.

Bud-K's customer service desk began looking for extras in their warehouse. If they were unsuccessful, they'd have me return the kit in exchange for a new one. A few days later, they advised that the manufacturer would ship out the missing components directly. After about a week, it arrived.

Completion of the kit requires the following ½-inch pipe parts:
- one ½-inch tee
- three ½-inch caps
- two 4-inch nipples
- one 3-inch nipple
- two 45-degree elbows
- one 90-degree elbow
- two jam nipples
- one 5-inch nipple

The only parts that were somewhat difficult to find were the so-called jam nipples. These are short nipples that are completely threaded. I found them under a variety of names such as zero nipples and flush

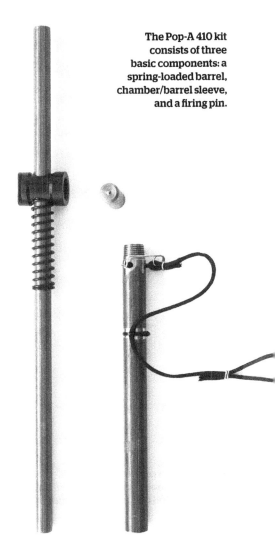

The Pop-A 410 kit consists of three basic components: a spring-loaded barrel, chamber/barrel sleeve, and a firing pin.

nipples. Perhaps jam nipples are a colloquialism in certain parts of the country or an older plumbing term, but I couldn't find them under that name in stores near me.

After a quick trip to Home Depot and $32 later, I had everything I needed to put the Pop-A 410 together.

Assembly took about 15 minutes, if that long. One of the trickier things to get right was ensuring that the angled pipe connectors aligned properly. They might line up perfectly while only grasping two or three threads, but then would be totally out of alignment when tightened all the way down. Lucas Oil Gun Grease and a small pipe wrench in conjunction with a vise got everything properly into position. I threaded as far as I could, backed off, and repeated in order to grasp more threads to make it sturdy and straight.

Once you have an idea on how everything lines up, you can make it semi-permanent by using plumbers' tape, Loctite, or another adhesive. Some builders have used JB Weld for a more permanent fix, but that might be excessive.

A crucial piece of this assembly is the ½-inch tee piece. This acts as your receiver, for lack of a better term, and the firing pin should be able to pass completely through it.

When finished, you have basically a two-piece shotgun composed of a chambered, spring-loaded barrel, a homemade receiver containing a fixed firing pin, a homemade stock, and pistol grips. A "safety" is included in the form of a clip that inserts between the firing pin and primer, attached to a short piece of cord so you don't lose it. There's no sighting system, but the forward pistol grip has a Weaver-style base so you can mount a red dot or visible laser. A short sheetmetal screw with a rounded head could make for an improvised bead sight.

You can leave the Pop-A 410 unfinished, "in the white," or you can break out some Krylon, Duracoat, or even Cerakote if you feel fancy and coat it in a protective finish.

Firing the Pop-A 410

To fire the Pop-A 410 you load the chamber, shoulder the shotgun, take hold of the forward grip, aim, and slam the barrel rearward. The impact of the firing pin against the primer of the shell causes ignition and fires the projectile.

For the cost of a completed Pop-A 410, a shooter can pick up a purpose-built shotgun in the same caliber, many made before 1968 also lack a serial number such as this single-shot Winchester Model 37 and an over/under Stevens Model 420.

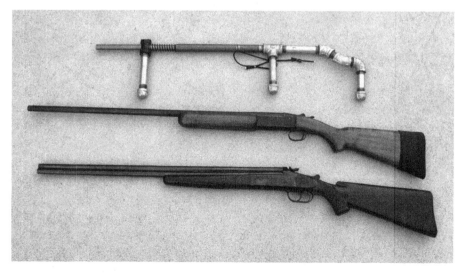

½-inch pipe parts:
(1) ½-inch tee: $2.95
(3) ½-inch caps: $1.95 each / $5.85
(2) 4-inch nipples: $3.35 each / $6.70
(1) 3-inch nipple: $1.95

(2) 45-degree elbows: $2.53 each / $5.06
(1) 90-degree elbow: $2.95
(2) jam nipples: $1.95 each / $3.90
(1) 5-inch nipple: $2.95
Total: $32.31

For less than $35 in pipe fittings, you can complete the Pop-A 410 kit and have a single-shot shotgun.

The first round was a bit of a doozy. The thought that kept going through my mind from the moment I loaded the chamber until I actually fired it was, *"Will that galvanized pipe fitting and that two-piece barrel assembly that I bought be enough to handle 12,500 to 15,000 psi?"*

It turned out that it was. The burst rating on this type of pipe is 21,000 to 26,000 psi, while pressurized. The short impulse of firing a single round of ammunition plays a role, too. Still, no one will get "millions of rounds out of this" weapon. I fired close to 150 rounds of assorted birdshot, buckshot, and buck and ball shot, without incident.

Beyond the fun factor, this is a firearm of last resort. For instance, if you had to build something out of scrap to forage for birds and squirrels in a survival situation. Or, in a darker scenario, if you needed to make something in order to take out the opposition and scavenge his weapon.

Alternatives

While this was a fun project, it's a bit expensive for what you get. It's basically a slam-fire .410. You can walk away with the satisfaction that you built a firearm on your own. Plus, putting it together may provide a better sense of how firearms work, along with the pride we all get whenever we build something with our own two hands.

If you're mainly intrigued by the fact that you can build a firearm without a serial number and wondering why you'd invest the time and money in one of these, there are other alternatives.

For example, there are untold numbers of firearms, mostly shotguns and rimfire rifles, built before 1968 that have no serial numbers and can be purchased for much less than what was invested in this project. These aren't just rusty single-shot cracked-stock scatterguns, either.

Over the years I've acquired single-shot shotguns made by Hopkins & Allen, New England Firearms, Harrington & Richardson, Iver Johnson, Savage/Stevens, and Winchester for less than $90 each — and in the case of the Hopkins & Allen and Stevens models, less than $40. An over/under Stevens 420 in .410 made 75 years ago set me back $110, and a bolt-action Sears 12-gauge cost me $60. None of these firearms have serial numbers; neither do a handful of 22 bolt-action and single-shot rifles I've acquired over the years.

Shooting the Pop-A 410 shotgun is a bit tricky due to the lack of a trigger, but not difficult. Shoulder it, take aim, and slam the shell rearward into the firing pin.

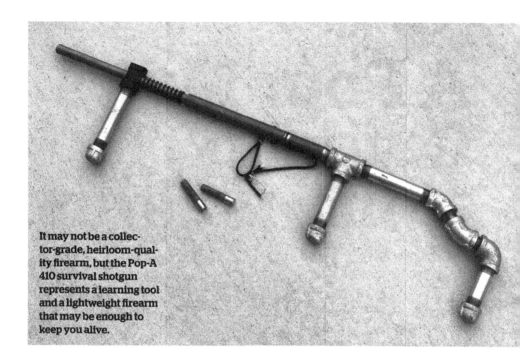

It may not be a collector-grade, heirloom-quality firearm, but the Pop-A 410 survival shotgun represents a learning tool and a lightweight firearm that may be enough to keep you alive.

Any prepared individual should have low-cost firearms on hand, because they're cheap, easy to learn how to use, and can be loaned, bartered, or otherwise utilized in the event of a large-scale long-term disaster.

The Pop-A 410 survival shotgun can fill this role, but it's more significant along the lines of a first-time gun-builder understanding how a firearm can be built, along with the inspiration for ideas on how to build your own, should you find yourself in a situation where making a firearm from scratch may be your only option.

Examine your ammunition types on hand and see how they fit in various pipes or tubes. Find pipes or tubes in a suitable grade of metal to contain the chamber pressure of the firing sequence and experiment. You can build something like the Pop-A 410 to gain an understanding of how the parts fit together properly and take those concepts to forge ahead on your own.

The key to preparing for a disaster and surviving is the knowledge we obtain and how we successfully apply it. A simple project like this can act as food for your mind.

RUNWAY SUB-CAL
Pop-A 410

CALIBER(S)
.410 gauge

BARREL LENGTH(S)
18 inches

OAL
28 inches

WEIGHT (UNLOADED)
3.9 pounds

CAPACITY
1

MSRP
$130

URL
www.budk.com

A Poor Man's Guide to Knife-making

DIY Bladesmithing Your Own Knife at Home

By Chad McBroom

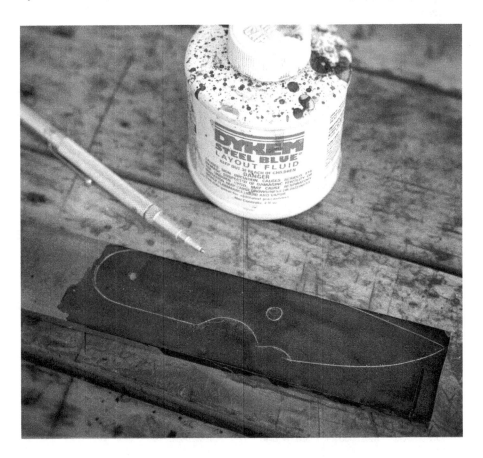

There's no doubt that every RECOIL OFFGRID reader understands the importance of a well-constructed knife. It's arguably the most valuable tool in any survival kit. Whether out of love of the blade or an innate desire for self-sufficiency, many have considered putting their own hands to the forge only to be dissuaded by the expensive equipment and technical skills employed by modern-day bladesmiths.

In this step-by-step instructional article, we'll guide you through the knife-making process from start to finish, using a stock removal method and basic hand tools.

STEP 1: Select A Steel

The foundation of the knifemaking process is steel, so consider your options carefully. Choosing a steel that has the right balance between hardness, durability (toughness), and corrosion resistance can be challenging, especially when you're working with limited resources and technology. Many of the steels you might find at the local salvage yard or hardware store are mild steels unsuitable for anything more than a prison shank, while the many "super steels" used in high-end cutlery must undergo hardening processes that require specialized equipment and extreme precision. It's best to stick with basic, high-carbon steels like 1095 or 1075. Some tool steels like O1 are also relatively easy to work with.

Whenever possible, you should purchase your steel from a reputable dealer that specializes in cutlery steels. This is the best way to make sure you're getting correct and uniform materials. Plus, you can purchase the steel in the width and thickness you wish to work with, which will save you a lot of time and effort.

Mystery steel (any steel with unknown properties) should always be a last resort. In the event of a global meltdown or zombie apocalypse, a car leaf spring would be a fair gamble, especially in older models where 5160 or similar spring steels were commonly used, but with modern cars it's still a crapshoot. Plus, repurposed steel, if not already flat, will require additional cutting, bending, twisting, and/or grinding to make it flat and usable.

STEP 2: Lay Out The Design

Once you've acquired your steel, the next step is to decide on the blade and handle design and then transfer that design onto the metal.

The easiest way to do this is to sketch your design on a piece of cardstock or cardboard with a pencil. Once you're happy with your design, cut out the design and then trace it onto your steel. You can use a steel layout fluid like Dykem to coat the surface and trace around the template with a metal scribe, or you can simply use a black marker on the bare steel surface.

STEP 3: Shape Your Blank

Shaping the knife blank with minimal tools will be the most tedious step in the process. This can be done with nothing more than a hacksaw and a file, but it'll take time and patience. If you can introduce an angle grinder or metal bandsaw into the mix, it'll be much faster with less tendonitis.

The process is the same regardless of the tools you're able to work with. Use a saw or grinder to cut along the lines of your

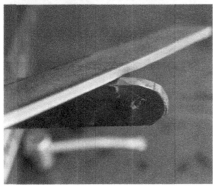

An angle grinder is an inexpensive power tool that can help you make quick work of shaping your knife blank. Use a file to smooth and straighten your cut lines. Different sizes and shapes of files to fit different areas will make this process much easier.

STEP 4: Smooth & Surface

Once you've finished shaping your knife blank, you'll need to smooth everything out and make sure the surface of the knife is even. This can be done using anything from a power sander to a homemade sanding block. The objective here is to make everything nice and even so you can grind your bevels.

design. Once you get to tight spots like the finger grooves, make a V-shaped cut to remove as much material as possible.

Once you've removed as much excess metal as possible, use a file to straighten your lines, round your corners, and remove everything else that isn't a knife. It's helpful to have a few different shapes and sizes of files so you can fit into those smaller grooves and odd-shaped crevices.

Don't forget to drill holes for your handle pins or cord wrap during this step of the process. It's much easier to drill your holes prior to hardening the steel.

Assuming you're working with minimal tools, a sanding block made out of mild steel with a piece of leather glued to the bottom works very well. Simply cut a sheet of sandpaper a little wider than your knife and fold it over the leather side of the block near the end of the strip. Pinch the sandpaper between you thumbs and index fingers to hold it in place. As the grit wears down, you can slide a fresh portion of sandpaper into place and continue until the entire strip is worn out.

It's recommended to start with 80-grit sandpaper for this step. Adding some WD-40 onto the sandpaper helps extend the paper's life and makes hand-sanding much easier and cleaner. You can use a bench vise to hold the knife while working on the outer edges. Once you begin working on the flat surfaces, you can place a long, flat board inside your vise so it extends out from the workbench, then clamp the knife onto the board to hold it in place. The back side of the jig we'll be discussing in the next section makes a great working surface.

STEP 5: Grind Your Bevels

Grinding the bevels into a knife is the most difficult task every knifemaker faces, whether they're using a $4,000 knifemaking grinder or the most primitive tools. This author discovered a highly effective way to grind perfectly uniform bevels using a simple homemade jig.

Jig Construction

To build the jig, you'll need three 2-foot-long ¾-inch by 3½-inch boards, wood glue, four or five eye bolts of different lengths, two nuts for the eye bolts, and a long screw with tight threading to use as a stop screw. You'll also need a table vise or other method to hold the jig in place when you start using it.

Using one of the boards as a base, glue and clamp the other two boards on top to form a "T" shape. Drill holes the size of your eye bolts down the center of the jig and holes the size of your stop screw down the center of the cross board. Use 1-inch spacing between the holes on both sections.

Using the Jig

To use the jig, begin by attaching a 2-foot metal rod to the back of a file with

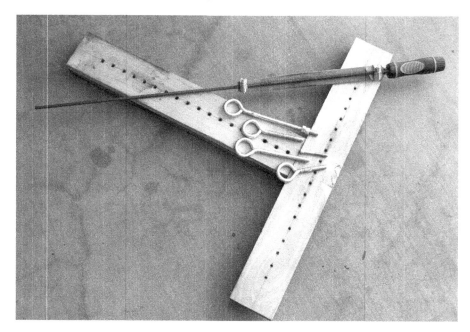

hose clamps. Insert a stop screw into one of the pre-drilled holes on the cross portion of the jig. The purpose of this screw is to create a consistent stopping point as you file your primary bevel.

Next, determine where you want to set your plunge line (where the grind stops) and orient the knife so the desired plunge line lines up with the stop screw. Once you have the proper alignment, clamp the knife to the board.

Screw an eye bolt into one of the pre-drilled holes on the jig to set your grinding angle and use the two nuts to lock the bolt in place. The angle should be set steep enough to achieve about a 30-degree bevel. The longer the bolt and the closer it is to the knife, the greater the angle.

Using the eye bolt to guide the file rod, grind down the bevel until you reach the midline of the edge, then repeat the process on the other side. Switch back to the

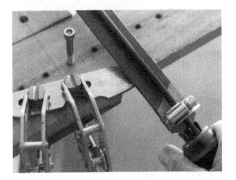
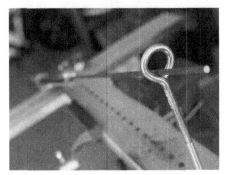

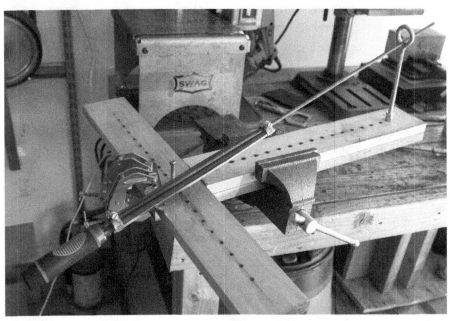

The homemade jig shown is cheap to build and, if used properly, will produce clean, uniform bevels.

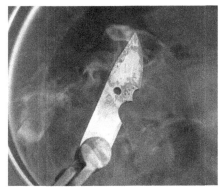

Heating the blade to critical temperature and quenching it in oil to harden the steel.

original side and decrease the grind angle. File until the bevel reaches the desired height and blends with the original bevel, then repeat on the other side. You may have to make slight adjustments to your angle along the way until you reach the desired effect.

STEP 6: Heat Treating

This is a multistep process used to change the molecular alignment of steel particles to create a hardened edge that isn't too brittle. The first step in this process is to heat the steel to a point where it temporarily loses its magnetic properties. The heating process can take place in a coal or gas forge, if available, but you can also make do with a propane or butane torch.

Heat the blade from the cutting edge up to at least the midline of the primary bevel. The heat should be applied until the steel reaches a cherry red color that's even throughout. The heating point can be confirmed by touching a magnet against the heated portion to check for magnetism. If the heated portion of the steel doesn't pull toward the magnet, then the critical temperature has been reached and the blade is ready to be cooled using a quenching solution. After performing a

Use a metal block with a leather surface and 80-grit sandpaper to surface the knife.

magnet check, be sure to apply additional heat to regain the temperature you just lost prior to quenching.

Dip the blade into the quench as rapidly as possible after removing the heat source. Be sure to move the blade back and forth so it cools evenly. Remove the blade and check the hardness with a file to make sure the quench was effective. The file should skate off the edge if the steel is hard.

The purpose of the quench is to cool the steel rapidly and force the rearrangement of atomic positions to produce martensite, which is an exceptionally hard phase of steel. Martensite is very brittle, so it's necessary to modify the mechanical properties by heat treating at a lower temperature range for an extended period of time, a process known as tempering.

Once the metal cools to the touch, place it in the oven for one hour at 400 degrees F (temperature can vary depending on the steel). Remove the knife and allow it to cool, then repeat the process for one additional cycle.

STEP 7: Resurface

After heat treating the blade, you'll need to remove the fire scale and carbon deposits from the surface. This is basically a repeat of Step 4, so there's no need to describe the process in detail. The amount of resurfacing you do is based on personal preference and how rough or polished you want the final product to be.

STEP 8: Add Handles/Wrap

Since handle-making and wrapping can itself be an art form, we won't go into detail here. A simple paracord wrap is the easiest method to start with. Wrap the cord around the top of the handle once, then cross and twist the cord each time the ends meet until the entire tang is covered. When you reach the end, feed the cord through the lanyard hole on the bottom and tie a knot on the other side. Cut and melt the ends of the cord to secure the knot.

STEP 9: Sharpen

The final step is to sharpen your blade. Depending on the thickness of your primary bevel, it may take some time to form a secondary bevel resulting in a cutting edge. Sharpening can be done using stones or mechanical sharpeners. The more consistent the angle, the finer the edge will be. For a polished, razor-sharp edge, work in stages and finish by running the edge backward along a leather strop. It's possible to improvise a strop from an old leather belt — look for one with a natural, suede-like inner surface — treated with automotive polishing compound or toothpaste.

Conclusion

The art and science of metalworking can take a lifetime to master, but it doesn't have to be a difficult arena to enter. No matter if you're motivated by the survivalist's code of self-reliance or a desire for artistic expression, the information presented here — though it only scratches the surface — is enough to get you started without breaking the bank. ⁂

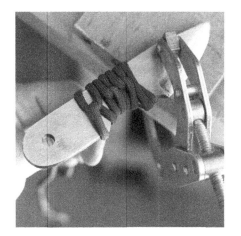

Applying a cord-wrap handle to the finished knife.